THE CAMBRIDGE COMPANION TO
JORGE LUIS BORGES

Jorge Luis Borges (1899–1986) was one of the great writers of the twentieth century and the most influential author in the Spanish language of modern times. He had a seminal influence on Latin American literature and a lasting impact on literary fiction in many other languages. However, Borges has been accessible in English only through a number of anthologies drawn mainly from his work of the 1940s and 1950s. The primary aim of this *Companion* is to provide a more comprehensive account of Borges's *œuvre* and the evolution of his writing. It offers critical assessments by leading scholars of the poetry of his youth and the later poetry and fiction, as well as of the "canonical" volumes of the middle years. Other chapters focus on key themes and interests, and on his influence in literary theory and translation studies.

EDWIN WILLIAMSON is the King Alfonso XIII Professor of Spanish Studies at the University of Oxford and a Fellow of Exeter College, Oxford. His books include *The Penguin History of Latin America* (updated and revised edition, 2009) and his acclaimed biography, *Borges: A Life* (2004), which has been translated into several languages.

A complete list of books in the series is at the back of this book.

D1599210

THE CAMBRIDGE
COMPANION TO

JORGE LUIS BORGES

EDITED BY
EDWIN WILLIAMSON

CAMBRIDGE
UNIVERSITY PRESS

University Printing House, Cambridge CB2 8BS, United Kingdom

Published in the United States of America by Cambridge University Press, New York

Cambridge University Press is part of the University of Cambridge.

It furthers the University's mission by disseminating knowledge in the pursuit of
education, learning and research at the highest international levels of excellence.

www.cambridge.org
Information on this title: www.cambridge.org/9780521141376

© Cambridge University Press 2013

First published 2013

Printed in the United Kingdom by Bell and Bain Ltd

A catalogue record for this publication is available from the British Library

Library of Congress Cataloguing in Publication data
The Cambridge Companion to Jorge Luis Borges / edited By Edwin Williamson.
pages   cm
Includes bibliographical references and index.
ISBN 978-0-521-19339-9 (hardback) – ISBN 978-0-521-14137-6 (pbk)
1. Borges, Jorge Luis, 1899-1986–Criticism and interpretation.   I. Williamson,
Edwin, editor of compilation.
PQ7797.B635 Z63546
868'.6209–dc23
2013020828

ISBN 978-0-521-19339-9 Hardback
ISBN 978-0-521-14137-6 Paperback

CONTENTS

CONTRIBUTORS

DANIEL BALDERSTON is Andrew W. Mellon Professor of Modern Languages at the University of Pittsburgh, where he chairs the Department of Hispanic Languages and Literatures. He is also the director of the Borges Center and editor of its journal *Variaciones Borges*. His most recent book on Borges is *Innumerables relaciones: Cómo leer con Borges*. He is currently working on a book on genetic criticism and compositional practices, *How Borges Wrote*.

ARTURO ECHAVARRÍA is Emeritus Professor of Comparative Literature at the University of Puerto Rico. He has been Visiting Scholar at Harvard and Visiting Professor at Yale, Brown, and several European universities. In 2010, he was appointed to the Cátedra Julio Cortázar (Guadalajara) and in 2012, to the Cátedra Carlos Fuentes (Universidad Veracruzana). He has published articles on Rubén Darío, Carpentier, Fuentes, García Márquez, among others, and two books on Borges: *Lengua y literatura de Borges* and *El arte de la jardinería china en Borges, y otros estudios*. He has also published short stories and a novel.

ROBIN FIDDIAN is Professor of Hispanic Studies at the University of Oxford and Fellow of Wadham College. He is the author of monographs on Fernando del Paso and Gabriel García Márquez, and articles on Julio Cortázar, Fernando del Paso, Carlos Fuentes, García Márquez, and Ignacio Solares, and of essays on *Brodie's Report* and "The Theme of the Traitor and Hero," which appeared in *Variaciones Borges* and *Modern Language Review*, respectively. He edited *Postcolonial Perspectives on the Cultures of Latin America and Lusophone Africa*.

EVELYN FISHBURN is Honorary Professor of Spanish American Studies at University College London and Professor Emeritus of London Metropolitan University. She has worked extensively on Borges and published numerous articles on him as well as editing *Borges and Europe Revisited* and *A Borges Dictionary* (in collaboration with Psiche Hughes). A collection of her revised articles on Borges will be published in book form by *Variaciones Borges* in 2013. Other publications include *The Portrayal of Immigration in Nineteenth-Century Argentine*

Literature (1845–1902) and *Short Fiction by Spanish American Women*. She has co-edited *Science and the Creative Imagination in Latin America*.

ROBERTO GONZÁLEZ ECHEVARRÍA is the Sterling Professor of Hispanic and Comparative Literature at Yale University. A member of the American Academy of Arts and Sciences, he received the National Humanities Medal from the President of the United States in 2011. His books include: *Alejo Carpentier: The Pilgrim at Home*; *Myth and Archive: A Theory of Latin American Narrative*; *Love and the Law in Cervantes*; *The Voice of the Masters: Writing and Authority in Modern Latin American Literature*; *Celestina's Brood: Continuities of the Baroque in Spanish and Latin American Literature*; and *Cuban Fiestas*. He is the editor of *The Oxford Book of Latin American Short Stories* and co-editor of *The Cambridge History of Latin American Literature*.

CLIVE GRIFFIN is Emeritus Fellow in Spanish at Trinity College, University of Oxford. His areas of research include: the history of the book in sixteenth-century Spain and its American colonies, and modern Spanish American literature. He has published studies of modern writing from Chile, Colombia, Mexico, and Peru. His most recent book is *Oficiales de imprenta: herejía e Inquisición en la España del siglo XVI*. He is currently working on the early Spanish colonization of the Philippine Islands. He is an Honorary Fellow of the Hispanic Society of America.

EFRAÍN KRISTAL is professor and chair of UCLA's Department of Comparative Literature. He is author of *Invisible Work: Borges and Translation*, editor of Jorge Luis Borges's *Poems of the Night*, and co-editor with John King of *The Cambridge Companion to Mario Vargas Llosa*. His forthcoming publications include an article on Yves Bonnefoy's translations of Shakespeare for *The Oxford Handbook of Shakespeare's Poetry*, and the essay on philosophical approaches to translation for *The Blackwell Companion to Translation Studies*.

SUZANNE JILL LEVINE has received many honors for her translations of Latin American literature, most recently the 2012 PEN Center USA Literary Award for Translation for José Donoso's *The Lizard's Tale*. Recent publications include her chapbook *Reckoning*, and a translation of Luis Negrón's *Mundo Cruel: Stories*. The author of *Manuel Puig and the Spider Woman: His Life and Fictions* and *The Subversive Scribe: Translating Latin American Fiction*, she is the general editor of the Penguin Classics Borges series, and director of Translation Studies at the University of California in Santa Barbara, where she has been teaching since 1988.

LUCE LÓPEZ-BARALT is Distinguished Professor of Spanish and Comparative Literatures at the University of Puerto Rico and a Harvard PhD in Romance Languages and Literatures. She has done extensive research and lecturing in Europe, America, and Asia. Recipient of an Honorary PhD from the University of Puerto Rico, of the Guggenheim Fellowship, and of the Cátedra Julio Cortázar (Mexico), she has served on the boards of prestigious literary journals. Her books and more than 200 articles on comparative Spanish and Arabic, *aljamiado*-Moorish, and Latin American literatures and mysticism have been published in eleven languages.

ALFRED MACADAM has been a professor of Latin American literature at Barnard College, Columbia University since 1983. His most recent book of criticism is *Textual Confrontations: Essays in the Comparative Study of Latin American Literature*. MacAdam is the translator of works by Carlos Fuentes, Mario Vargas Llosa, Juan Carlos Onetti, Alejo Carpentier, and Alfredo Bryce Echenique, among others. He has also published the anthology *Jorge Luis Borges: On Argentina*.

FLOYD MERRELL is Professor Emeritus from Purdue University. His fields of investigation include Latin American cultures and literatures, Borges studies, Charles S. Peirce studies, and semiotic theory. He has taught at the Pontifícia Universidade Católica de São Paulo and the Universidade Federal da Bahia. His books include *Signs Becoming Signs*; *Unthinking Thinking: Jorge Luis Borges, Mathematics, and the "New Physics"*; *Semiosis in the Postmodern Age*; *Simplicity and Complexity*; *Sobre las culturas y civilizaciones latinoamericanas*; *Complementing Latin American Borders*; *Capoeira and Candomblé*; *Becoming Culture*; and *A semiótica de Charles S. Peirce hoje*.

RAFAEL OLEA FRANCO has PhD degrees from Princeton University and El Colegio de México, where he is now a professor. His books include *El otro Borges: El primer Borges* and *Los dones literarios de Borges*. He is editor of *Borges: desesperaciones aparentes y consuelos secretos*; *Fervor crítico por Borges*; and *In memoriam Jorge Luis Borges* as well as the articles "Borges en la constitución del canon fantástico" and "De la ansiedad de influencias: Borges en Pacheco." Recently, he has been visiting professor at the Hebrew University of Jerusalem and the University of Beijing.

PHILIP SWANSON is Hughes Professor of Spanish at the University of Sheffield. His major publications include *Latin American Fiction*, *The New Novel in Latin America*, *José Donoso: The Boom and Beyond*, *Cómo leer a Gabriel García Márquez*, and the edited volumes *Landmarks in Modern Latin American Fiction*, *The Companion to Latin American Studies*, and *The Cambridge Companion to Gabriel García Márquez*.

EDWIN WILLIAMSON is the King Alfonso XIII Professor of Spanish Studies at the University of Oxford and a Fellow of Exeter College. He has published numerous articles reflecting his interest in both Latin America and the Golden Age of Spain. His books include *The Halfway House of Fiction: "Don Quixote" and Arthurian Romance*, and the edited volumes *Cervantes and the Modernists* and *Autoridad y poder en el Siglo de Oro*. His *Penguin History of Latin America* (updated 2009) has been translated into Spanish and Portuguese, and his biography *Borges: A Life* has been translated into Spanish and six other languages.

JASON WILSON is Emeritus Professor at University College London. His publications include: *Octavio Paz: A Study of his Poetics*; *Octavio Paz*; *Traveller's Literary Companion to South and Central America*; *Buenos Aires: A Cultural and Literary Companion*; *Jorge Luis Borges*; *A Companion to Pablo Neruda*; and *The Andes*. He has translated Alexander von Humboldt's *Personal Narrative of a Journey to the Equinoctial Regions of the New Continent*, Octavio Paz's *Itinerary*, and Bernardin de Saint-Pierre's *Journey to Mauritius*. He is writing a biography of W. H. Hudson for Constable & Robinson.

MICHAEL WOOD is Professor Emeritus of English and Comparative Literature at Princeton University. He is the author of, among other works, *García Márquez: One Hundred Years of Solitude*; *The Magician's Doubts*; *Children of Silence*; *The Road to Delphi*; *Literature and the Taste of Knowledge*; and *Yeats and Violence*. He is a Fellow of the British Academy and the Royal Society of Literature as well as of the American Academy of Arts and Sciences and the American Philosophical Society.

NOTE ON EDITIONS AND QUOTATIONS

In all chapters, unless otherwise indicated, quotations in English from Borges's work refer to the following three editions by Viking Penguin. Page references are given in brackets after quotations in the main text, as shown in bold below:

- *Collected Fictions*, trans. Andrew Hurley, New York, Penguin, 1998:

(**CF** and page number).

- *Selected Non-Fiction, 1922–1986*,* ed. Eliot Weinberger, New York, Viking Penguin, 1999:

(**SNF** and page number).

* The title of the British edition is *The Total Library: Non-Fiction, 1922–1986*, London, Allen Lane, the Penguin Press, 2000, but the page numbers are the same as for the US edition.

- *Selected Poems*, ed. Alexander Coleman, New York, Viking Penguin, 1999:

(**SP** and page number).

Unless otherwise indicated, other quotations refer to the four volumes of the *Obras completas*, Buenos Aires, Emecé, 1996, and have been translated into English either by the editor or by the author of the chapter. Page references will be given in brackets after quotations in the main text, thus: (**OC** followed by volume and page number). The English titles of Borges's works follow the style of the Viking Penguin editons above. Titles from the *Obras completas* and other sources have been translated into English; Spanish titles are give, or added in brackets, only when appropriate for identification of the original texts.

CHRONOLOGY

1899	Born on August 24 in Calle Tucumán 840, in the center of Buenos Aires, to Jorge Guillermo Borges, a half-English lawyer and aspiring writer, and Leonor Acevedo Suárez.
1900	Family moves to Palermo, a poor district bordering the pampas, inhabited by immigrants and once notorious for knife-fighters and brothels.
1914	Family goes to Europe and settles in Geneva until end of World War I. Attends secondary school, and learns French, Latin and German.
1919–21	Family spends time in Majorca, Seville, and Madrid. Joins an avant-garde group of poets known as the Ultra.
1921	Returns to Buenos Aires. Forms a group of *ultraístas* and introduces avant-garde ideas through "mural magazine" *Prisma* and little review *Proa (Prow)*.
1923	*Fervor de Buenos Aires* (poems).
1923–24	Second visit to Europe. Becomes disillusioned with Spanish *ultraísmo*. On return to Buenos Aires, relaunches *Proa* with a group of young writers and develops a left-of-center cultural nationalism called *criollismo*.
1925	*Moon Across the Way* (*Luna de enfrente*) (poems) and *Inquisitions* (essays). Frequent clashes between Borges's *criollista* group around *Proa* and an avant-garde group associated with the "cosmopolitan" review *Martín Fierro*.
1926	*The Extent of My Hope* (*El tamaño de mi esperanza*) (essays, many on *criollismo*).
1927	Creates a "Committee of Young Intellectuals" with a group of *criollistas* to campaign for the re-election to the presidency of the Radical party candidate, the populist Hipólito Yrigoyen. Increasingly opposed by right-wing nationalists.

1928	*The Language of the Argentines* (essays). Yrigoyen elected president.
1929	*San Martín Copybook* (*Cuaderno San Martín*) (poems). Meets Nicolás Paredes, a former Palermo gang boss, who will inspire his first story, "Man on Pink Corner."
1930	*Evaristo Carriego* (biography of a Palermo poet, plus essays on folk themes). President Yrigoyen overthrown in military coup d'état by right-wing nationalists. Disillusioned, Borges abandons *criollismo*.
1931	Invited by Victoria Ocampo to join board of new cultural journal *Sur*.
1932	*Discusión* (essays). Contributes to various literary magazines.
1933	Co-editor of the Saturday color supplement of mass daily newspaper *Crítica*, where he publishes stories, essays, reviews, and sketches, until 1934. Becomes a leading opponent of right-wing Argentine nationalism and repeatedly denounces fascism and Nazism in Europe.
1935	*A Universal History of Iniquity* (fictionalized biographical sketches).
1936	*A History of Eternity* (essays). Edits fortnightly books section of popular weekly magazine *El Hogar* (*The Home*), for which he writes reviews and capsule biographies of writers.
1938	Employed as library assistant in a municipal library, his first full-time job. Father dies. Accident on Christmas Eve leads to life-threatening septicemia.
1939	Writes "Pierre Menard, Author of the *Quixote*" while recuperating. Loses job at *El Hogar*. Publicly supports the Allies in World War II, and will condemn Nazism and its many sympathizers among Argentine nationalists throughout the conflict. Joins *Unión Democrática*, a coalition of Radicals, socialists, and communists opposing the pro-Axis nationalists.
1940	Begins collaboration with Adolfo Bioy Casares, which will produce stories, film scripts, and translations over the years. They compile, together with Silvina Ocampo, an *Anthology of Fantasy Literature* and an *Anthology of Argentine Poetry*. Begins contributing regularly to *Sur*, where he will first publish many of his famous texts.
1941	*The Garden of Forking Paths* (fiction).
1942	*Six Problems for Don Isidro Parodi* (detective stories), with Bioy Casares under common pseudonym H. Bustos Domecq.

1943   *Poemas (1922–43)*. First edition of his collected poems, but the three collections of the 1920s considerably revised, a process continued until tenth edition in 1978. Military coup by nationalist officers sympathetic to Mussolini, including Colonel Juan Domingo Perón.

1944   *Fictions (Ficciones)*, consisting of *The Garden of Forking Paths* (above), and *Artifices*, comprising six new stories.

1946   Perón elected president of Argentina. Borges resigns post as library assistant when offered dubious promotion by Peronist authorities. Becomes an implacable opponent of the Peronist regime. Earns living by giving lectures on literature. Editor of *Los Anales de Buenos Aires* but resigns in 1947.

1948   Mother and sister arrested and latter briefly imprisoned for demonstrating against Perón.

1949   *The Aleph* (fiction).

1950   Elected president of SADE, the Society of Argentine Writers, a focus of opposition to Perón.

1951   French edition of *Fictions*, first book to be translated into a foreign language.

1952   *Other Inquisitions* (essays). Death of Perón's wife, Eva. SADE closed down after Borges refuses to comply with official mourning decreed by Peronist authorities. In Paris, Roger Caillois publishes *Labyrinthes*, an anthology.

1954   Accident damages his congenitally weak eyesight and can no longer read or write.

1955   Perón overthrown in a military coup and goes into exile. Borges strongly supports the new junta in its campaign to root out Peronism from public life. Appointed Director of the National Library. Elected to the Argentine Academy of Letters. Jean-Paul Sartre publishes eight essays by Borges in *Les Temps modernes*. *La biblioteca di Babele*, a collection of his *ficciones*, appears in Italian.

1956   Appointed to a professorship of English and American Literature at the University of Buenos Aires. Receives honorary doctorate from the University of Cuyo, Mendoza, the first of many. Awarded the National Prize for Literature.

1957   *Manual de zoología fantástica* (sketches of fantastic animals), with Margarita Guerrero. *Book of Imaginary Beings* is an expanded version published in 1967. *Other Inquisitions* published in French as *Enquêtes*.

1960   *The Maker* (*El hacedor*) (prose and poems).

1961	Awarded International Publishers' Prize, jointly with Samuel Beckett.
1961–62	Semester at the University of Texas at Austin. Innumerable trips abroad henceforward until the end of his life. *Ficciones* (1962), first book into English.
1963	First lecture tour of Britain.
1964	*Obra poética 1923–1964* (new title for collected poems). Includes new poems in a section called *The Self and the Other (El otro el mismo)*, later published as separate volume in 1969.
1965	*For Six Strings* (lyrics for *milongas*).
1967	Marries Elsa Astete Millán. *Chronicles of Bustos Domecq* (spoof essays), with Bioy Casares.
1967–68	Nine months at Harvard as Charles Eliot Norton Professor of Poetry.
1969	*Brodie's Report* (fiction). *In Praise of Darkness* (poems).
1970	Legal separation from Elsa Astete.
1971	*The Congress* (novella), later included in *The Book of Sand*. Begins relationship with Japanese-Argentine María Kodama. Peronist guerrillas start campaign of bombings and kidnapping against the ruling military junta.
1972	*The Gold of the Tigers* (poems).
1973–74	Resigns as Director of National Library after a Peronist wins the presidency. Borges calls those who voted for him "six million idiots." In September Perón himself elected president but dies in office in July 1974 and succeeded by wife, María Estela. Guerrillas escalate violence in face of counter-terror by death squads.
1974	First edition of *Obras completas*.
1975	*The Book of Sand* (fiction). *The Unending Rose* (*La rosa profunda*) (poems). Mother dies at the age of ninety-nine. Returns to Geneva for the first time since 1923, and visits frequently thereafter.
1976	*The Iron Coin* (poems). María Estela Perón's government overthrown by military coup. Borges makes controversial statements in the media supporting the new Argentine junta as well as General Pinochet in Chile. Armed forces pursue a "Dirty War" against the guerrillas through torture and "disappearances" of opponents.
1977	*The History of the Night* (poems). *New Stories by Bustos Domecq* (fiction), with Bioy Casares.

1977–78   Borges criticizes Argentine military junta for nationalis-
           tic saber-rattling against Chile over islands in the Beagle
           Channel.

1979   *Borges oral* (lectures given at the Universidad de Belgrano).
           Dispute with sister and a nephew over joint bank account.
           María Kodama named his sole heir in new will.

1980   *Seven Nights* (lectures at Teatro Coliseo, Buenos Aires).
           "Shakespeare's Memory" (story) published in *Clarín* news-
           paper; subsequently the title story of a collection incorporated
           in *Obras completas*, 1989. Supports "Mothers of the Plaza
           de Mayo" and calls on junta to provide information on the
           "disappeared."

1981   *The Limit* (*La cifra*) (poems).

1982   *Nine Dantesque Essays on Dante* (five previously published
           in 1948, one in 1951). Argentine invasion of the Falkland
           Islands/Malvinas. Publishes poems regretting the ensuing
           war with Britain. Calls himself a pacifist and an "inoffensive
           anarchist."

1982–83   Fall of military junta. Denounces torture and "disappear-
           ances." Calls for investigation into crimes by both sides dur-
           ing the "Dirty War" and for punishment of military officers.
           Writes the poem "Los conjurados" ("The Confederates"),
           praising Swiss Confederation for enabling citizens to "forget
           their differences and accentuate their affinities," and claiming
           Geneva as "one of my *patrias*."

1983   *"August 25, 1983" and Other Stories* (fiction). Welcomes
           return of democracy. Celebrates election of Radical candidate
           Raúl Alfonsín as president.

1984   *Atlas* (travel pieces), with María Kodama.

1985   *Los Conjurados* (*The Confederates*), (poems and prose). In
           September diagnosed with cancer. In November secretly leaves
           Buenos Aires with María Kodama.

1986   Receives medical treatment in Geneva. Dispute with nephews
           and housekeeper over property and remuneration, respect-
           ively. In April marries María Kodama in Geneva, after obtain-
           ing divorce from Elsa Astete and marriage license by proxy in
           Paraguay, as divorce illegal in Argentina. Dies June 14. Buried
           in the Plainpalais cemetery in Geneva.

EDWIN WILLIAMSON

Introduction

Jorge Luis Borges was one of the great writers of the twentieth century and the most influential author in the Spanish language of modern times. He had a seminal influence on Latin American literature and a lasting impact on literary fiction in many other languages. Although a poet and essayist, he was best known for his *ficciones* – short stories or prose texts whose brevity condensed mental play into reverberating images and situations. Rejecting the constraints of psychological or social realism, Borges encouraged writers to accept fiction as a self-conscious artifact, susceptible to fantasy and to overtly intellectual, and even philosophical, concerns. Borges challenged the supremacy of the novel in the hierarchy of modern literature: he favored modes of storytelling which had long preceded the novel – fable, epic, parable, and folktale – as well as subgenres such as thrillers, science fiction, and detective stories. He also blurred generic categories by bringing book reviews, scholarly essays, and footnotes within the bounds of fiction. Even metaphysics and theology, he famously observed, could be regarded as branches of the literature of fantasy.

Borges's interest in metaphysics and literary ideas fostered the impression that his work belonged in a kind of literary utopia, divorced from personal experience or historical reality. This impression was underscored by the blindness which afflicted him a few years before he became famous, and which lent him the aura of an otherworldly, sightless bard. He was, however, no disembodied, bloodless intellectual, but rather a man riven by inner conflicts, including amorous and sexual conflicts, and far from living in an ivory tower, he was deeply imbued with a sense of history, and was indeed a leading public intellectual in Argentina for most of his literary career.

Borges was born at the height of Argentina's golden age, when the country was among the most prosperous in the world, but he was to witness its descent into appalling violence and economic failure. This may account for his erratic political allegiances in the course of his life. In his youth he was an enthusiastic advocate of liberal democracy and a progressive nationalist – indeed, he was among the earliest cultural nationalists in Latin America; in the 1930s he became a public critic of fascism in Argentina and Nazism in Europe, and supported the Allied struggle against Hitler during World War II; he opposed Juan Perón's authoritarian regime in the 1940s and 1950s, but as Peronism continued to dominate Argentine politics after its leader's overthrow in 1955, his unyielding anti-Peronism led him to adopt conservative and, for a while, anti-democratic positions, including support for the military juntas that ruled Argentina in the 1970s. This pro-military stance, aggravated in 1976 by unwise declarations in favor of General Pinochet's brutal regime in Chile, reputedly cost him the Nobel Prize. However, the Falklands/Malvinas war in 1982 and the consequent fall of the military junta were to bring about a change of heart. When the atrocities committed during the vicious "Dirty War" against Marxist guerrillas came to light in the media, Borges publicly denounced the "disappearances" and torture of opponents by the military regime and called for the punishment of the officers responsible for those crimes. He welcomed the return to democracy in 1983, and in his last years described himself as a pacifist and an "inoffensive anarchist" who hoped for the eventual disappearance of the state and of frontiers between states.

Borges's international reputation still rests largely on three collections – *Fictions* (1944), *The Aleph* (1949), and *The Maker* (1960) – together with a book of critical essays, *Other Inquisitions* (1952). In other words, his best-known work dates from the 1940s and 1950s. The work from the mid 1960s, both in fiction and in poetry, still remains comparatively neglected and undervalued. His writing before the mid 1930s has received even less attention. This was largely due to the fact that he preferred to play down, if not disown altogether, this phase of his career. He revised the texts of the three poetry collections of the 1920s for the publication of his collected poems in Spanish in 1943, purging them of local color and even omitting a good number altogether, and he kept on changing them in successive editions of the *Obras completas* until these early books became all but unrecognizable in relation to the originals of the 1920s. As for the three books of essays which he published in that decade, he opted for total suppression, steadfastly refusing to have them reprinted in his lifetime. To add to the confusion, he had a habit of appending additional texts to later editions of his books, texts which had often been written years before, or indeed after, those books had first been published.

The reception of his work has been affected by the vagaries of publication and translation. For many years, the *Obras completas* that the Argentine publishing house Emecé had published in successively expanding editions since 1974, omitted the original texts of the work of the 1920s, giving only the later revised versions. Things began to improve when, in the early 1990s, the three collections of essays of the 1920s (but not the three original collections of poetry) were reprinted, and in the last couple of decades most of Borges's articles and reviews for magazines and newspapers have begun to be collected and published under various imprints. In English, except for an early edition of *Ficciones* and *El hacedor* (translated as *Dreamtigers*), Borges is accessible only through a number of anthologies put together from more or less random selections of his work, largely from the middle period, although Penguin's *Collected Fictions* does contain the volumes of his stories in the form and sequence in which they were originally published in Spanish. The situation with regard to French is much better thanks to Gallimard's two-volume Pléiade edition, which offers most of the books in the chronological order of their original publication.

Given the patchy availability of Borges's output, there has been little sense until recently of the evolution and range of his writing. Criticism, scholarship, and commentary have tended to concentrate on the middle period, an emphasis which has produced a somewhat restricted and arguably distorted view of Borges: it is still difficult to see him whole. The primary aim of this *Companion*, therefore, is to provide a more comprehensive account of Borges's *œuvre* than has generally been available so far. Thus, in addition to critical assessments of the "canonical" volumes of the middle years (1935-60), there are chapters that deal with the poetry of his youth and with the later poetry and fiction. Another aim of this *Companion* is to reflect the extraordinary diversity of his writing. The first chapter, by Clive Griffin, discusses his strikingly innovative use of philosophical ideas. Some of these stories, as Floyd Merrell shows in Chapter 2, are remarkable for the ways in which their inventive treatment of philosophical issues suggest scientific or mathematical ideas. In Chapter 3, Michael Wood discusses how French poststructuralist theorists and critics found in Borges's fictions and essays an anticipation of some of their key concerns. Suzanne Jill Levine writes in Chapter 4 about his revolutionary impact on contemporary translation theory. There follow two chapters which focus on Borges's idiosyncratic incorporation of theological concepts and religious symbols in his writing. Evelyn Fishburn deals with the Jewish, Christian, and Gnostic themes that recur in his work, studying their subversive and countercultural intent, and the way in which they are used to convey the mysterious character of the universe. Luce López-Baralt demonstrates his extensive knowledge and subtle use of Islamic culture. In Chapter 7 Philip Swanson sheds light on his interest in popular culture, ranging from the hoodlums of old Buenos Aires to the movies of Hollywood's heyday. In Chapter 8 Robin Fiddian considers his work in the light of post-colonial theory, given his peripheral relation as an Argentine to the dominant cultures of Europe and North America.

The following chapters discuss the main collections of stories. Daniel Balderston analyzes the intellectually dazzling ways the great stories collected in *Fictions* play on the relations between fiction and non-fiction. Roberto González Echevarría approaches *The Aleph* as a "kaleidoscope" of Borges's major themes, stressing the underlying coherence of this collection, rooted as it is in a stance of stoical courage and ironic humor. Alfred MacAdam shows how the miscellaneous prose vignettes and poems of *The Maker* revolve around questions about writing and the self. Arturo Echavarría reveals the sophistication underlying the more direct, "realistic" style of *Brodie's Report*, a collection which represents a critique of Argentine society. Efraín Kristal questions whether the stories of *The Book of Sand* and *Shakespeare's Memory* show evidence of declining powers, and makes a case for their being regarded as his most accomplished and emotionally intense works of fiction. The next two chapters concentrate on the poetry, which is still not sufficiently well known or appreciated either in the Spanish-speaking world or beyond. Rafael Olea Franco shows the young poet in the 1920s selectively adapting avant-garde techniques in his search for a specifically Argentine voice. After 1929, Borges virtually gave up poetry but returned to it in the late 1950s and wrote prolifically until the end of his days. In Chapter 15 Jason Wilson brings out the predominant concerns of this large, heterogeneous body of later poems. The final chapter argues that Borges's writing, and its evolution, were influenced by personal circumstances.

The critical views represented in this *Companion* may at times conflict with one another, but these disagreements testify to the continuing vitality of Borges studies, for the Argentine master has lost none of the power to fascinate and provoke his readers that marked his career as a writer.

I

CLIVE GRIFFIN

Philosophy and fiction

Borges was not a philosopher, and never considered himself to be one. His father was particularly interested in metaphysics and introduced the young Borges to the basic tenets of idealism, as well as to Zeno the Eleatic's paradoxes (see p. 13 below). As a youth in Switzerland Borges learned German and, after finding Kant intractable, read for the first time the philosopher whom he would come to regard above all others, Schopenhauer.[1] He subsequently read, or read about, many major thinkers, claiming in later life that there was a good deal in their writings that he did not understand and describing himself, in "A New Refutation of Time," as "an Argentine adrift on a sea of metaphysics" (*SNF* 317). Largely self-taught, he acquired a broad knowledge of philosophy from general guides, such as Lewes's *Biographical History of Philosophy*, Mauthner's *Wörterbuch der Philosophie* (*Dictionary of Philosophy*), and Russell's *History of Western Philosophy*, from reading works of the philosophers themselves, and from discussions with his father's friend Macedonio Fernández.[2] Nevertheless, he returned time and again to the same thinkers – Heraclitus, Zeno, Plato, Spinoza, Berkeley, Hume, Schopenhauer, and Nietzsche – and to the same, predominantly metaphysical, problems: substance (matter or reality), time, identity, the limits of human understanding, language, infinity, eternity, death, causality, determinism and chance, and the question of design in the universe, as well as to mathematical and theological questions (he was particularly interested in Buddhism and in Swedenborg's mysticism). He published a number of essays on philosophical issues, the longest and best known being "A New Refutation of Time," and he planned a book on Spinoza which he never wrote.[3]

His enquiries into metaphysics were quirky, and he invariably treated philosophers, and the systems they proposed, with irony. Indeed, the humor that characterizes much of his writing reflects his agnosticism and skepticism; he is especially ironic about his own enquiries. In "A New Refutation of Time," for

I thank my colleague Mike Inwood for his helpful suggestions about this chapter.

5

instance, he builds upon the arguments of the British empiricists Berkeley and Hume to question the objective existence of the material world, the self, and the continuum of time. Yet he teasingly states from the outset that, as this is his second version of the essay in which he questions time, it therefore presupposes it, for without time there could not be an earlier or a later version. He ends this essay recognizing his failure to achieve his aims: "To deny temporal succession, to deny the self, to deny the astronomical universe, appear to be acts of desperation and are secret consolations … Time is a river that sweeps me along … The world, unfortunately, is real; I, unfortunately, am Borges" (*SNF* 332).

He included philosophical meditations, notably "The Nothingness of Personality" and "Berkeley's Crossroads," in his first book of essays, *Inquisitions*, which appeared in 1925, several years before he published any fiction. Nevertheless, philosophy for him was not a question of personal belief. He famously admitted that he tended to be "interested in religious or philosophical ideas for their aesthetic value and even for their strange and marvelous elements," and had some of his invented philosophers treat metaphysics as "a branch of the literature of fantasy."[4] Rather than using his stories as vehicles for philosophical ideas, he often used those ideas as the starting point for fiction, and the literary use he made of them is more important than the ideas themselves.

It was principally Berkeley, Hume, and Schopenhauer whom Borges referred to when discussing the idealism that was so important for his imaginative writing, and they stimulated his interest in three questions: substance, identity (or self), and time. As early as 1923, in his poem "Break of Day," from the collection *Fervor de Buenos Aires*, he wrote:

> Curious about the shadows
> and daunted by the threat of dawn,
> I recalled the dreadful conjecture
> of Schopenhauer and Berkeley
> which declares that the world
> is a mental activity,
> a dream of souls,
> without foundation, purpose, weight or shape. (*SP* 23)

The speculation that the material world does not exist outside the mind of the perceiver (solipsism) underlies many of his stories. In "The Shape of the Sword" John Vincent Moon misleads the narrator and the reader by maintaining that he was the victim of treachery when, it transpires, Moon himself was the traitor. He is a liar: the story he tells does not reflect any reality outside his own mind, and so it should come as no surprise to learn that the farm on which the events of his story take place is owned by a fellow Irishman called Berkeley (the philosopher George Berkeley was Bishop of Cloyne, in County Cork, Ireland). In "Averroës' Search" Borges tries to conjure up the medieval Arab philosopher Averroës, but is aware that this Averroës is merely a shallow product of his mind and so, when he ceases to imagine him, Averroës simply disappears. Even though Borges's characters may think that they are real, they can turn out to be the figment of others' imaginations. For example, the magus of "The Circular Ruins" dreams into existence a son, hoping to conceal from this invented offspring his invulnerability to fire, which would alert him to his fictiveness. However, when a fire breaks out, the magus discovers that he, too, is invulnerable and must also be the product of somebody else's dream.

Dream and reality can merge in Borges's stories, so that any notion of an objective reality outside the mind is questioned. This is what happens in "The Wait" where the character who adopts the name Villari incorporates his pursuers into his dream. In a more enigmatic tale, "The South," we are never certain whether Juan Dahlmann dies in the gaucho knife fight that, as a second-generation immigrant, he conceives as being a truly Argentine death or whether such an end was the effect of hallucination as he lay dying in an operating theatre in Buenos Aires.

Borges thus finds it intriguing (if not convincing) to question the objective existence of things, and this is important not only for his own imaginative writing but also for his ideas about literature. If the world exists only in our minds, then mimetic realism is based upon a false premise. This provides him with a philosophical underpinning for his predilection for fantasy and for the rejection of realism in most of his fiction; it is not for nothing that he entitled his major collection *Fictions* and one section of it *Artifices*. It could even be argued that literature is intrinsically idealist: writers of fiction use words to convey something conjured up in their imaginations and, when we read those words, we in turn create from them events and characters which have no real substance. Writing and reading fiction is philosophical idealism put into practice. Indeed, Borges's particular emphasis on the role of the reader in shaping the meanings of texts parallels idealist thought. In the prologue to one of his collections of poetry he writes:

> This preface might be termed the aesthetics of Berkeley, not because the Irish metaphysician … actually ever professed it, but because it applies to literature the same argument Berkeley applied to the outer world. The taste of the apple (states Berkeley) lies in the contact of the fruit with the palate, not in the fruit itself; in a similar way (I would say), poetry lies in the meeting of poem and reader, not in the lines of symbols printed on the pages of a book.[5]

In his earliest essays, such as "The Nothingness of Personality" (*SNF* 3–9), Borges challenged the notion of the self, and a continuing desire to do so runs through much of his writing. His argument starts from Berkeley and leads on to Hume's more radical conclusion: if, as Berkeley maintained, the world exists only insofar as it is perceived, then the mind exists only as a series of successive acts of perception. This casts doubt upon any continuum of identity we could call the "self" lying behind those momentary and shifting perceptions, and has direct consequences for Borges's fiction. He is skeptical of psychology – in particular that of Freud – which he associates with the nineteenth century and realist novels: if the very notion of identity is unfounded, then psychology is an empty study.

Such an argument provides a philosophical basis for Borges's stated antipathy toward psychological portraits in literature and the scarcity of credible individuals among Borges's own characters. This antipathy can be seen in several ways in his stories. First, Hume's argument that we are merely a series of perceptions is illustrated by the Mayan priest Tzinacán of "The Writing of the God," who is depicted as clusters of apparently random perceptions when he undergoes a mystical experience. Second, while authors often use names to characterize or particularize their creatures, many of Borges's figures share the same ones: for example, Otálora in "The Dead Man" and Otárola in "Ulrikke"; Nolan from "The Other Duel" and "The Theme of the Traitor and the Hero"; Runeberg in "Three Versions of Judas" and "The Garden of Forking Paths." Third, he sometimes leaves his characters' names vague: the brutish brothers of "The Interloper" are the Nelsons or the Nilsens; the narrator of the story "The Encounter" cannot remember whether one of the characters is called Acevedo or Acébal; the "real" name of the corrupt British official in "The Man on the Threshold" is kept from us, the narrator choosing to refer to him as David Alexander Glencairn because the names David and Alexander are symbolic of ruthless rulers. Fourth, some characters exist only insofar as they are doubles or rivals of somebody else rather than having any being in their own right. Although the two enemies in "The Theologians" believe that the theological opinions which characterized them are so different that one has the other burnt as a heretic, God is unable to distinguish between them. Finally, the archetypical nature of many of Borges's characters is all of a piece with his questioning of identity, as well as recalling his interest in Platonic archetypes. Baltasar Espinosa, of "The Gospel according to Mark," is not only "a Buenos Aires youth like so many others" (CF 397), but a reincarnation of one example of the self-sacrificing god, Jesus, whose fate we are led to believe Espinosa will share. Perhaps the most striking example of his portrayal of characters as archetypes is to be found in the stories "The South" and "The Man on the Threshold" where Borges uses exactly the same words to describe two old men, one an archetypical gaucho and the other an archetypical Indian. He draws our attention to this by emphasizing in both cases that his description is "essential" in the sense both of important and describing an essence. His speculations on pantheism, reflecting his reading of Spinoza and Schopenhauer, lead to a further dissolution of identity as he suggests that all men are one man, and one man all men.

Again, philosophical speculation not only underlies Borges's own practice, but also his more general theories about literature. His questioning of self parallels a downplaying of the importance of authors and their lives, stressing from his *ultraísta* period onward how unimportant are the innovations introduced by any one author and how much literature owes to tradition. He concentrates instead on texts and how they are read. So in "Pierre Menard, Author of the *Quixote*," emphasis is once more laid on the reader's role in forging meaning in a text.

Of all the metaphysical questions that absorbed Borges, the most important for him was time. He frequently refers to Heraclitus when invoking the inexorability of change, and he quotes the Greek philosopher's image likening time to a flowing river into which no person can step twice because that river is constantly transformed (Borges notes that so is the bather). However, speculation that questions the lethal onrush of time mitigates its horror for Borges. Building upon idealism, he suggests that time, like substance and identity, is subjective. In "The Secret Miracle," the Czech writer Jaromir Hladík is condemned to death. As he counts the days left him before his execution, he unsurprisingly shares his author's desire – and for both this is emotional as much as intellectual – to deny the successive nature of time. His conjectures, based as they are on wishful thinking, are those that Borges would discuss at greater length in his essay "A New Refutation of Time," but the story is principally an illustration of the subjective nature of time. As Hladík faces the firing squad and the order to shoot him is given, time freezes for a whole year during which he finishes the mental composition of a play. At the moment that he finds the final epithet, time unfreezes and the bullets kill him. The year's grace has passed in his mind only. Borges's original epigraph to this tale was: "The story is well known of the monk who, going out into the wood to meditate, was detained there by the song of a bird for 300 years, which to his consciousness passed in only one hour."[6]

A somewhat similar idea is posited in a footnote which appears in the story "Tlön, Uqbar, Orbis Tertius": the hypothesis borrowed from (and rejected by) Russell that the world sprang into being five minutes ago, peopled by those who "remembered" a wholly unreal past (*CF* 74). This, yet again, parallels the process of writing and reading literature. Writers create characters and, when they do so, they invent a fictitious past for them. The events recounted in a story may cover hours, days, weeks, or years, but that period is often reconstructed in the reader's mind in only a few minutes.

A consequence of the notion of subjective time is the suggestion that it exists only in the present, the past consisting of present memories and the future of present hopes or fears. Borges investigates this in his story "The Other Death," which alludes to the thesis propounded by the medieval theologian Pier Damiani that, as God is omnipotent, he can make what once existed never to have been. Borges playfully suggests that if the past is constituted solely of memories, then it changes as those memories change. His character Pedro Damián, an Argentine farm laborer, broods all his life on his youthful cowardice during the heat of battle. Borges hypothesizes that in old age Damián managed to change his shameful past: the only surviving witnesses of that battle forget his cowardice and later recall his heroic death leading a charge as a young soldier.

Not all of Borges's meditations on time have their roots in idealism, but they invariably challenge successive time. In his "The Garden of Forking Paths" the English sinologist Stephen Albert suggests that the Chinese author Ts'ui Pên "did not believe in a uniform and absolute time: he believed in an infinite series of times, a growing, dizzying web of divergent, convergent and parallel times" (*CF* 127). Yet Borges ironizes this speculation by placing it in a story the plot of which is rigidly linear. In "The Theme of the Traitor and the Hero" and "The Plot," on the other hand, there is a suggestion that time may be cyclical as the Pythagoreans and, later, Nietzsche postulated.

The hypothesis that time is circular again has repercussions not only for Borges's own practice but also for his ideas about literature. He suggests that authors do not invent new stories but recycle old ones, and that there is no sense of progress in literature. As for idealist time, his substitution of linear by subjective time parallels his suggestion that it matters less when works were written than the order in which we read them. A further consequence of his questioning of successive time is that as, according to one hypothesis, the past exists only as it is perceived in the present, he can subvert our usual assumption that past writers influence their successors and claim instead, as he does in "Kafka and His Precursors," that writers create their own precursors in the present.

Borges's fascination with idealism is central to one of his longest stories, "Tlön, Uqbar, Orbis Tertius." It is a "what if?" think-piece: if the idealists' speculations really were true, what would a world based upon them be like? It is an imaginary place written into existence by a secret society of such philosophers, an early member of which was Berkeley. The project grows over the generations thanks to the munificence of Berkeley's near namesake, one Buckley, an American millionaire. The story begins with a mirror and an entry in a rogue copy of an encyclopedia, both idealist images: the mirror because what we see in mirrors has no substance but is a just a product of our perception, and the encyclopedia because, rather than a work which describes something real, this rogue encyclopedia invents a fictional region called Uqbar. Borges has much pseudo-philosophical fun summarizing this entry and the volume of a subsequent encyclopedia that describes a whole invented planet called Tlön. We are given a synopsis of thought on Tlön, its languages, its heresies, the refutation of those heresies, its mathematics, its literature, and so on. We learn that objects there depend upon being perceived so, in a *reductio ad absurdum* of idealism, an amphitheater exists only because some birds or a horse visit it. The southern languages of Tlön contain no nouns because this is a radically anti-materialist world. Things there have no objective existence, but can, somewhat illogically, be manufactured by being imagined. There is no causality on Tlön because separate perceptions cannot be linked in time; thus a smoldering cigarette, a bush fire, and smoke are not related causally, any connection between them being considered merely an association of ideas. The philosophers of Tlön invent paradoxes in the style of Zeno in which, playing Devil's advocate, they conjecture that things really do exist independently of the mind, and then find sophisticated arguments to disprove such an outlandish heresy. Borges's humorous account of the Tlönian philosophers logic-chopping in an attempt to prove what appears to them as common sense gives us pause as we are invited to question the assumptions we, in turn, make about our own world. In Tlön, as there is nothing outside the perceiving mind, psychology lies at the heart of its culture. This is an interest not in individual psychology but in the idea that mind is all there is, and the mind in Tlön is just clusters of perceptions. Indeed, one school of Tlönian thought postulates that everybody is really the same single mind. The absence of self on the planet has various repercussions; for example, in the planet's languages the only verbs used are impersonal ones. There is a range of opinion on Tlön about time: for some Tlönian schools of thought time exists, predictably enough, only in the mind and exclusively in the present. "Tlön, Uqbar, Orbis Tertius," then, provides a test bed for idealist philosophy, humorously showing how different from our world is a world based on a philosophy that purports to describe ours.

I maintained at the beginning of this chapter that Borges drew upon philosophy as a springboard for his fiction. "Tlön, Uqbar, Orbis Tertius" opens with a first-person narrator in a reassuring world of real places and real people, many of whom were Borges's own friends, and it is to that world that the reader is returned after the account of Tlön, to be informed in a postscript of the fictional origins of the imaginary planet. If the story had ended at that point we would be left with a neatly rounded tale which took us from the real Buenos Aires, to an invented land, and back again. However, the postscript subverts that structure and is far from reassuring.

Borges published "Tlön, Uqbar, Orbis Tertius" in May 1940, as Hitler began his western offensive. Borges's postscript, futuristically dated 1947, predicts how the world would have changed by then: it is a terrifying place in which the imaginary planet of Tlön, which seemed to have no existence outside the pages of an invented encyclopedia, invades reality: people die in agony, and all our languages, history, and methods of intellectual inquiry based on materialism disappear, as Tlön with its one big idea takes over. Reality gives way; "the truth is, it wanted to cave in. Ten years ago [i.e. 1937], any symmetry, any system with an appearance of order – dialectical materialism, anti-Semitism, Nazism – could spellbind and hypnotize mankind. How could the world not fall under the sway of Tlön, how could it not yield to the vast and minutely detailed evidence of an ordered planet?" (CF 81).

Borges implies that we constantly search for explanations because we are uncomfortable with the messy unknowability of the world. In the 1930s he saw the rise of seductively simple political philosophies. They were, of course, man-made and therefore, like Tlön which is also the product of human intelligence, they were neat and rendered the world comprehensible. That was their fatal attraction. In the face of totalitarian ideologies, like that of Tlön, of Nazism, and of communism which subordinate the individual to the masses, the first-person narrator in the story resists by reasserting an identity which had been progressively eclipsed in the story. He celebrates doubt – the essence of intelligence for Borges – and different languages, with all their unsatisfactory, untidy idiosyncrasies: "As for me, I pay no attention to all this; during quiet days in my hotel in Adrogué, I go on revising (though I never intend to publish it) a hesitant translation in the style of Quevedo of Sir Thomas Browne's *Urn Burial*" (my translation; see also CF 81). This is his way of keeping totalitarian barbarians at bay.

Not all the philosophical themes in Borges's stories are metaphysical. Sometimes, he parodies bad argument; at others he dramatizes problems of argumentation. In "Death and the Compass," the detective Erik Lönnrot attempts to solve a murder. On examining the victim's room, he happens upon a potential piece of evidence and decides that it holds the key to the crime. It turns out that, although his sleuthing is from then on impeccable, he is wrong. Caught in a trap that Red Scharlach, the criminal, has laid for him and about to be murdered in his turn, he arrogantly suggests that the trap could have been more elegantly devised:

> There are three lines too many in your labyrinth ... I know of a Greek labyrinth that is but one straight line. So many philosophers have been lost upon that line that a mere detective might be pardoned if he became lost as well. When you hunt me down in another avatar of our lives, Scharlach, I suggest

that you fake (or commit) one crime at A, a second crime at B, eight kilometres from A, then a third crime at C, four kilometres from A and B and halfway between them. Then wait for me at D, two kilometres from A and C, once again halfway between them. Kill me at D. (*CF* 156)

This "Greek labyrinth" is not a physical but an intellectual one; it alludes to Zeno's dichotomy paradox which denies the possibility of motion. As Borges explained it in "Kafka and His Precursors": "A moving body at point A … will not be able to reach point B, because it must first cover half the distance between the two, and before that, half of the half, and before that, half of the half of the half, and so on to infinity" (*SNF* 363). The paradox lies in our knowing that this defies common sense, yet the premise on which it is based makes it difficult to disprove. Although Borges's stories are not parables from which an unequivocal message can be deduced, any more than the famous metaphors he uses in them – labyrinths, mirrors, libraries – are symbols that can readily be deciphered, in "Death and the Compass" it is Lönnrot's erroneous premise at the beginning of his investigation that determines its development and its fatal outcome. But how can a detective begin to investigate a crime, or a philosopher a problem, without starting from a premise, without treating some pieces of evidence as irrelevant and others not? The opposite situation is to be found in "Funes, His Memory," where Funes accumulates facts and impressions without prioritizing or categorizing any of them. As the narrator points out, Funes cannot abstract, cannot see the wood for the trees, and he is therefore incapable of thought. Borges offers no solution to the argumentative bind evoked in these two stories, but merely presents it. This parallels his recourse elsewhere to paradox as a response to insoluble intellectual problems.

In his "A New Refutation of Time" Borges stated, "I do not exaggerate the importance of these verbal games" (my translation; see also *SNF* 318), but he does not always treat philosophy so lightly. In the immediate aftermath of the Second World War he published his chilling tale "*Deutsches Requiem*." The narrator is Otto Dietrich zur Linde, a member of a German military dynasty who explains, on the eve of his execution by the victorious Allies, how he came to run a Nazi concentration camp where he tortured and executed Jewish prisoners. He presents himself as a sensitive and cultured nationalist who found spiritual refuge in music, literature, and metaphysics, although, as often with Borges's first-person narrators, we become aware that he is deceiving himself as well as us. Zur Linde's interest in Schopenhauer led him to abandon Christianity, and when he read Nietzsche – or at least the Nietzsche of the Nazis – he not only made some of that philosopher's views his own, but acted upon them, cultivating ruthlessness. His account is shot through with the language used by Schopenhauer, Nietzsche, and Spengler, and with his selective understanding of their writings which, like a religious zealot, he applies uncritically to his own life. For example, he maintains that everything we do and experience is preordained and willed by us; he considers himself a superman; his attitudes are those of a warrior caste, and he learns to exalt war and violence; he admires strength of will above all else, despising and overcoming the weakness of compassion which he claims was natural to his character and which Nietzsche had identified with a "slave mentality"; and, perversely, he exults in the destruction of what he holds most dear: Germany. He finds justification for this in an apocalyptic vision, partly absorbed from Nietzsche and Spengler, in which violence and destruction are to be welcomed because a new order will arise from the ashes.

Borges paints a disturbingly human portrait of a man who claims that his philosophical beliefs are at odds with his nature, but who nevertheless convinces himself of their truth and so persuades himself to embrace Nazism and the opportunity to act monstrously. We appreciate, as he does not, that a combination of that ideology and his personal inadequacy – his fear of cowardice, his intellectual rather than militaristic bent, the loss of a limb which prevented him from soldiering as his forebears had done, and in particular his suggested sexual impotence – lie behind zur Linde's cruelty, and that he is the victim of his own convictions. In this story Borges tries to understand how a country he himself loved succumbed to an ideology he despised. A lesson emerges from it: philosophy is intellectually engaging, but it is perilous when read unintelligently; that is, without appropriate detachment, for the reader may then come to believe in its conclusions and even act upon them. After the horrors of the War and as news of the Nazi concentration camps reaches him, Borges's advocacy of skepticism is urgent. This least didactic and most metaphysical of writers adopts an ethical stance.

Borges's engagement with philosophy lies at the heart of the "fiction" (ficción), the genre he develops which lies somewhere between the essay and the story, and which has a close affinity to the eighteenth-century French *conte philosophique*. The influence of philosophy can be detected in the weft and warp of his stories: in their imagery and metaphor, their structure, their narrators, their characters, and even their language. Despite his skepticism toward the ideas he uses as the mainspring of many of his stories, the reader senses that those ideas did not just induce an aesthetic thrill in him, and that the systems of philosophy he investigated did not merely provide him with examples of fun and fantasy. When proposing his implausible theory that the seemingly chaotic world he inhabits may, just possibly, be ordered, the desperate narrator of "The Library of Babel" says, "my solitude is cheered by that elegant hope" (*CF* 118). Borges may not be convinced by the philosophical speculations that intrigue him, and he may caution against their danger, but they do appear to afford him solace.

NOTES

1 "An Autobiographical Essay," in *The Aleph and Other Stories 1933–1969*, ed. and trans. Norman Thomas di Giovanni in collaboration with the author, New York, Dutton, 1970, 215–17.
2 "An Autobiographical Essay," 227–30.
3 J. L. Borges and O. Ferrari, *Diálogos últimos*, Buenos Aires, Sudamericana, 1987, 59.
4 "Epílogo," in *Otras Inquisiciones* (OC II 153), and "Tlön, Uqbar, Orbis Tertius" (*CF* 74).
5 *Selected Poems 1923–1967*, ed. with an introduction and notes by Norman Thomas di Giovanni, Harmondsworth, Penguin, 1985, 294.
6 "El milagro secreto," *Sur*, 101 (1943), 13–20 (13).

2

FLOYD MERRELL

Science and mathematics in a literary mode

Although Jorge Luis Borges occasionally expressed his ignorance regarding matters of physics and the sciences in general, mathematics was one of his lifelong passions.[1] He considered it a branch of fantastic literature. Indeed, one might speculate that "reality," in light of quantum theory and relativity, has also become a branch of fantastic literature, for it is not merely stranger than we think, but stranger than we are capable of thinking.

There are two perennially conflicting doctrines common to both mathematics and the sciences, and they have a bearing on many of Borges's tales: *realism* and *nominalism*. Briefly, one brand of *realism* involves the effort to know the objective world as it *is*. According to this interpretation, objects (and names and abstract concepts accounting for them) exist in "reality," independently of our knowing them. *Nominalism*, in contrast, tells us that things have no "thingness." The particulars of our world, which we see, name, and talk about as if they belonged to a general class of "things," have no "real" existence outside our talk – I can talk about a particular human, but the general term "humanity," as the class of all humans, has no "real" existence.

What *is*, and what *isn't*?

Borges's Funes, of "Funes, His Memory," is an inveterate *hyper-nominalist*, for whom every perceptual grasp and acknowledgment of every aspect of his world are committed to memory in all their particulars, and for whom at every moment what he perceives is fresh, spontaneous, and new. If he sees a "dog" from the front, and later sees the same "dog" from behind, it is for him a completely different "dog"; the idea of diverse mental grasps of this particular "dog" placed in a pigeon-hole labeled the "general category dog" would be for him impossible. Each instantiation of everything "out there" is for Funes what *is*, for the moment, and then in another moment it is something else. Funes's problem is that he can forget nothing; hence he can't think, for to think is to abstract, to forget almost everything in order to focus on some things as generalities – "dogs," "trees," "houses," and so on – that have relatively fixed identity over time. In other words, *realism* remains beyond Funes's comprehension.

We have those inhabitants of Borges's imaginary planet Tlön, in "Tlön, Uqbar, Orbius Tertius." If for Funes everything that *is* for the moment *is* what it *is*, for the Tlönians, inveterate *hyper-nominalistic idealists*, everything *is* according to the figment of their imagination. They are capable of mentally conjuring up bits and pieces of their world wherever and whenever they so desire, in contrast to Funes, whose world is "out there," ready and waiting for his perceiving it. But alas, each and every individual Tlönian is destined to live in her/his own world: they are helpless and hopeless *solipsists*.

And then there is the fanciful object in "The Zahir," which, as a serial signifier, is capable of linking up with all the items of the world in one-to-one fashion. The Zahir is a small coin the protagonist received as change in a bar, and it can signify now a "chair," now a "book," now a "house," and, through time, virtually anything and everything. The Zahir evokes a name for whatever there *is*, right here and now in *nominalist* fashion. The problem is that the Zahir's owner can use his remarkable tool to name the objects of his "reality," but there is no conceivable end of the task, for that "reality" is too rich, given its myriad particulars.

In sum, we have: (1) a *nominalist* for whom what you see "out there" is what you get, for the moment, (2) *nominalists* for whom what is "out there" is what you want to make it, and (3) a *nominalist* instrument with which to arbitrarily assign names to particular objects. So much for Borges as *nominalist*. Now for his *realist* side.

What *is* just as it *is*, in spite of what we want to think of it?

"Death and the Compass" tells us about Lönnrot, a *hyper-logical realist* detective out to catch Scharlach, the criminal and assassin, in a trap of the detective's own making by forcing "reality" into his logically sublime, symmetrically precise, rationally clear and distinct conceptual scheme. He assumes that his conceptual scheme, which he believes patterns the objectively "real" world, is foolproof.

Thus, a third homicide, by the assassin's own declaration in a note he left, is supposed to be the last; but Lönnrot reasons that the number four is more symmetrical than three, so he opts for a fourth homicide. The first three murders were separated by 31 days (3 + 1 = 4), and so also must be the fourth murder; the first three were equidistant in space on the city map, and so also must be the fourth, in order to yield a rhombus. He pinpoints the time and the place of the fourth homicide, and goes there to catch his antagonist. But Lönnrot fails miserably, because he is by no means objectively omniscient; he is in fact all too human, and a fallible human at that. Scharlach beats him at his own game by setting a trap for Lönnrot, who ironically becomes Scharlach's fourth victim. Lönnrot's conceptual scheme turned out to be false to itself.

Borges's enterprising *realist* "Emma Zunz" nurtures none of Lönnrot's totalistic dreams. As a *realist*, she is supremely pragmatic. She reconstructs her "reality" to suit her purposes. She wants to avenge her father's death which was due in large part to his boss's exploitative and repressing ways. So she loses her virginity to a sailor and later shoots her father's boss, telling the police he raped her and she was only defending herself. Emma's "reality" is painfully "real," for sure, but unlike Lönnrot, she constructs no grandiose conceptual scheme in her relations with her antagonist. Rather, she uses her world as best she knows how; she conforms to it, and she rebels against its injustices in order to attain her goal.

Realism, as embodied in descriptions, loses patience with mere words as "names" of things. It pays homage to "texts," that hopefully mirror "reality." And just as "reality" becomes perceived and conceived differently through the years, so also do "texts." Take the case of "Pierre Menard, Author of the *Quixote*." After a few miscarriages, Menard succeeds in reduplicating a few paragraphs of Cervantes's celebrated novel without having read it: he writes it by somehow bringing his mind in tune with that of Cervantes. And how do the literary critics take his text? *Intertextually*, relating it with the times and texts from Cervantes's day to the present. They marvel at how Menard's enriched text bears allusions to works by Bertrand Russell, William James, and others, while Cervantes's relatively impoverished novel does no more than make reference to early seventeenth-century Spain. Nevertheless, even though Menard was somewhat unfamiliar with Cervantes's milieu and his writings, they influenced him, and even though Cervantes knew nothing of Menard's milieu, it influenced the interpretations of Menard's faithful reiteration of Cervantes. The message? *Realists'* perception and conceptualization of texts and *reality* change, and so also does *reality* itself.

Then there is that medieval Islamic philosopher, Averroës, of "Averroës' Search." He is caught in a bind, incapable of coming up with a viable translation of "tragedy" and "comedy" in Aristotle's *Poetics*, because in his culture, theatres, tragedies, and comedies are non-existent. After a number of hits and misses, he finally arrives at what he thinks is a comfortable solution. Then, as he prepares to retire for the night, he catches a peek of himself in his mirror, and his entire physical world, including himself, disappears, dissolving into the vast sea of "reality." His world vanished, because it had merged with Aristotle's "reality," and Aristotle's world had merged with his; Averroës was no longer who he was, nor was Aristotle who he had been. Borges intercedes at the end of his story with a confession:

> I felt that Averroës, trying to imagine what a play is without ever having suspected what a theater is, was no more absurd than I, trying to imagine Averroës ... I felt ... that my story was a symbol of the man I had been as I was writing it, and that in order to write that story I had had to be that man, and that in order to be that man I had had to write that story, and so on, *ad infinitum*. (CF 241)

We have, then, dreams of *reality* as: (1) the imposition of the subject's grandiose construct, (2) pragmatic manipulation of what there is at hand, (3) the sheer product of "textuality," and (4) translation by way of a fusion of minds and cultural worlds.

Nominalism's failure has over the centuries been *realism*'s hope, and vice versa. All to no avail, Borges seems to suggest. And now, finally, what does all this have to do with mathematics and physics?

Everything is here, working like a clock

Nominalism and *realism* have their counterparts in both mathematics and physics. Funes's teeming world, and the myriad collection of particulars with which the Zahir establishes links, make up a *nominalist* physical "reality," or, mathematically speaking, a "reality" empirically grounded in numbers and their interrelations as experienced by the mathematicians. This branch of philosophy of mathematics lends itself quite comfortably to scientific "empiricism." Physics talks about "electrons" to explain how light bulbs work, so "electrons" are a name for something empirically unseeable used for describing what physicists can see; since physicists use numbers to demonstrate how "electrons" work when they make light bulbs work, so also numbers are handy for describing what physics can't directly see but can write about. Cryptically put, what you experience, and how you describe it, is what there is.

Funes and the Zahir tell us something important about *empiricism* and *nominalism*, whether in mathematics or in physics; yet both are severely limited. The Tlönians experience and talk about their experienced "reality," equally in *nominalist* fashion. But it's all in their mind. Their "subjective idealism" allows each one of them to create the "reality" s/he wants, which should imply that everything can be fine and dandy. But it isn't. The Tlönians, in their own way, are as limited as Funes and the "reality" the Zahir indicates. Indeed, the two hemispheres of the planet Tlön have no nouns in their language, thus there are no genuine objects, only happenings, and "reality" is not spatial, but successive, through time. In one hemisphere, instead of the noun "moon," the Tlönians would use a verb which might be translated into English as "to moon." Thus, for "The moon rose above the river," they would say "Upward, behind the onstreaming it mooned" (*CF* 73). In the other hemisphere, they have adjectives in place of nouns, so "moon" would be expressed more or less as "aerial-bright above dark-round" (*CF* 73), and the nouns in "The moon rose above the river" would be replaced by strings of adjectives.

However, as *idealistic nominalists*, the Tlönians are caught up in their equivalent of our Zeno paradox. Zeno argues that if an arrow is shot from a bow, at a given instant it is where it is and nowhere else; in the next instant it is where it is and nowhere else, and so on. Hence, at each discontinuous instant the arrow is fixed within an increment of space. Since nothing transpires from one increment to another, the arrow is never in motion, so there is no time during which the arrow moves; hence there is neither time nor motion. The Tlönians express a charming counter-Zeno quandary as follows:

> On Tuesday, X is walking along a deserted road and loses nine copper coins. On Thursday, Y finds four coins in the road, their luster somewhat dimmed by Wednesday's rain. On Friday, Z discovers three coins in the road. Friday morning X finds two coins on the veranda of his house. (*CF* 75)

We in our anti-Tlönian world believe the arrow is what it is during each instant of time, that it occupies a portion of space during each instant, and so it exists. The Tlönians believe the coins have no existence unless they are seen – what exists, exists only insofar it is experienced. Thus if the coins are lost on a deserted road, there's no reason to believe they can be found there and there only. They can be found anywhere one wishes to experience them. In this sense the Tlönians are tantamount to "formalist mathematicians," or, in philosophy, George Berkeley's "idealists," with respect to their physical descriptions of their world. Their "truths" aren't "truths" about something, but about nothing at all, unless they fabricate it.

The narrator of Borges's tale tells of a radical upstart – counterpart to Zeno – who tried to convince the Tlönians that the coins enjoyed continuous existence, and from the moment of losing them to finding them had some secret form of "reality" (but a "reality" quite natural for us). Needless to say, the author of this interpretation was considered as absurd as we tend to consider Zeno. Thus the Tlönians' stark limitations, which Borges elucidates with remarkable aplomb.

Lönnrot's world is that of Platonic *realism*, and *logicism*. Platonic *realism* tells us that even mathematical entities exist, eternally and unchangingly.

They are "out there" in Platonic heaven, and it is the mathematician's and the physicist's task to find them. *Logicism* tells us that mathematics is reducible to logic. Virtually the same can be said of Lönnrot's physical "reality": it exists, as replicas approximating Platonic forms, and it is reducible to logical, geometrical, and mathematical formalisms. We're now familiar with Lönnrot's fate, due to the limitations of his dogmatic belief. Emma Zunz, however, exists in stark contrast to Lönnrot. Yet Zunz, as a pragmatic opportunist – or "unscrupulous opportunist," as Einstein once put it[2] – reworks her "reality" quite effectively. She intuits what needs to be done within this "reality," and she does it.

In this respect, the world she fabricates is comparable to Menard's world of "textuality." Mathematically or scientifically speaking, this involves what is called *constructionism*, an exercise of human intuition coupled with experience and a remaking of what is experienced in collaboration with intuition. *Constructionism* is no game played with meaningless symbols; rather, it is about entities created through mental activity and signs. It involves invention rather than discovery, worlds fashioned rather than merely found.[3] But how far can *constructionism* go toward solving any and all problem situations? It obviously worked in Zunz's particular case, but its success was based on deception, and deception is the offspring of lies, scientific falsehoods, and failed mathematical proofs, at best, and disastrous catastrophic consequences, at worst.[4]

A catastrophic case is that of the aged shaman of "The Circular Ruins," who wishes to dream a son and interpolate him into "reality." After an aborted attempt, he feels he has succeeded, and when his son reaches the proper age the shaman sends him away for a period of initiation. But he later becomes apprehensive, fearing that his son might come into contact with fire, which cannot harm him, and hence he will know he is a phantasm. While the shaman is caught up in meditation, a concentric blaze threatens to engulf him. He decides to walk into the flames and bring an end to his inevitable demise, but when the flames don't consume him, he realizes that he, too, is someone else's dream. The message? We are not masters of our *constructions*. We are in them and they are in us; we *co-participate* in the universal process of becoming – a topic to be taken up later.

The Library: finite or infinite?

Is the universe finite or infinite? That question has intrigued scientists and mathematicians over the centuries. Borges has a unique slant on this problem in "The Library of Babel." This Library is composed of a monstrous number of hexagonal galleries, with a ventilation shaft in the center allowing visitors to see the floors above and below, in endless sequence. Each wall of each hexagon holds 32 books of equal size; each book has 410 pages; each page 40 lines; each line approximately 80 letters. The books consist of all possible combinations of 25 orthographic symbols. Every conceivable book has been written.

William Goldbloom Bloch computes the number of books in the library according to this data: 410 pages times 40 lines times 80 symbols equals 1,312,000 symbols in each book. Since there are 25 orthographic symbols, the total number of possible books is: $25^{1,312,000}$! Putting this unfathomable figure in the power of 10 gives us: $10^{1,834,097}$![5] The universe is currently estimated to be 1.5×10^{26} meters across, and if we filled the entire universe with sand there would be no more than a paltry 10^{90} grains, a sum that doesn't even begin approximating the number of books in the Library. To give a more concrete feeling for the magnitude of the Library, if we walked 60 miles a day for 100 years, we would travel a distance slightly less than what light covers in two minutes. For light to cross the entire universe, which is minuscule in comparison to the Library, it must travel for at least 15 billion years! Obviously, no less than an immortal librarian would be able to inspect all the Library's books.

An observer of the Library once speculated that, rather than constructing this massive edifice, one infinite book would be sufficient. Such an infinite book is precisely what Borges describes in "The Book of Sand." The owner of the book hands it to the narrator, who begins looking for a particular page. What are his chances of finding it? If we had a book of 100 pages and we wanted to open it to page 17, our chances would be 1/100. If there were 1,000 pages our chance would be 1/1,000. If there is an infinite number of pages, the probability of our opening it to a particular page would be $1/\infty$; in other words, zero probability! Now what if we turn this book over to inspect the back side? What do we see? Nothing! Emptiness! There is nothing there to see.

Yet, the "The Library of Babel" and "The Book of Sand" are there for our impoverished imagination. We read Borges's captivating tales, and we are in them and they are in us. In fact, Borges mentions that the writer of "The Library of Babel" is somewhere within the Library, which is the "reality" of which he writes, toiling away at his laborious task. This tells us that we, too, are here, reading the short story, striving to understand the consequences of our reading; at the same time we are within the Library, that is, within our own "reality." This notion invites us to contemplate, as have mathematicians and physicists since early in the twentieth century, our condition as subjects and what we consider our objective "reality."

We are co-participants

Borges's "The Aleph" tells us that Carlos Argentino Daneri is privileged to gaze upon the mysterious Aleph, a golf-ball-size sphere allowing a look at the entire universe, past, present, and future. Daneri's vision is akin to mystical insight. However, given a superficial reading of the short story, his experience appears to be *objectivism* in the purest possible sense, as he plays the role of a neutral onlooker of "reality."

On second thoughts, Daneri cannot but be part of the universe, and so also is the Aleph. Daneri is *both* detached observer *and co-participant* with(in) his universe; the Aleph is *both* the object of observation *and co-participant* with the *co-participating* subject in the self-organizing process that includes *both* Daneri *and* the *Aleph*. Both are *neither* entirely detached and "out there" *nor* are they simply *co-participants* within the universe. This is the crux of what is called the part/whole and many/one paradox, which demands detachedness and prohibits it; it demands oneness and wholeness, and prohibits them. This is the paradox of which physicist Erwin Schrödinger eloquently writes regarding quantum theory: "Subject and object are only one. The barrier between them cannot be said to have broken down … for this barrier does not exist"; and elsewhere: "The reason why our sentient, percipient and thinking ego is met nowhere without our scientific world picture can easily be indicated in seven words: because it is itself that world picture. It is identical with the whole and therefore cannot be contained in it as a part of it."[6]

Arthur Eddington writes complementary words along the same lines: "We have found a strange foot-print on the shores of the unknown. We have devised profound theories … to account for its origin. At last, we have succeeded in reconstructing the creature that made the foot-print. And Lo! it is our own"[7] – words true to form regarding Daneri's condition when gazing upon the Aleph! The Aleph: it is everything, including itself within everything else and itself within itself, as a self-contained, self-sufficient whole. The Aleph must be none other than a minuscule four-dimensional hypersphere: everything rolled up into one. It is a mere point in space, a timespace singularity (of 10^{-33} centimeters!), or better, what physicists call a "naked singularity," which, unlike a "black hole," is of somewhat less than absolute gravitational pull such that it lets a little light leak out so as to bare itself to anyone who wishes to take a peek.[8] As no more than a point, the Aleph is nothing, like zero, which gives rise to the engenderment of an infinite number of integers. This observation draws attention to Borges's "*Everything and Nothing.*" An actor spends his life playing at being others before crowds of people who play at taking him for those others. At the end of his life he realizes he has been so many others that he no longer knows who he is. He finds himself before God, and implores: "I, who have been so many men in vain, wish to be *one*, to be myself." To which God responds from a whirlwind: "I, too, am not I; I dreamed the world as you, Shakespeare, dreamed your own work, and among the forms of my dream are you, who like me are many, yet no one" (*CF* 320).

Everything, and nothing. Let's boot this equation up to the most particular and the most general level to include ourselves as minuscule singularities within the universe. In this condition, are we like Funes? In part yes, and in part no, depending on our particular timespace context. Are we like the owner of the Zahir? Yes, and no. The Tlönians? Yes, and no. Lönnrot? Yes, and no. And we can say the same of the other Borges characters we've considered. We are all of them – at least during particular moments of our lives – and we are none of them – at all moments of our lives. It is as if in the most general sense and in the most particular sense we emerged from a mere point, nothing, and, like Borges's Shakespeare, we are on our way toward becoming everything – though, finite individuals that we are, of course we will never reach that goal.

We are many, and we are one; we are always becoming one from many and we are becoming many because the one is perpetually subdividing into two, three, and many, within the stream of life within which we find ourselves. We can intermittently become *realists* or *nominalists*, *objectivists* or *idealists*, *relativists* or *determinists*, or in Einstein's words, we can become "unscrupulous opportunists," depending on the context and the circumstances. Mathematicians and scientists, as Borges intimates, hardly fare much better. Let us turn to that topic.

From a magnificent machine to giant thought to absurdity?

The Cartesian–Newtonian view of the machine-like universe was that of clockwork precision, and God was the supreme agent who originally wound it up. The universe as a machine model, however, was put into question during the latter decades of the nineteenth century.

More than a half-century later, Robert Oppenheimer could write: "Despite all the richness of what men have learned about the world of nature, of matter and of space, of change and of life, we carry with us today an image of the giant machine as a sign of what the objective world is really like."[9] However, a few years earlier, physicist James Jeans had lamented that physicists nurture a bias toward mechanical interpretations, but that actually "the universe begins to look more like a great thought than like a great machine."[10] God, one might wish to say, is a Great Mathematician. Galileo said as much centuries ago.

The mechanical model was destined to fall, however. Max Born was elated that modern physics abandoned it, as were Werner Heisenberg, Niels Bohr, Eddington, and Einstein, to mention the most prominent physicists.[11] The "universe as thought" places the physicist, and by extension all of us, in the role of *actors* not merely *spectators*, or in John Archibald Wheeler's conception, as *co-participants* with the universe.[12]

Twentieth-century physics reveals that the physicist can't observe nature without disturbing it. Born compares the observer "not with the audience of a theatrical performance, but with that of a football game where the act of watching, accompanied by applauding or hissing, has a marked influence on ... the players, and thus on what is watched."[13] According to Louis de Broglie: "Science thus loses a part of its objective character; no more is it the passive contemplation of a fixed universe; it becomes a hand-to-hand struggle where the scientist succeeds in matching from the physical world which he would like to understand, certain information, always partial, which would allow him to make predictions that are incomplete."[14] No physicist defends the "mind within nature" concept more vehemently than Wheeler. What he calls his "delayed-choice" thought-experiment, later verified experimentally, illustrates how the physicist not only disturbs what some aspect of the quantum world will *have been doing*, but she decides what it *has done* in the past and *is doing* in the present.[15]

Wheeler extrapolates his thought experiment to our concrete world, arguing that the "cosmological anthropic principle" applies. The "anthropic principle" has a "weak" and a "strong" version. Wheeler prefers the "weak" version, which says that if intelligent life exists in the universe, it exists insofar as its intelligence is capable of falling in line with the nature of the universe, hence the universe as it is couldn't exist without intelligent life, and intelligent life couldn't exist without the universe.[16] Steven Weinberg comes close to this notion when he says that "the world is the way it is, at least in part, because otherwise there would be no one to ask why it is the way it is."[17] As far as Wheeler is concerned, we, as *co-participants* with the universe, wouldn't be able to imagine a universe that didn't somewhere, and from some length of time, contain knowers (ourselves and other living organisms), because knowing and known, or *co-participancy*, is the only way the universe can perpetuate its process of becoming. (Remarkably, this would seem to mirror some form of an enchanting combination of Tlön, Funes, and the Zahir, and Lönnrot, Emma Zunz, Averroës, and Menard.)

All told, it is we who make "reality" what it is, and it is "reality" that makes way for our own creation. Surely there is a massive dose of humor in this conception of ourselves and the universe. Either that, or the universe is patently absurd. Indeed, Richard Feynman, somewhat in jest, describes the world of quantum theory as "absurd from the point of view of common sense. And it fully agrees with experiment. So I hope you can accept nature as she is – absurd."[18] If absurd, nothing is certain, as Feynman intimates elsewhere: "[W]hat we call scientific knowledge today is a body of statements of varying degrees of certainty. Some of them are most unsure; some of them are nearly sure; but none is absolutely certain. Scientists are used to this."[19] These words would have fascinated Borges.

Quantum parallel worlds, and the garden

Nowhere do we find the implications of uncertainty, apparent absurdity, and our *co-participancy* more than in "The Garden of Forking Paths." It is a spy story, and it is also much more.

Dr. Yu Tsun, an agent for the Germans during World War I, is in England expecting execution, for he knows that British intelligence is in hot pursuit. His objective is somehow to inform Berlin of the name of the city the British are preparing to attack: Albert. There happens to be a person with the same name as the city. Yu decides to kill this person, knowing that he will be caught and executed, and that the name of the victim and his own name will appear in the newspapers, giving a clue to the Germans regarding the target of the British attack. He arrives at the home of that person, Stephen Albert. However, rather than kill him on the spot, he engages Albert in a discussion of an extraordinary Chinese book by Ts'ui Pên, *The Garden of Forking Paths*, which consists of a temporal rather than a spatial labyrinth. Albert claims he has discovered the key to this enigmatic novel that apparently consists of a multitude of time lines:

> *The Garden of Forking Paths* is an incomplete, but not false, image of the universe as conceived by Ts'ui Pên. Unlike Newton and Schopenhauer, your ancestor did not believe in a uniform and absolute time; he believed in an infinite series of times, a growing, dizzying web of divergent, convergent, and parallel times. The fabric of times that approach one another, fork, are snipped off, or are simply unknown for centuries, contains *all* possibilities. In most of these times, we do not exist; in some, you exist but I do not; in others, I do and you do not; in others still, we both do. In this one, which the favouring hand of chance has dealt me, you have come to my home; in another, when you come through my garden you find me dead; in another, I say these same words, but I am an error, a ghost. (*CF* 127)

Wheeler's student, Hugh Everett, republished his 1957 PhD dissertation, along with a collection of papers on the "many worlds interpretation of quantum mechanics," with Princeton University Press, in 1973. Most appropriately, the above quote appears in the volume as an epigraph. In the words of Bryce DeWitt, who has worked extensively with Everett's interpretation, the universe of the "many worlds interpretation," like the passage depicting Ts'ui Pên's labyrinth, "is constantly splitting into a stupendous number of branches, all resulting from measurement like interactions between its myriads of components. Moreover, every quantum transition taking place on every star, in every galaxy, in every remote corner of the universe, is splitting our local world on earth into myriads of copies of itself."[20]

Indeed, quantum theory – comparable to Borges's tales – is based on the idea that all possible events, no matter how fantastic or silly, might occur. There exists the imaginary possibility, albeit of virtually zero probability, of your walking through a brick wall and rematerializing on the other side. Borges, of course, deals with imaginary situations within the human condition. Many of these imaginary situations are of inconceivable improbability; and yet, they tell us something about mathematics, physics, and ourselves and our world. We feel, we sense, and we try to think them and conceptualize them, but we always fail, at least in part, and then we begin anew. The task is unlimited, but fortunately we have an unlimited number of possibilities for failure, and hopefully a few drops of success. Heisenberg once mused along these lines that in "every act of perception we select one of an infinite number of possibilities and thus we also limit the number of possibilities for the future."[21]

Borges wrote about the infinite and the infinitesimal, possibility and possible "realities," geometry and symmetry, continuity and discontinuity, all of which bear on twentieth-century physics and mathematics. Reading Borges in this light affords satisfaction, and ultimately hope, rather than despair, regarding our place in our world.

NOTES

1 For admiring comments on Borges from mathematician-physicists, see P. Morrison, "The Physics of Binary Numbers," *Scientific American*, February 1996, 130; H. A. Makse, *et al.*, "Dynamics of Granular Stratification," *Physics Review*, 58 (1998), 33–57; A. J. Leggett, *The Problems of Physics*, Oxford University Press, 1987, 172; J. S. Bell, *Speakable and Unspeakable in Quantum Mechanics*, Cambridge University Press, 1986, 133; and A. di Marco, "Borges, the Quantum Theory and Parallel Universes," *The Journal of American Science*, 2 (1) (2006), 1–30.

2 A. Einstein, "Reply to Criticisms," in *Albert Einstein: Philosopher-Scientist*, ed. P. A. Schilpp, LaSalle, IL, Open Court, 1949, 665–88 (684).

3 N. Goodman, *Ways of Worldmaking*, Indianapolis, Hackett, 1978.

4 M. Gardner, *Science: Good, Bad and Bogus*, New York, Prometheus, 1996; R. L. Park, *Voodoo Science: The Road from Foolishness to Fraud*, New York, Oxford University Press, 2001.

5 W. G. Bloch, *The Unimaginable Mathematics of Borges' Library of Babel*, Oxford University Press, 2008, 17–18; R. Rucker, *Infinity and the Mind: The Science and Philosophy of the Infinite*, New York, Bantam, 1983, 101–2.

6 Erwin Schrödinger, *What is Life?*, Cambridge University Press, 1967, 137 and 138.

7 A. S. Eddington, *New Pathways in Science*, New York, Macmillan, 1935.

8 K. S. Thorne, *Black Holes and Time Warps: Einstein's Outrageous Legacy*, New York, W. W. Norton, 1994, 23–58.

9 J. R. Oppenheimer, *Science and Common Understanding*, New York, Simon and Schuster, 1954, 14–15.

10 James Jeans, *The Mysterious Universe*, New York, Macmillan, 1948, 166.

11 M. Born, *Physics in My Generation*, New York, Pergamon, 1956, 45; W. Heisenberg, *Physics and Philosophy*, New York, Harper and Row, 1958, 197–98; N. Bohr, *Atomic Physics and Human Knowledge*, New York, John Wiley, 1958, 94, 96; A. S. Eddington, *New Pathways in Science*, 72–74; A. Einstein, *Out of My Later Years*, New York, Philosophical Library, 1950, 109–10.

12 John Archibald Wheeler, *At Home in the Universe*, New York, American Institute of Physics, 1994, 271–94.

13 Born, *Physics in My Generation*, 39–40.

14 Louis de Broglie, *Physics and Microphysics*, New York, Pantheon, 1955, 131.

15 Wheeler, *At Home in the Universe*, 112–31.

16 J. D. Barrow, *The World Within the World*, Oxford University Press, 1990; J. D. Barrow, F. J. Tipler, and J. A. Wheeler, *The Anthropic Cosmological Principle*, Oxford University Press, 1988.

17 Steven Weinberg, "The Cosmological Constant Problem," *Reviews of Modern Physics*, 61 (1989), 1–246.

18 In B. Greene, *The Elegant Universe: Superstrings, Hidden Dimensions, and the Quest for the Ultimate Theory*, New York, W. W. Norton, 1999, 111.

19 R. Feynman, *Meaning of It All: Thoughts of a Citizen Scientist*, Reading, MA, Addison-Wesley, 1998, 27.

20 B. S. DeWitt and R. N. Graham, *The Many-Worlds Interpretation of Quantum Mechanics*, Princeton University Press, 1973, 161.

21 W. Heisenberg, *Philosophical Problems of Nuclear Science*, New York, Pantheon, 1952, 28.

3

MICHAEL WOOD

Borges and theory

The word "theory" is very old; it has definitions ranging from spectacle to system to speculation, and even in one rare sense signifies a messenger. Literary theory flourished among the ancient Greeks and Romans, in the European Renaissance, and in the Enlightenment, and notable theorists in the twentieth century included Jean-Paul Sartre and Northrop Frye. But in English in the late 1960s the word acquired a very particular set of meanings, representing a phenomenon that could come alive, threaten us or save us (one could be for it or against it), and finally die, as various recent and forthcoming books suggest it has.[1] The phenomenon was a mixed affair, and this is not the place to unmix it, only to evoke a sense that I believe is fading but still useful. "Theory" meant overt reflection on the practice and study of literature where such reflection was taken to have been either implicit or non-existent; a turn to thinkers and writers outside the Anglo-American critical tradition; and an interest in extra-literary disciplines or movements like philosophy, psychoanalysis, anthropology, feminism, Marxism. Not all this work was theoretical and some was intensely practical, but it all stood outside what the "literary" was then felt to mean to English speakers. In effect, this produced an engagement with structuralism (and then post-structuralism) as it was defined in France in particular by the writing of Claude Lévi-Strauss, Roland Barthes, Jacques Lacan, Jacques Derrida, and Julia Kristeva; then moving backward in the chronological order of history, with the early twentieth-century elaborations of poetics by the Formalists Viktor Shklovsky, Boris Eichenbaum, and Roman Jakobson; and finally, shifting halfway forward again in time, with the socially inflected work of members of the Frankfurt School of Critical Theory, notably Walter Benjamin and Theodor Adorno. Many other figures were involved, but these were the chief, recurring protagonists when "theory" was mentioned in English and American criticism and scholarship.

The word is sometimes used even now to mean only or mainly French theory, which is an impoverishment of the concept generally, but fairly apt in the case of the perceived relation of Borges to the topic. It is in France and through France that we can trace the major travels of Borges into the realms of "theory" in its special, recent sense – although there is at least one route that takes us to Italy.[2]

Borges and his admirers – Foucault, Lacan, *et cie*

In Borges's "The Approach to Al-Mu'tasim," the title character is repeatedly named and everywhere intuited, but never seen. The narrative describes a search for a soul through the "reflections this soul has left in others" (*CF* 84), which is certainly how we find Borges in France.

There are clear French traces of Borges, ones that have his name visibly attached to them. The most lucid and ample of them opens Michel Foucault's *The Order of Things*:

> This book first arose out of a passage in Borges, out of the laughter that shattered, as I read it, all the familiar landmarks of my thought.[3]

The text is Borges's essay "John Wilkins' Analytical Language," and more specifically his description there of "a certain Chinese encyclopedia," with its dizzying and utterly unmanageable classification of animals as, among other categories, belonging to the Emperor, embalmed, tame, sirens, fabulous, included in this classification, innumerable, and which from a distance appear to be flies (*SNF* 231). What makes us laugh, Foucault says, is our abrupt arrival at the limits of our thought: "the naked impossibility of thinking *that*." But then what exactly is it, he goes on to ask, that we can't think? It's not the fabulous animals or quirky categories, since we have models for those in various literatures, nor is it even the strange encounters the taxonomy mobilizes for us. What is vanishing before our eyes, Foucault suggests, is the conceptual ground on which any sort of coherent thinking about these creatures could occur: "The common ground on which such meetings are possible has itself been destroyed. What is impossible is not the propinquity of the things listed, but the very site on which their propinquity would be possible" (xvi). Classifications are forms of convenience for the mind, Borges says, "*des commodités pour l'intelligence*."[4] All the more reason, then, to be interested in them when they are designed to make things difficult for the mind.

Destruction or, more literally, ruin is an important metaphor for Foucault, and an indication that our laughter is only part of the story. "That passage from Borges kept me laughing a long time," he writes, "though not without a certain uneasiness that I found hard to shake off " (xvii). The laughter and the unease have the same origin: what Foucault now calls the destruction

not of a common space but of syntax – and not just the syntax that constructs sentences but "that less apparent syntax which causes words and
things … to 'hold together'" (xviii).

The subtitle of Foucault's book is "An Archeology of the Human
Sciences" – three years later he wrote a more broadly theoretical account of
his method called *The Archeology of Knowledge* – and what Borges's mock-
classification allows Foucault to elaborate is what we *can* think, what lies
within the limits of our thought, precisely what an unruined syntax looks
like, first that of the classical age, which he dates from the middle of the
seventeenth century, and second that of the modern age, which begins for
him in the early nineteenth century:

> What I am attempting to bring to light is the epistemological field, the epis-
> teme in which knowledge … manifests a history which is not that of its grow-
> ing perfection, but rather that of its conditions of possibility; in this account,
> what should appear are those configurations within the space of knowledge
> which have given rise to the various forms of empirical science." (xxii)

The key phrase here is "conditions of possibility." Foucault is interested not
in what people have or have not thought but in what they have found it
possible to think, and in this sense his episteme strongly resembles Thomas
Kuhn's conception of the paradigm, as articulated in *The Structure of
Scientific Revolutions* (1962). In both Kuhn's and Foucault's view, the interesting and important movements in history are not gradual or cumulative,
but abrupt and radical: wholesale shifts of conceptual scenery. Hence the
notion of an archeology, or history as archeology: a set of mind is to be
reconstructed not described.

But of course Foucault's allusion is not an academic acknowledgement.
The archeology and the historical interest do not belong to Borges, and we
need to pause over Foucault's language, and especially the phrases "arose
out of" (literally "had its place of birth in") and "for a long time." What
does it mean for a book to born in another text, and how long has Foucault
been thinking and laughing over the Chinese encyclopedia? It is Borges the
writer who matters here, the inventor of several crucial forms of the modern imagination, whose fictions are essays and whose essays are preludes to
fiction. Foucault is both naming and continuing to use Borges's work not as
a prompt for a research but as the location of a memorably shaped preoccupation – a preoccupation that cannot be only Foucault's, even if he is the one
who at this moment is evoking it most directly.

This Borges became known in France through, among other publishing
events, the translation of *Ficciones* in 1951 (the first translation into English
came 11 years later) and the appearance of eight essays, including the one

on John Wilkins, in Sartre's journal *Les Temps modernes* in 1955. Foucault's "*longtemps*" therefore can mean quite some time before 1966, the year of *The Order of Things*; and when Jacques Lacan refers to Borges in the printed version of his 1955 seminar on Poe's "Purloined Letter," he is thinking of the Wilkins essay in *Les Temps modernes. Otras Inquisiciones* appeared in French in 1957 as *Enquêtes.*[5] This Borges is not the whole of Borges, far from it; but the selection does represent the basis of what "Borges" came to mean "for a long time" outside Latin America.

Lacan's tribute is grandiose and ambiguous. He refers to Wilkins's "semiotic utopia" as "the very one to which Jorge Luis Borges, in works which harmonize so well with the phylum of our subject, has accorded an importance which others have reduced to its proper proportions."[6] Lacan's joke about classification creates a distance from Borges even as it brings him into the picture: a phylum is a division of the animal kingdom's five categories more general than a species. The idea that Borges exaggerates the importance of Wilkins's work seems to be another joke, a recognition of Borges's tone disguised as a misrecognition. If it is a joke, and not a bit of miscellaneous pompousness, it is completely in harmony with the rest of the seminar, which is all about failing (for good reason) to recognize the obvious. Lacan has settled on Wilkins's word "nullibility," which Borges does not cite, to designate that which can't be found although the seeker has looked "everywhere" – an object, in other words, that changes the meaning of "everywhere," since it is neither present nor absent as objects are supposed to be, but both present and absent. "Everywhere" in this instance means everywhere a reasonable person would hide something, and everywhere a reasonable person would look. But who better than Borges to teach us that there are other places and, *pace* Lacan, what better reader of Poe is there?

Lacan's seminar is littered with suggestions that, if they do not stem from Borges, are perfectly consistent with his work, or find in his work their wittiest and most mischievous avatars. It's true that Borges is not interested in psychoanalysis and does not use the word "signifier" (or any word remotely like it). But it is also true that what Lacan means by a signifier – a mark or a sound that has floated free of its ostensible meaning, a form of fiction, and finally a materialization of death[7] – has several counterparts in the recurring figures Borges finds for what he calls his "basic skepticism."[8] Borges's very name becomes a traveling signifier, for example, in stories where it identifies a narrator or a character who is and is not the person of the historical record, and most notably in the brief essay "Borges and I," where "the other one" runs away with the complete sign (signifier and signified), leaving the notional "I" of the piece with two impossible options: to secede from what "Borges" has come to mean or to accept that such a secession is meaningless.

When we read the last words of the essay – "I am not sure which of us it is that's writing this page" (*CF* 324) – we may think we know how to decode them, but our interpretative certainty can't long survive Borges's implacable impersonation of doubt. We are at first inclined to say, "Of course it's the other Borges who's at work here," since the piece is written and published and we are reading it. But this Borges would know for sure he had written the page; it would be one of his performances. Is he actually impersonating the first Borges, the one who is trying to say "I"? Or is that "I" really speaking, after all, through the small miracle of grammar, which allows even invisible men to make themselves seen in the use of a phrase like "it's Borges, the other one, that things happen to" (*CF* 324).

We may seem to be a long way from the shifting signifier here, but we are still within reach of the idiom's implications and relatives. The world of Borges's fiction, in its most ample and philosophically mischievous measures, maps very convincingly on to a number of preoccupations we find in (French) critical theory, associated in particular with the names of, respectively, Michael Foucault, Louis Althusser, Roland Barthes, and Jacques Lacan. I am thinking of *discourse* (rather than material event) as the source of meaning in history; *ideology* as ubiquitous and unavoidable (rather than representing any given set of chosen political assumptions); *mythology* as an aspect of everyday contemporary life; and the realm of the *symbolic* as that of shared social existence. These notions differ from each other in important ways, of course, but each has a touch of Borges about it, and each involves a system of meaning which allows for the investigation of realities felt to be (often distressingly) out of reach or caught up in complicated mediations.

The illusory library

Borges's relation to the work of these different thinkers is itself different in each case, easily perceptible, like the name of the always hovering Al-Muta'sim, but variable. If his writing forms an attractive provocation for Foucault, and a half-denied parallel project for Lacan, for other Europeans it is something like an indispensable reference, the mark of a stylish and informed modernity, and an acknowledgment that playfulness too must be part of any sophisticated skepticism. Should we be saying modernity or postmodernity? The only credible answer to this question is the unhelpful "both," and I shall not pursue further complications. I will say, though, since I believe this proposition to be a crucial aspect of Borges's "situation" in Europe (and in the United Kingdom and North America to the extent that they followed European intellectual fashions), that if we take Lyotard's view of the postmodern not as a style or a period but as an extrapolation of aspects of the modern – it is what we would have if modernity ever ended and if anything came after it – then Borges becomes the exemplary figure of a modernity that sees beyond itself. What could be more modern *and* postmodern than the suggestion that we know literature not through texts but through perceptions of texts: "If I were able to read any contemporary page – this one, for example – as it would be read in the year 2000, I would know what literature would be like in the year 2000."[9] Borges is writing in 1951.

The third part of Derrida's essay, "Plato's Pharmacy," has two epigraphs from Borges. The first comes from the essay "Pascal's Sphere" and the second from "Tlön, Uqbar, Orbis Tertius." Between them is a quotation from Joyce's *Portrait of the Artist as a Young Man*, in which Stephen Dedalus thinks anxiously of the Greek labyrinth-maker whose name he bears and also of Thoth, the Egyptian god of writers ("A sense of fear of the unknown moved in the heart of his weariness, a fear of symbols and portents"). The first of the Borges quotations evokes the 42 or 20,000 or 36,525 books supposedly dictated by Hermes Trismegistus and the corresponding illusory library – the translation Derrida is using calls it a *"bibliothèque imaginaire"* – and the second describes conflicting interpretations of time and the universe on the planet of Tlön. Since Derrida doesn't comment on these quotations but simply allows their placing to do its work, we are invited to see them as enlarging or qualifying his own argument.

Derrida's concern in this section of the essay is with the god Thoth – he makes an appearance in two dialogues of Plato, which is one of the reasons for his importance here – and with his variously deconstructive activities in the theology he belongs to. The god "had several faces, belonged to several eras, lived in several homes."[10] This multiplicity might be his identity, Derrida says, if his function were not to undermine the very notion of identity. Thoth is "the god of second language and of linguistic difference,"[11] the son not the father, the moon not the sun, the substitute not the authority itself, the always subordinate delegate of writing, seen as a mere replacement or record, what we have when speech is not available. But then he is also not as subordinate as he looks. As we know from *Of Grammatology*, Derrida sees this mythical structure, this ubiquitous preference for the spoken word, as the repression and inversion of a truth: that speech, insofar as it follows the intricate rules of any language, is already a form of writing.[12] We see this repression and an all but secret confession of it in Plato's *Phaedrus*, where Socrates applauds the decision of the Egyptian god Thamus not to take up Thoth's new invention but also speaks twice of a discourse "inscribed" in the soul – that is, not the opposite of writing but a better form of writing.[13]

Thoth then for Derrida is the joker in the theological pack, "the father's other, the father, and the subversive movement of replacement"[14] – the usurper, let's say, who was already secretly the legitimate ruler and who will always repeat the double gesture of authority and revolt. It's hard not to think here of Borges's ironic suggestion in "The Lottery in Babylon" that an impostor might be the real thing without knowing it if the grounds for truth were uncertain enough: "Besides, who will boast of being a mere impostor?" (*CF* 106). And although Borges talks constantly of books, in the essay "On the Cult of Books" and elsewhere, those books are often fragmentary, like the illusory library in Derrida's first quotation, or incoherent, like a number of books in the infinite library of Babel. In this sense they are in Derrida's terms more like writing ("*écriture*") than like books as we used to understand the word, since although they may glance at a transcendent totality, that totality is always absent.[15] In his conversations with Georges Charbonnier, Borges clearly replaces Mallarmé's idea of the book ("Everything in the world exists in order to end up in a book") with his own "idea" that "everything in the universe is a form of writing."[16]

In the second of Derrida's quotations from Borges three dizzying possibilities follow in rapid succession: that time is already over and we are living in its crepuscular aftermath; that the history of the universe is the writing a minor god uses to communicate with a demon; and that the universe is like one of those codes in which not all the symbols count – the French translation says, slightly differently, a code in which not all the symbols have the same value. Taken together with the evocation of the illusory library and Stephen Dedalus's myth-haunted fears, these propositions serve to turn all writing into indispensable but variously fallible script, an image of knowledge that is, once again, irremediably oblique.

Julia Kristeva's chief allusion to Borges is similar in style to Derrida's: a swift evocation and a trail of associations. The question is again writing, but pointed not toward an anxiety about codes but toward Lacan and Kristeva's own earlier work on the "*chora*" – the confused and all-welcoming stage of child development that for a certain branch of psychoanalysis precedes our entry into the orderly symbolism of integrated social life. Her subject is abjection, a condition in which the wholeness of the self is threatened or unavailable, in which we ourselves become what we cannot contain or contemplate, and which is variously defined in her work as "a resurrection that has gone through death (of the ego)"; "a border"; the result of an encounter with "a deep well of memory that is unapproachable and intimate"; and "inseparable, contaminated, condemned, at the boundary of what is assimilable, thinkable."[17] She begins to illustrate her theme through brief, impressionistic comments on aspects of the work of Dostoevsky, Proust, Joyce, Borges, and Artaud – later in the book she devotes considerable attention to Céline.

What's most intriguing about Kristeva's reflection on Borges is her choice of instances, a most unusual conjugation. For her the Aleph in the story of that name evokes abjection because of its exorbitant nature, its relation to "rampancy, boundlessness, the unthinkable, the untenable, the unsymbolizable" (23), and because – her argument moves very quickly here – such exorbitance can be articulated in a non-mediocre way by narratives of infamy. This thought leads her straight to "The Cruel Redeemer Lazarus Morell," in *A Universal History of Iniquity*, from which she quotes at some length. In this story of the American South the master criminal encourages slaves to escape so that he can sell them again – and again and again. In the combination of the Aleph's unsayability and Morell's sinister ingenuity Kristeva finds an allegory of modern writing, cut off from the sacred:

> The writer cannot but recognize himself, derisive and forfeited, in that abject character, Lazarus Morell, the frightful redeemer, who raises his slaves from the dead only to have them die more fully, but not until they have been circulated – and brought a return – like currency. (24)

She ends the section on a frightening political possibility: "Just imagine [Morell's] imaginary machine transformed into a social institution – and what you get is the infamy of fascism" (25).

The suggestion, of course, is not that writers are infamous but that a threat of infamy may haunt all writing, may float up from the sense of hollowness that lurks among words that are treated like slaves or money, among words that are only ever words. Kristeva is close to one of Borges's deepest intuitions – the suspicion of the void beneath the most beautiful artifices – but of course the accents of horror are hers, not his. Borges certainly looks into this void, and his elegant, worldly irony recognizes, or glances at, all kinds of horrors. But he doesn't sink into them. His writing is a way of navigating the space between the dark and the light.

The secret sharer

We have already evoked Roland Barthes's notion of the death of the author – well, more precisely, his notion of the birth of the reader – and it's time to look more closely at this critic's relation to Borges. The relation is obvious in many ways – a shared interest in fictionality, a suspicion of realism, a susceptibility to the play of syntax and diction – and can initially seem more encompassing than some of the other embraces of Borges we have seen. But here's the odd thing. There is no literal, textual embrace of Borges in Barthes's work that I can find or recall; not even a mention. Of course this is no impediment to anyone who has been reading "Kafka and his Precursors," but it is striking. It is possible but very unlikely that Barthes had not read Borges. Perhaps he felt the very fashion for citing Borges was something to shy away from: he needed to be fastidious.

The chief ground on which Borges and Barthes seem to meet is, as it happens, not exactly that of the death of the author, which in its many forms is an enduring question tracked by poets and novelists and critics since the end of the nineteenth century. Mallarmé thought the poet should "cede the initiative to the words"; Proust thought real writing is accomplished by a secret self, quite separate from the visible being who has a biography and a social life; Yeats was sure the poet "is never the bundle of accident and incoherence that sits down to breakfast."[18] Henry James wrote a short story, "The Private Life" (1892), about a writer who seems literally to have no time at all to write but turns out not to need any such time, since he has a ghostly second self, a version of Proust's secret self (*moi profond*), who stays in his room and does the work. Closer in period and mood to Barthes, Foucault wrote an essay on the author as a function of the institution of literature,[19] and Calvino invited us to think of the writer as a machine. A little earlier a (relatively) famous American academic essay on "The Intentional Fallacy" had told us in no uncertain terms that an author's intention was "neither available nor desirable as a standard for judging the success of a literary work."[20] If we want to know what a poem or a novel is about, or how good it is, we have only to read it; there is no point in trying to consult what the authors of the essay call "the oracle." This is all very general, though, and what really connects Borges and Barthes, makes them "precursors" of each other, so to speak, is the sense not that the author is hidden or ghostly or inaccessible or not needed but that the reader *creates* the author. This proposition is familiar to us now in various nuanced forms, but in Borges and Barthes it rings with a strong sense of discovery.

Of Pierre Menard, the belated French Symbolist who has decided to write – not rewrite or copy – a *Don Quixote* that will turn out to be word for word the same as the text of Cervantes, Borges says the man has imposed upon himself an "unreal" destiny, and indeed he has. We smile at the desperate fantasy, partly accepting the sophisticated argument that Menard's text – he completed two chapters and a fragment of another – really is different from Cervantes's, although verbally nothing has changed. After all, Menard is not a native speaker of Spanish, and he lives in the wrong country and the wrong century; many of the words both writers use have changed their connotations. At the same time we're shaking our heads, laughing like Foucault. If the texts are different in one light, they are stubbornly the same in another. Borges cites a passage from Cervantes ("Truth, whose mother is history, rival of time, depository of deeds, witness of the past, exemplar and adviser to the present, and the future's counselor"), which he regards as "mere rhetorical praise of history", in contrast with the startling relativistic modernity of Menard's thought. He then quotes precisely the same words as written by Menard. His use of the phrase "on the other hand" (*"en cambio"*) to introduce the second (perfectly identical) quotation is a master stroke, perhaps the best single-phrase joke in literature (*CF* 94). But this comic, half-truthful, unreal destiny of the writer is an ordinary activity for readers, who, whatever their nationality or century, become Cervantes as they read him – while fully remaining themselves. Borges's casual tone at the end of the story – "Menard has (perhaps unintentionally) enriched the slow and rudimentary art of reading" (*CF* 95) – and his mischievous suggestion that we might want to attribute *The Imitation of Christ* to Joyce or Celine, should not mislead us. Pierre Menard, the unreal writer, is a perfect, dizzying portrait of the real reader.[21] As Gérard Genette pointed out: "Pierre Menard is the author of the *Quixote* for the sufficient reason that every reader (every true reader) is" (my translation).[22]

Barthes's line is more polemical and historically situated than Borges's mischief. He was writing in Paris in the 1960s and he had a mission. The fictions he had been calling *"mythologies"* were for many people still firmly in force as received truths, and the existence of the Author was one of them: "The author still reigns in histories of literature, biographies of writers, interviews, magazines … The image of literature to be found in ordinary culture is tyrannically centred on the author, his person, his life, his tastes, his passions."[23] What better tactic than to claim that the figure in the myth is dead, like Nietzsche's God: that is, revealed to have been non-existent all along. If he was a real God, he couldn't die – or be born, for that matter.

The Author, however, unlike God since the days of scripture, keeps leaving material traces; indeed, keeps publishing. This is where Barthes's argument joins those of Foucault and Calvino. The Author is not the writer; the former is a construction, exactly like Nietzsche's God, a figure created out of interpretative and institutional need. If there were no Authors, how could professors tell their students they were wrong about literary intentions? The writer is not a constructed figure in this sense; he or she is the material arranger of sequences of words. The writer doesn't have to die – or only as a person, not as function. In fact, the reader can welcome the writer as a companion once the old authorial deity has been fired. "The reader is the space on which all the quotations that make up a writing are inscribed without any of them being lost; a text's unity lies not in its origin but in its destination."[24]

In a later work, *The Pleasure of the Text* (1973), Barthes is even ready to let the author, as well as the writer, back into the scene of reading – "in the text, in a way, I desire the author, I need his figure … as he needs mine."[25] But of course this figure is now tame and diminished, shorn of his capital A and the baggage of the old mythology. Barthes's self-deprecating irony here approaches the tone of Borges when he invents authors too improbable to oppress us – authors who are themselves expressions of the reader's power and freedom. In "The Approach to Al-Mu'tasim" he evokes, from a pair of imaginary book reviews, a work that seems to combine the influences of Wilkie Collins and Farid Attar, the Victorian thriller and the Persian work of mysticism. And the inhabitants of Tlön don't believe in authors except as forms of fantasy. One of their modes of literary criticism is to choose two disparate works – a Chinese *Tao* and the *Arabian Nights*, say – and attribute them to a single writer. The critic's task is to "determine the psychology of that most interesting *homme de lettres*" (CF 77).

The very idea

I want to pause briefly over, and to end with, two instances where reading and writing are intimately linked, and where fiction is theory, or is immediately theorized. This is also where the trail leads us, as promised, to Italy.

Italo Calvino reminds us that *Ficciones* first appeared in Italian in 1955 (under the title *La biblioteca di Babele*), and underlines the importance of Borges's influence "on … literature in Italian, on literary taste and even on the very idea of literature."[26] This "very idea" recalls Lacan's sense that fiction itself is made possible by the adventures of the signifier, and Calvino spells his thought out eloquently by means of an analysis of the story "The Garden of Forking Paths."

He suggests that the spy-narrator of the tale can commit his "absurd and abominable crime" – the murder of an innocent man whose name is that of a strategic site in Belgium during World War I – because he possesses a concept of "ramifying time" in which "all possibilities are realized in all possible combinations" (242). We could read the story another way: the spy's crime is all the more desperate and his "endless contrition and … weariness" (CF 128) all the worse because he knows so well the difference between the actual and the virtual, the one life we all have and the many lives we might have. But Calvino's point holds in either interpretation. Ramified time, he says, "is the condition which makes literature possible" (242), and he quotes an eloquent passage from Borges on Dante:

> In real time, in history, whenever a man is confronted with several alternatives, he chooses one and eliminates and loses the others. Such is not the case in the ambiguous time of art, which is similar to that of hope and oblivion. ("The False Problem of Ugolino," *SNF* 279)

Borges is rephrasing a remark made by the man about to be murdered in "The Garden of Forking Paths":

> In all fictions, each time a man meets diverse alternatives, he chooses one and eliminates the others; in the work of the virtually impossible-to-disentangle Ts'ui Pên, the character chooses – simultaneously – all of them. He creates, thereby, "several futures," several *times*, which themselves proliferate and fork. (*CF* 125)

"In all fictions" means in all ordinary, linear fictions, those which submit to the logic of clock and calendar time. Ts'ui Pên's "almost inextricable" novel (the novel that is also a labyrinth) understands, defines, and creates the freedom of fiction, the condition of literature, the time of art. This freedom, like almost everything else in Borges, is both very real and quite unreal. It will save us, again and again, from dogmatism, madness, superstition, determinism, despair, and enclosure in the self: it is a very considerable, treasurable freedom. But it will not save us as historical, corporeal persons, because nothing can, and neither reading nor writing promises anything better than metaphorical immortality. "Those pages will not save *me*," as we read in "Borges and I" (*CF* 324).

The sadness of the second thought is too much for some readers, and they see in Borges a partisan only of ramifying time. But Borges is surely smiling either way. In his novel *The Name of the Rose* Umberto Eco rather startlingly glances at Borges through the person of the grim blind librarian, Jorge of Burgos, enemy of all change and invention, and above all the enemy of laughter. Deborah Parker has plausibly argued that with this characterization Eco is attacking not Borges the writer but Borges the symbol of isolated, unworldly bookishness, although perhaps this is to take a playful literary allusion more morally than we need to.[27] Calvino, however, worried about the same thing, and in a letter to Eco, having wondered why the novelist makes these negative associations with Borges's name, arrives at a remarkable definition of a modern, philosophical laughter which takes us back to Foucault and his long, troubled amusement over the Chinese encyclopedia. There would be two kinds of laughter, Calvino says: a carnivalesque, Bakhtinian, bodily variety, and a "mental one, the laughter of Schopenhauer when he thought of some geometrical figure or other, the laughter of Borges and – I believe – our own."[28] Calvino is right. Borges's laughter is ours – in theory and in practice.

NOTES

1 See, for example, Thomas Docherty, *After Theory*, Edinburgh University Press, 1997; Valentine Cunningham, *Reading After Theory*, Oxford, Wiley-Blackwell,

2002. Terry Eagleton, *After Theory*, New York, Basic Books, 2004; Nicholas Birns, *Theory After Theory*, London, Broadview Press, 2010; Judith Ryan, *The Novel After Theory*, New York, Columbia University Press, 2011; Jane Elliott and Derek Attridge, eds., *Theory After "Theory,"* London, Routledge, 2011.

2 For a brilliant, generous and many-faceted French response see *Jorge Luis Borges*, Paris, Cahiers de l'Herne, 1964.

3 Michel Foucault, *The Order of Things*, translator unnamed, London, Routledge, 1989, xv. Further quotations are taken up into the text.

4 Georges Charbonnier, *Entretiens avec Jorges Luis Borges*, Gallimard, Paris, 1967, 124.

5 For these details and others see Edwin Williamson, *Borges: A Life*, New York, Viking, 2004, 346.

6 Jacques Lacan, "Seminar on 'The Purloined Letter'," trans. Jeffrey Mehlman, *Yale French Studies* 48 (1972), 53.

7 Cf. "a pure signifier – the purloined letter"; "it is that truth [the decisive orientation which the subject receives from the itinerary of a signifier] which makes the very existence of fiction possible"; "the signifier … materializes the agency of death." *Yale French Studies*, 45, 40, 53.

8 "Postscript," *Other Inquisitions*, trans. Ruth L. C. Simms, Austin, University of Texas Press, 1964, 189.

9 "Note on Bernard Shaw," ibid., 164. See also Jaime Alazraki, "Borges and the New Critical Idiom," in *Borges and his Successors*, ed. Edna Aizenberg, Columbia and London, University of Missouri Press, 1990, 105–6.

10 Jacques Derrida, "Plato's Pharmacy," in *Dissemination*, trans. Barbara Johnson, Chicago, University of Chicago Press, 1981, 86.

11 Ibid., 89.

12 Cf. "language is first … writing"; "this stock of writing, noted or not, that language is." Jacques Derrida, *Of Grammatology*, trans. Gayatri Chakravorty Spivak, Baltimore, Johns Hopkins University Press, 1976, 37, 53.

13 Plato, *Phaedrus*, trans. W. C. Helmhold, Indianapolis, Bobbs-Merrill, 1956, 77, 73. See also Derrida, *Of Grammatology*, 14.

14 Derrida, "Plato's Pharmacy," 93.

15 "The idea of the book, which always refers to a natural totality, is profoundly alien to the sense of writing." Derrida, *Of Grammatology*, 18.

16 Charbonnier, *Entretiens*, 130, my translation.

17 Julia Kristeva, *Powers of Horror: An Essay on Abjection*, trans. Leon S. Roudiez, New York, Columbia University Press, 1982, 15, 96, 18. Further quotations are taken up into the text.

18 Stéphane Mallarmé, "Crise de vers," in *Poésies et autres textes*, Paris, Librairie générale française, 2005, 358. Marcel Proust, *Against Sainte-Beuve*, trans. John Sturrock, London, Penguin, 1998, 15. W. B. Yeats, "A General Introduction to My Work," in *Essays and Introductions*, London, Macmillan, 1961, 509.

19 Michel Foucault, "What is an Author?" trans. Donald F. Bouchard and Sherry Simon, in *Language, Counter-Memory, Practice*, Ithaca, NY, Cornell University Press, 1977. Italo Calvino, "Cybernetics and Ghosts," in *The Literature Machine*, trans. Patrick Creagh, New York, Vintage, 1997.

20 W. K. Wimsatt and Monroe Beardsley, *The Verbal Icon: Studies in the Meaning of Poetry*, Lexington, University of Kentucky Press, 1954, 3.

21 See Gérard Genette, *Figures*, Paris, Seuil, 1966, 132.
22 Gérard Genette, *Palimpsestes*, Paris, Seuil, 1982, 296.
23 Roland Barthes, "The Death of the Author," in *Image-Music-Text*, ed. and trans. Stephen Heath, New York, Hill and Wang, 1977, 142–48, 143.
24 Ibid., 148.
25 Roland Barthes, *The Pleasure of the Text*, trans. Richard Miller, New York, Hill and Wang, 1975, 27.
26 Italo Calvino, *Why Read the Classics?*, trans. Martin McLaughlin, New York, Pantheon Books, 1999, 237. Further quotations are taken up into the text.
27 Deborah Parker, "The Literature of Appropriation: Eco's Use of Borges in *Il Nome della Rosa*," *Modern Language Review*, 85 (1990), 842–49.
28 Italo Calvino, *Lettere*, Milan: Mondadori, 2000, 1442. My translation.

4

SUZANNE JILL LEVINE

Borges on translation

Not an impossible task

Borges did not consider translation an impossible task: "In prose, the colloquial meaning is the most valid, and finding its equivalent tends to be easy."[1] Translation is not only possible but also essential to the understanding of literature: "No problem is as consubstantial to literature and its modest mystery as the one posed by translation," he wrote in "The Homeric Versions" (*SNF* 69). Translation is not only intrinsic to the reading process, but, as he asserts in the same essay, it is "destined to illustrate aesthetic debate." Written from a peripheral Argentina that looked toward Europe as the center of culture (with Paris as its capital), Borges's statement reverberates far and wide: not only is translation a literary practice motivated by aesthetic goals and choices, but it is itself a facet of reading and writing, the link between and across languages and literatures.

Borges first made this statement, as well as the now famous dictum at the end of the first paragraph of his essay on versions of Homer – to wit: that the concept of "definitive text" is relevant only to religious dogma or exhaustion – in his prologue to the Spanish translation of Paul Valéry's *Le Cimetière marin* (*Sea Cemetery*) published a few months before "The Homeric Versions." Borges would often recycle his material, expanding, evolving, supplementing ideas and citations, thereby showing in practical terms that no enunciation is definitive or exhaustible. In "The Homeric Versions" he repeated not only a phrase but the first two paragraphs of his discussion from the Valéry prologue where, in effect, he had redefined the categories of original and translation by placing both kinds of texts on an equal plane as "drafts." In the same text, he praised the bilingual Nestor Ibarra as not only a great translator of Valéry into Spanish, but also the best translator of Borges into French. As Borges wrote later about Ibarra in the preface to the French edition of his poetry published in 1965: "Ibarra does not misinterpret the connotations of irony, tenderness and nostalgia that nuance each word in my poems ... he understands the affinities and differences of the two poetic languages."[2] This time speaking not of prose but of poetry, Borges affirms that the gifted ear, the translator who intimately knows the culture and language of the text's origins as well as the language into which he is translating it, can produce a successful recreation.

Borges is also a pragmatist in that he does not trust general theories, but rather evaluates "particular" translations and originals alike, case by case: hence the work itself matters more than its author. He criticizes author-centric modern readers (the today he spoke of was the twentieth century) who read the writer rather than the work. Art matters more than the individual artist, and translation dramatizes the error readers make upon thinking, for example, that they're reading Borges or Valéry when, in fact, the aesthetic experience has been produced by Ibarra in conjunction with a Borges or Valéry – the collaborative or non-authorial spirit of Borges's perspective here was at the very heart of his own many collaborations with his friends, most notably with Bioy Casares.

These ideas illustrate how essential Borges's broad understanding of translation (both as a writerly activity and as a text) was to his poetics and practices as a writer. The implications, as we shall see, of translation as a paradigm for reading, writing, and critical interpretation bear fruit not only in his numerous translations but also in almost every essay, poem, review, prologue, and story he wrote from the 1920s through to the 1980s. To follow such a fertile path would require an entire book. Thus, while glancing over a range of texts, I will highlight those four essays whose principal theme is translation – "Two Ways to Translate" (1926, see endnote 1), "The Homeric Versions" (1932, *SNF* 69–74), "The Translators of *The Thousand and One Nights*" (1936, *SNF* 92–109), "The Enigma of Edward FitzGerald" (1951, *SNF* 366–68) – as well as his quintessential *ficción*, "Pierre Menard, Author of the *Quixote*."

Borges's views on translation have trickled down to literary thinkers such as George Steiner and Umberto Eco, and have been analyzed at length in numerous essays, dissertations, and books.[3] Steiner called "Pierre Menard, Author of the *Quixote*" "arguably ... the most acute, most concentrated commentary anyone has offered on the business of translation."[4] Menard is an imaginary author who recreates word for word excerpts from *Don Quixote*, passages which, though identical to the original, signify something entirely different from anything Cervantes may have imagined. Translation, like reading, always follows an original, whether or not its origins are known, and is by its very nature anachronistic. As I have discussed in *The Subversive Scribe*, my book on the creative and critical act of translation,

I believe Borges provides the most lucid perspectives for the understanding of literary translation.[5]

Invisible work

Efraín Kristal's *Invisible Work* (the title alludes to the way Borges's narrator refers to Pierre Menard's "fantastic" feat) summarizes the three aspects of Borges's engagement with translation which informs the essays we will explore. Kristal observes that the obscure books (better known in the Edwardian era) which Borges perversely celebrates in his many essays and fictions became "secret masterpieces" thanks to the invisible workings of Borges himself. Creation in Borges emerged organically, systemically, and simultaneously along with his elaborations as a translator, and the notion of what a writer is, indeed, emerged out of Borges's version of what a translator is, or can do, especially when that translator is Borges. The first chapter, "Borges on Translation," takes on the slippery challenge of Borges's translation theory (theory in a uniquely Borgesian mode, that is) by leading us through numerous essays and stories to show how Borges subtracts from the history of translation and its theoretical positions those elements which most help him construct his ideas and especially his practices as a reader and writer. Kristal illustrates, for example, that translation mistakes are sometimes more valuable than so-called accurate translations: texts are inevitably appropriated by readers, and become for the creative mind pretexts for the act of writing and, ultimately, the resurrection of a kindred imagination.

Borges precisely avoids the pitfalls of taking theoretical positions such as in the debate between Matthew Arnold and the linguistic scholar Francis Newman on translating Homer. Borges exposes the insights and blindness of both gentlemen to show, ultimately, how both positions are valid, depending on the function or effect of the version at hand (*SNF* 71). In Borges's portrayal, either is right, depending on text, context, and reader, depending particularly on the emphases that matter in a given context. Their seemingly ironclad positions melt away but what remains is the continuing elaboration of the work of art despite the intentions of individuals. Borges sees the other side always, and tells us both sides simultaneously with his famous insight that there is no such thing as a "definitive text" (*SNF* 69). And yet, who loves the great classics we consider definitive more than the man who utters these seditious words?

In his chapter on Borges as translator, we get to study the specific transformations in Borges's translations of writers such as Walt Whitman, Edgar Allan Poe, and Franz Kafka, and how Borges, by improving upon and enriching the originals, was developing his own strategies as a writer. The book's final chapter, "Translation in the Creative Process," reveals how translation scaffolds Borges's fictions in our now increased and detailed awareness of the presence of other writers' works in Borges's texts. Furthermore, Kristal discusses at length the now visible presence throughout Borges's works of the trope, or metaphorics of translation, the word whose etymological meaning is metaphor.

In the context of his early career as an avant-garde poet, Borges's first essay on translation, written in 1926, came out in *Inquisitions* and was called, no doubt with some irony, "Two Ways to Translate." By the mid 1920s, young Borges (who by age nine had experienced and published his first translation, of Oscar Wilde's story "The Happy Prince") was well aware of translation (and particularly Anglophone) controversies centered on the ideological and linguistic complexities of the Bible, Dante, and Homer, most notably the Arnold–Newman debate about Homer – "more important," he observes, "than either of its two participants" (*SNF* 71).

He had already concluded that a "literal" formula for fidelity to an original was by definition absurd, and would lay this idea to rest most effectively via the "invisible" work of the intrepid and phantasmal Pierre Menard. But beyond questioning accepted notions about originals and authors, Borges, as the creative reader, was also arguing that, as there are endless interpretations by diverse readers of any given text, there is no *one* way to translate. To begin with, countless works throughout history have been translated, many of them repeatedly, hence Borges's close reading of generations of English poets who had translated Homer's epics, as a way into understanding Homer's contributions to Western culture.

"Two Ways to Translate"

"Two Ways to Translate" highlights the dialectic shape of translation arguments of which the above-mentioned Arnold–Newman debate is typical, opposing "spirit" to "letter" or "literary" to "literal." By setting forth to define two ways, with the usual ironic sleight of hand, he not only summarizes the historical dueling duets over translation, but opens the floodgates beyond dialectics into the ineffable world of chance and imagination. There is always more than one way, and by inference there are multiple ways, of translating any text, just as there are many different interpretative approaches to any literary work. While appearing to summarize what's been said, Borges steps out of his own frame to reflect implicitly on his inevitable limitation as yet another reader. His genial discussion, apparently objective and supposedly didactic, soon reveals, as with all intelligent critics, his own interests, aesthetic preferences, ethical stances. The underlying thrust of "Two Ways to Translate" brings to the foreground a paradox: while preferring a classical Aristotelian approach to writing and translating, Borges has a problem with the sacred concept of "classic" for the very reason that any work, classic or eccentric, is the product of contingencies and of a progression of readings. Here he takes issue, from the cultural context of an urban Argentine writer in the early twentieth century, with the canonization of Argentina's national poem *Martín Fierro*, which has its virtues but also its defects.

In this article, whose ideas would be further refined in "The Homeric Versions" and "The Translators of *The Thousand and One Nights*," he defines the "two ways" in terms of aesthetic positions, that is, the art-centered classical approach and the artist-centered romantic approach, revisiting, as mentioned, the famous nineteenth-century debate of the classicist man of letters Matthew Arnold, who favored a "plain" and "noble" Homer in his attack upon polyglot linguist Newman, who favored a literal rendering which would make transparent all the linguistic quirks of the poetry. While "Classical" and "Romantic" pertain to precise historical periods of Western art, Borges uses them generically as the aesthetic tendencies they have come to signify. However, as with all categories Borges places in question, he reveals how their definitions, beyond the strictly historical contexts, are ultimately in flux – thus, of course, showing us by example how important it is to deal with the particular as opposed to attempting general principles. For example, in a mischievous 1930s essay, "The Postulation of Reality," he makes us realize that while Gibbon's history of the Roman Empire proposes to be classical, the results are romantic – one of numerous instances where these terms cross each other's boundaries as if they were Tweedle Dee and Tweedle Dum.

Nonetheless, the two categories serve as a convenient departure in this first stab at a discussion of translation. Again, by the time the young poet Borges was in his twenties, his poetic tastes and strategies were already formed, and whether the object of discussion was originals or translations, in a subversive modernist way his "classical" focus places the work in the spotlight by placing the master in the shadows – in line with T. S. Eliot's "Tradition and the Individual Talent" (1920).

Borges writes in 1926 about two ways of translating:

Universally, I suppose there are two kinds of translations, the literal and paraphrase. The former corresponds to the romantic mentality, the second to the classical. I'd like to explain this statement in order to diminish its aura of paradox. The classical way of thinking is interested only in the work of art, never the artist. The classics believe in absolute perfection and seek it out. They despise localisms, oddities, contingencies. Poetry must be a beauty similar to the moon, eternal, dispassionate, impartial. The metaphor, for example, is not considered by classicism as either emphasis or personal vision, but as the attainment of poetic truth which, once engineered, can be (and should be) seized by all. Each literature possesses a repertory of these truths, and the translator knows how to take advantage of it and to pour the original not only into the words but into the syntax and usual metaphors of his language. This procedure seems sacrilegious to us, and sometimes it is. Our condemnation, nevertheless, suffers from optimism, since most metaphors are no longer representations, but merely mechanical. Nobody, upon hearing the adverb "spiritually" thinks of breath of air, or of the spirit; nobody sees any difference (not even of stress) between the phrases "dreadfully poor" and "poor as a church mouse."

Conversely, romantics never seek the work of art, but rather the man himself. Man (we already know) is neither timeless nor an archetype, he's Jack So and So, not John Doe; he possesses a way of being, a body, an origin; he does something, or nothing, has a present, past, future and even his death is his. Beware of twisting one word of those he wrote!

That reverence for the I, for the irreplaceable human difference which is any I, justifies literal translations. Besides, the faraway, the foreign is always beautiful. Novalis clearly articulated this romantic sentiment: distant philosophies resound like poetry. Everything becomes poetic in the distance: faraway hills, faraway men, faraway events, and so on. From such derives the poetic essence of human nature. "Poems of the night and of the penumbra" (*Werke*, III, 213). Delight in the faraway, homey voyage through time and space, vestuary of foreign destinies, promised to us by the literary translations of ancient works, a promise that generally remains in the prologue. The announced purpose of truth makes the translator a charlatan since to maintain the strangeness of what he's translating he finds himself obliged to thicken the local color, to roughen the rough edges, to sweeten the sweetness and to emphasize everything including the lie. (My translation)[6]

Where this discussion begun in "Two Ways" might take us, beyond Borges's move away from author-centered values, is to the creative reader, which is maybe why he ceased, in his later essays, to speak of such categories as classical and romantic, irrelevant if what matters is the reception of texts – that is, the reader. Regarding this creature, Borges was not so much defending or attacking approaches to translation as he was proposing to de-classify a classic, that is, *Martín Fierro*, the nineteenth-century romantic gaucho poem which was so greatly revered by his fellow Argentines.

Anonymous classics: Homer and "*The Thousand and One Nights*"

Homer's epic poems and "*The Thousand and One Nights*" the classics of world literature to which Borges dedicated essays that explicitly examine the field of translation history, share in common their popularity with readers through the ages, and their questionable authorship. Both apparently began as oral traditions and cannot be traced to a single author whose identity is indisputable. Moreover, the *Nights* were translated from different sources at different times and, as they passed into various European languages acquired additions which, ironically, became the tales for which they were most known, especially the framing story of Scheherazade. The survival and transformations of such literary monuments over centuries and languages no doubt contributed to Borges's own very original and ironic "theory" of translation, which he expounds in "The Homeric Versions," namely, that the only difference between an original and a translation is that a translation can be measured against a visible text – a point both obvious and previously unnoticed, like the purloined letter, and worthy of that joker, Pierre Menard.

Rather than taking the pessimistic view that we will never know intimately the original language, never know whether Homer's images like the "wine-dark sea" and epithets like the "wily" Odysseus were his inventions or the everyday speech of ancient Greece, Borges takes his "ignorance" as an opportunity to discover the poetry of the English language. Translation is not what you lose but what you gain. In the same light, Borges spoke of the contribution of the Celtic monk the Venerable Bede, who wrote in Latin and who translated the Bible. Borges mused: "It is beautiful to think that he died translating – that is, achieving the least vain and most self-effacing of literary tasks – and translating from Greek or Latin into Anglo-Saxon which, in time, would become the vast English language."[7]

Homer becomes a rich library of marvelous books, all those versions by one seafaring culture which felt affinities with that other ancient one. Ezra Pound preferred the lyrical emotion of Chapman's version, but for Borges, epic exaltation was essential. His own aesthetic preference is Pope's "speeches and spectacles," in part because Pope's Homer is reminiscent of the hyperboles of the Baroque poet Luis de Góngora in the Spanish Golden Age. Any reading is contextual, Borges again reminds us.

As in "Pierre Menard," "The Garden of Forking Paths," and his later meditation "The Enigma of Edward FitzGerald," "The Translators of *The Thousand and One Nights*" explores, among other things, Borges's fascination not only with books but with men who are fascinated by and submerge themselves in other cultures, times, and languages. His essay reveals, in particular, how his interpretation of this labyrinthine chapter in literary history uses the subject of translation to discuss his own intricate relationship with literature and its producers. Of particular interest are the curious mistranslations which seem unavoidable in cultural exchange, as well as the reception of this ubiquitous book in its various reincarnations in the Western canon. Aside from his childhood in his Anglo-Argentine father's library, a key to Borges's fascination with the *Nights* was his innate cosmopolitanism.[8] Though not a popular attribute in certain intellectual circles during the 1930s and 1940s, such a spirit was central to characterizations of Argentine cultural identity. "The universe is our birthright," (*SNF* 427), Borges pronounced in his famous lecture "The Argentine Writer and Tradition", a title which pays homage to T. S. Eliot's modernist manifesto "Tradition and the Individual Talent."

For Borges, growing up in his father's English library, in the bosom of an Anglo-Argentine family steeped in European liberalism and Victorian morals, the *Nights* were his childhood entry into the forbidden world of sex. His father, a frustrated novelist, significantly destroyed a book of Oriental stories he had written inspired in the *Arabian Nights*. Hence, it shouldn't surprise us that this book often appears in his stories (for example "The South") as an icon or displacement for erotic content, as well as a literary terrain to be explored by a son created to fulfill his father's desires. For the writer Borges, *The Thousand and One Nights* (that *One* extra night and *mise en abyme* in the title intrigued him the most) offered, moreover, like Part II of *Don Quixote*, a template for an infinite textuality, an endless stream of stories which can be read and reread in order to be rewritten anew. Furthermore, for the Argentine Borges, that the book was a translation, arriving in a form assumed by a classic "Oriental" text in a European language, made it germane to his region's marginality in the Western literary tradition. In its misinterpreted though familiar exoticism, the Arab world could be and was often associated with Latin America under the colonial gaze of Europe and Anglo-America. Sir Richard Burton's "adventures" in both Africa and Latin America exemplify such a positioning.

Regarding this realization, it is interesting to note how Borges embarks on the *Nights*, discussing the literary figure whose version he apparently preferred but also who, among all the European translators, most intrigued him as a flesh and blood individual. This writer was Sir Richard Burton, British consul in Trieste, a linguist who knew some of the most obscure languages in the world, a scholar and adventurer who discovered the source of the Nile and who fought in wars in South America, a libertine who scandalized Victorian England with his exploits and with his pen: in brief, the kind of man Borges, a bookworm with unfulfilled yearnings for a more active and sexual life, could certainly admire and even perhaps envy.

The Argentine immediately speculates about a "secret aim" of Burton's famous 1872 translation, namely, to annihilate his predecessor, the Orientalist Edward Lane, who in 1839, Borges continues, had in turn, translated against his predecessor, Antoine Galland, the French translator.[9] Borges implies here that translation is a polemical tool, an act of literary criticism in which one informed reader imposes his interpretation upon another's. His argument also suggests that through translation one writer duels against another, that translation is a perfect weapon to kill a father figure, to assert one's own paternity. Borges may also be telling his reader that his own "secret aim" may be to damn with praise and to pay homage with ironic reservations: for while Burton's was the best version of the *Nights* in his view, Burton's version was often awkward and inconsistent, and the man himself was an ingenuous positivist who did not recognize that while he thought he succeeded where Lane failed, his appropriation of the cultural Other was problematic: Burton was too naïve to realize that even great translations, like many originals, are brilliant failures.

Rather than beating a dead camel – that is, the Lane–Burton debate – at this point in his essay Borges covers his tracks, as it were, and goes back to his job as literary historian: "Let me begin with the founder," he says, meaning Antoine Galland (74). In the eighteenth century Galland brought from Istanbul a copy of the book along with a supplement from someone "said to be Hanna" – and Borges notes both the questionable origin of the supplementary stories and the fact that these are among the stories which were to become most popular, such as "Aladdin's Lamp" and "Ali Baba and the Forty Thieves." Always the ironist, Borges remarks that this translation, filled with "jewels and magic spells," was both the "worst and the most read" – and praised – by writers who would have significant impact on literary culture, such as Coleridge, De Quincey, Stendhal, and Poe (74). These writers, particularly Coleridge, De Quincey, and especially Poe, would in turn be significant precursors of Borges, of course.

Galland's version was much criticized, Borges notes. One reason was because it suffers – perhaps inevitably – from anachronisms: Weil, a German scholar whose translation Borges would peg as the most pleasant of the four uninspiring German translations, points out, for example, that a *"valise"* should be a "saddlebag" (74). More serious was Galland's so-called decorum, suppressing, as the Victorian Lane will later do, scenes, descriptions, and stories (such as kings who had many wives) that a Western reader of that era might consider obscene. Borges remarks mischievously, defending Galland against the criticisms of André Gide who favored Mardrus's version, that the repression of these elements makes the book actually more obscene, since more is left to the reader's imagination.

Moving on to the scholarly Lane, Borges delights in the paradox that while his translation was "an encyclopedia of evasion," Lane was admirably faithful, resorting – unlike Galland, who simply practiced the art of omission – to explanatory and scholarly footnotes (76). Lane, unlike his successor Burton, had no polemical or ulterior motive other than that of bringing the wonders of the Orient to Western readers, but Borges is quick to point out – without using jargon – that ideology is never absent despite an author's visible intentions. Lane becomes for Borges exemplary of the notion of censorship not only as a predictable aspect of translation between cultures whose moral codes were so different, but as a form of creation. Comparing this "creativity" sarcastically with certain procedures of Hollywood, where husbands and wives slept only in twin beds until the Hayes code was defrocked by the sexual revolution of the 1960s, Borges is suggesting that such creative processes are not alien to him. Censorship is seen in an affirmative light through the Borgesian looking glass, or rather it is considered, at the very least, unavoidable in the act of interpretation.

While Galland and Lane "disinfected" the *Nights*, however, Borges points out that they also invented the concept of the "marvelous" – an adjective missing from the original book which, as Borges comments, was in its own culture, only an "adaptation" of smutty jokes and stories well known to "Cairo's middle classes" (77). Citing Enno Littman, the German translator whom Borges would criticize for being the most faithful and least inspired, Borges stresses that the book which Galland introduced to the Western reader was, on the contrary, a "collection of marvels," projecting a "magical atmosphere." This defining factor made it a more popular and much greater commercial success than it had been for its original readers who, after all, already knew the original characters and customs which those stories portray.

At this juncture of the essay Borges returns to Burton, who claimed to have a command of thirty-five languages and wrote seventy-two volumes, and who apparently experienced every kind of sexuality and cuisine, not to mention, in his African wanderings, cannibalism. Borges sums all this up – as if following Lane's prudish example – with his best stuffy British librarian tone: "the attractions of the forbidden are his" (79). Certainly by alluding to Burton's friendship with the poet Algernon Swinburne, well known for his homosexuality, Borges means to leave tantalizing trails for his reader's imagination – once again proving the vicarious joys of censorship.

What exactly did Borges like about Burton's version? He criticizes Burton for a "lack of ear" in his verses, and for an inconsistency in the language ranging from the literal to the colloquial. It would appear that he praised most of all the erotic erudition, the copious copulating footnotes as it were – hence not so much the pleasure of the text as of the sex – and the fact that this translation was somewhere between a recreation and an act of literary criticism. To wit, Burton had created a heterogeneous genre – one might say like Borges's *ficciones* – somewhere between narrative, essay, and poetry.

The one other element in both Burton and Mardrus which was decisive in Borges's mind was the title, *The Thousand and One Nights*, which, following Galland, added that "One Night," which represented the framing tale of Scheherazade, valued by Borges as the gateway to the infinite *mise en abyme* of storytelling reaching from the picturesque past into the unfathomable future.

From his discussion of the enterprising Burton, whose motives were to glorify his reputation as an Arabist and to gain readers, Borges traveled chronologically and back across the Channel to the French version of "doctor Mardrus." Here he slapped Gide on the hand, not for preferring Mardrus, but rather for using the wrong reasons to play Mardrus against Galland, claiming the latter to be more unfaithful than the former. On the contrary, this 1899 French version was the most readable after Burton's, but also because, once again, it was not faithful. Borges tells us why: Mardrus was an illustrator, providing the reader with "art-nouveau" flourishes, "visual Orientalism." Rather than a literal translator, Mardrus was an inter-semiotic translator; hence Borges compares Mardrus's "interpolations" – not without his usual tongue-in-cheek tone – to the biblical extravaganzas of the Hollywood classic filmmaker Cecil B. DeMille.

While with his discussion of Dr. Mardrus he reaches the climax of the essay, a celebration of felicitous "creative infidelity," perhaps he saves for last his most important critique of the German versions. The summary of this critique could be: each literature, each culture, each era appropriated the *Nights* according to its own deforming mirror; the better translations were better because they, in turn, in Poundian spirit, brought something new into the target literature and language. In the case of Germany, a country which had generated such a prolific body of fantastic literature in the nineteenth century, Borges was disappointed by the relatively "tranquil" results. He concluded that "the exchange between the *Nights* and Germany should have produced something more" (86). Finally, referring to Germany's *Unheimlichkeit*, the "uncanny" (Freud lurks in this remark as well as Germany's vast library of fairy tales), Borges ended his essay with a tantalizing question that was also an answer: the creative translator to transport the *Nights* into German would have to be Kafka himself.

Translation and reincarnation

"The Enigma of Edward FitzGerald" pays homage to the curious fate of this minor Victorian poet whose fame was due to his translation of Omar Khayyam's *Rubaiyat*, a quintessential love poem from old Persia. For Borges, FitzGerald was a kindred spirit but, even more, a precursor of his father

Jorge Borges, that anarchist lawyer and frustrated novelist, who translated into Spanish FitzGerald's version of the *Rubaiyat*, and whose son would fulfill his dreams of literary glory. Like Pierre Menard, FitzGerald was an avid reader of *Don Quixote*; the Englishman was separated by seven centuries from the Persian poet and was "less intellectual than Omar, but perhaps more sensitive and sadder," Borges writes. And yet, a kind of miracle occurred in the textual encounter between these two dissimilar beings:

> From the fortuitous conjunction of a Persian astronomer who condescended to write poetry and an eccentric Englishman who peruses Oriental and Hispanic books, perhaps without understanding them completely, emerges an extraordinary poet who resembles neither of them. (*SNF* 368)

The transmigration of Khayyam's obscure quatrains into FitzGerald's great "English poem with Persian allusions" (*SNF* 368) becomes, in Borges's recounting, almost identical to the odyssey of the *Nights* – an obscure book from the East turns into a canonical work in the West. Borges's obsession, whether admiration or rivalry, vis-à-vis Burton seems displaced, however, by a sympathetic sense of communion in this tale of FitzGerald and Khayyam, a nostalgic communion with phantoms sought throughout his life as reader, writer, and translator, seeking the spirit through the letter. His communion with writers included not only those he read and rewrote but, again, those friends he collaborated with, such as Bioy Casares, with whom he created a third writer, Bustos Domecq (and other pseudonyms). This third writer did not resemble either of them and was nicknamed "Biorges" by Emir Rodríguez Monegal. In Borges's world, collaboration and translation were, in a way, two sides of the same coin, as he concludes in his meditation on FitzGerald:

> All collaboration is mysterious. That of the Englishman and the Persian was even more so, for the two were quite different, and perhaps in life might not have been friends; death and vicissitudes and time led one to know the other and make them into a single poet. (*SNF* 368)

NOTES

1 "Two Ways to Translate," in J. L. Borges, *On Writing*, ed. with an introduction and notes by S. J. Levine, Penguin Classics, New York, Penguin, 2010, 54; "Las dos maneras de traducir," in *J. L. Borges: Textos recobrados 1919–1929*, Buenos Aires, Emecé, 1997, 256.

2 J. L. Borges, "Préface a l'Édition Française," *Œuvre poétique (1925–1965)*, trans. Nestor Ibarra, Paris, Gallimard, 1965, 8. My translation.

3 See Efraín Kristal, *Invisible Work: Borges and Translation*, Nashville, TN, Vanderbilt University Press, 2002, and Sergio Waisman's postcolonial discussion in *Borges on Translation: The Irreverence of the Periphery*, Lewisburg, PA, Bucknell University Press, 2005.

4 In *After Babel: Aspects of Language and Translation*, Oxford University Press, 1975, **p. 70**.

5 See Suzanne Jill Levine, *The Subversive Scribe: Translating Latin American Fiction*, London, Dalkey Archive Press, 2009.

6 See also, "Two Ways to Translate," in Borges, *On Writing*, 54.

7 "Beda el Venerable," *Literaturas germánicas medievales* [1966], in *Obras completas en colaboración*, J. L. Borges with María Esther Vázquez, Buenos Aires, Emecé, 1995, 882–4. My translation.

8 Dominique Jullien, "In Praise of Mistranslation: The Melancholy Cosmopolitanism of Jorge Luis Borges," *Romanic Review*, 98 (2007), Special Issue: Jorge Luis Borges (ed. with intro. by S. J. Levine), 205–24.

9 "The Translators of *The Thousand and One Nights*," in *Borges: A Reader*, Emir Rodríguez Monegal and Alastair Reid (eds.), New York, E. P. Dutton, 1981, 73. My discussion of Borges's ideas on translation began in the 1970s with Rodríguez Monegal, hence I would like to use this edition to cite this essay on the *Nights*. Subsequent page references are given in the main text. The essay first appeared in its entirety in *A History of Eternity* (1936) (see *SNF* 92–109).

5

EVELYN FISHBURN

Jewish, Christian, and Gnostic themes

Borges was a self-confessed non-believer for whom God was at best an unknowable entity beyond human comprehension. His often quoted opinion that he considered theology and religion branches of the literature of the fantastic is usually taken as a witty quip, dismissive of them both, but this overlooks the value that Borges places on the literature of the fantastic. What he ridicules is not religious thought *per se* but its claims to universal truth, yet what he is implicitly, though indirectly, praising is its special value as a source of literary metaphors. It should be borne in mind that for Borges, the literature of the fantastic is not one of escape, but a means of approaching and expressing the mysterious character of the universe. This explains, in part, the widespread presence of religious motifs in his writings, particularly his fiction.

Borges was knowledgeable about most major religions but he referred most frequently to Judeo-Christian elements. The teachings of a devoutly Catholic mother and a Presbyterian grandmother who knew her Bible intimately were offset by the influence of a free-thinking father, and the tension between these oppositional influences can be felt in Borges's handling of religion in his fiction. This could be summarized as being invariably accurate, learned, though not rigorous or scholarly, and perhaps even sensitive at times, but what distinguishes it above all is its subversive and countercultural thrust. In this introductory discussion of Jewish, Christian, and Gnostic elements I shall focus principally on a few representative texts from the canonical fiction since I believe this is where their controversial use is most imaginative. Their division into separate categories is not meant to be in any way exclusive but should be seen as simply a convenient device to identify the presence of certain concepts in a particular context.

Jewish themes

Borges's interest in Judaism is extensive, encompassing a preoccupation with the Wandering Jew and the Jewish diasporic condition, with matters of Jewish identity, particularly in an Argentine context, and with questions of anti-Semitism. His Jewish characters adhere to no stereotype and include outlaws as much as peace-loving, bookish intellectuals. Though far from idealized, they are mostly sympathetically portrayed, even in the case of the murderess Emma Zunz, discussed below. Ultimately, Jews and all things Jewish are but a point of departure to convey motifs that transcend a single allegiance.

Borges found in the Old Testament a rich source for fictional inspiration, as evidenced by the many biblical quotations used as epigraphs, and by the reworkings of stories such as Cain's fratricide into a number of different fictions of oppositional rivalry. These are as varied as "*Deutsches Requiem*," "The Interloper," or "The End," in addition to the ones discussed below, while "The Circular Ruins" re-tells the Golem legend, and is also a gloss on the first chapter of Genesis. However, the Kabbalah is Borges's preeminent fount of inspiration and the closest to the essence and substance of his own creative writing. In his essay "A Vindication of the Kabbalah," he makes clear that it is not the doctrine itself that interests him, but its emphasis on the symbolic nature of language and the hermeneutic and cryptographic elements associated with it. His writing has much in common with the Kabbalists' understanding of the universe as a system of symbols.[1] The essay's title is deliberately provocative: Kabbalah presupposes a faith in the possible revelation of the true word of God and, therefore, the hidden meaning of the universe, but this is an idea that Borges, far from vindicating, consistently undermines and derides. That is why every epiphanic instance in the fiction must be measured against its possibly ironic presentation. This applies to all the stories discussed in this section and arguably to all others.

Kabbalah derives from its Hebrew meaning, "tradition," and refers to a system of Jewish theosophy or intuitive knowledge of the Divine developed in Spain in the eleventh and twelfth centuries. Its principal concepts are compiled in the *Zohar* (Book of Splendour) and the *Sefer Yetzirah* (Book of Creation). Given Borges's attraction to the marginal, it may be worth pointing out that Kabbalist ideas, mystical and speculative, are not part of mainstream Judaism, which views them with considerable misgivings. Borges admits to having but dabbled in these impenetrable texts, and his information is largely from secondary sources, which he read not with the fervor of a Kabbalist but as a fabulist with an interest in esoterica.

Some themes that have found their way into Borges's fiction are distilled versions of Kabbalah's extremely complex cosmogony, for example the belief that the universe is the enactment of a pre-existing text, crafted from the thirty-two paths of wisdom, that is, from the combination of the ten primordial numbers and the twenty-two letters of the Hebrew alphabet.

These are supposedly endowed with magical properties lending a metaphysical dimension to language, so that its meaning can never be grasped in its plenitude. This, however, has not dissuaded Kabbalists from attempting to decipher God's text through speculative exegetic efforts.

The two stories that engage with these themes most directly are "The Library of Babel" and "The Writing of the God." In the first of these the eponymous Library, a clear metaphor for the universe, is laid out in repeating hexagons holding a series of equally repeating texts whose contents are predictable yet unintelligible to the human mind. Yet the librarians, variably referred to as "pilgrims," "infidels," or "inquisitors," persist in their Kabbalah-driven search for The Book that may hold the elusive clue to Revelation. But, as in the Bible story of the Tower of (precisely) Babel, where man's presumption to attain knowledge was punished by chaos and confusion, the search leads to mayhem: "These pilgrims squabbled in the narrow corridors, muttered dark imprecations, strangled one another on the divine staircases, threw deceiving volumes down ventilation shafts, were themselves hurled to their deaths by men of distant regions" (*CF* 115). Fittingly, the story ends with "an elegant hope" of survival, but of the Library, not its inhabitants.

"The Writing of the God" tells the story of Tzinacán, his incarceration, and his search for the forgotten magic formula which brings him the revelation that God's cryptic message is encoded in the spots of a jaguar held in a cell next to his, ending with his dismissive refusal to utter the remembered fourteen syllables that would give him his power and his freedom. "The Writing of the God" is unusual in that it blurs cultural boundaries, intermingling not only Maya, Aztec, and Quiché elements with Kabbalistic themes, but also passing references to Hindu and Buddhist ideas. Needless to say, it could be read from any one of these perspectives, but given that in the epilogue to his collection *The Aleph* Borges draws attention to the fact that he has put Kabbalistic arguments in the mind of a Mayan priest, it does not seem inappropriate to offer an interpretation based on such arguments.

The priest's fervent conviction of the textuality of the universe (as suggested in the title) fictionalizes one of the fundamental concerns of Kabbalah. Moreover, his belief in a secret message which he had once possessed, and in its recovery by means of mystical exegesis, echoes the Kabbalist idea that Adam was born with total wisdom which was lost at the time of the Fall and which we are forever trying to retrieve. Needless to say, these Kabbalistic arguments are presented against the grain, and this becomes apparent from the tension between the protagonist's account of his epiphanic experience and the less trusting meanings that may be deduced from it. Tzinacán's refusal to speak the magic words he sees on the jaguar's coat is explained by him as a mystical "overcoming" of the self and a dissolution into the Divine presence. (This is a prime case of Kabbalah overlapping with Gnosticism and Neo-Platonism.) But his refusal can also be interpreted as an inability to communicate the mystical experience, thereby illustrating the *aporia* or logical contradiction in a belief that language originated the world yet seems unequal to the task of talking about its meaning. An even more cynical reading of the priest's vision of "plenitude" would observe that he remains incarcerated in his cell, liberated only from his compulsive obsession with Revelation. As in the story of that name, Tzinacán's is a "secret miracle," one that does not alter the hard reality of the outside world. In "The Writing of the God" we read "ecstasy does not use the same symbol twice" (*CF* 253); quite so, but Borges, the master craftsman, does. Blinded by the profusion of esoteric allusions, few readers, if any, have built on the information that Tzinacán was imprisoned for refusing to *reveal* the location of a *hidden treasure* (my emphasis). The aesthetic implications of this stylistic nicety lie beyond the remit of this discussion, but I suggest that this structural circularity reframes, irrevocably, the import of the ending: his refusal, once again, to reveal his hidden treasure.

The bliss of plenitude is similarly undermined in "The Aleph." The title alludes to the first letter of the Hebrew alphabet, believed to contain all others, and by extension, the universe. The shape of the Hebrew letter, א – two inverted commas attached at opposite ends to a diagonal dividing line, the one pointing to heaven and the other to earth – suggests their specular relationship. Here, the eponymous Aleph is a small disk, a microcosm of the universe. The narrator is invited by his rival to contemplate the mystical Aleph in its transcendent glory, and the passage describing his extraordinary experience ranks among Borges's most poetic writing. But the majesty of the vision is disturbed on a number of counts: first, it takes place in grotesque surroundings and includes sordid details of lust and betrayal; secondly, it has no spiritually uplifting effect, as shown in the "Borges" character's pettily vindictive reaction in denying the experience, and thirdly, the uniqueness implied in the name of the microcosmic disk is severely compromised by a long list of other universal mirrors and finally when another more genuine Aleph is suggested.

In his essay on the Kabbalah Borges points out that the sacred text is eternal and perfect, every one of its words purposefully chosen. No detail can be altered, but it can be interpreted in different, even contradictory, ways, and Borges expresses admiration for the ingenuity of what he understood as being the Kabbalists' way of dealing with a changing world. In "Emma Zunz" he fictionalizes this hermeneutic tradition with a story in which two, and even three, conflicting motivations for revenge are played out by a central plot which significantly remains intact in its execution. It is an impious story making ironic use of the notion of piety, lending a piquant touch to the connection that I make between it and a sacred text.

The story is set in the Jewish atmosphere of Buenos Aires in the 1920s and, devoid of any fantastic elements, appears to be realistic. Yet the protagonist's near-palindromic name, the zeal of her sense of mission, her belief in a secret pact with God, as much as the story's careful narrative structure, are details which invite consideration of possible metaphysical meanings. To avenge her father's suicide, Emma conceives a plan: she resolves to seek sexual intercourse with a stranger, shoot her boss, the culprit of his death, and, when interrogated, accuse him of rape, pleading self-defense. However, the impact of the first stage of the plan – the trauma suffered by the virginal Emma during intercourse – completely changes her resolution. Instead of avenging her dishonored father, she incriminates him in her mind, now feeling the need to avenge her mother for having had to suffer during her marriage the humiliation she has just tasted. But even more, she wants to avenge her own humiliation, one dishonor replacing another as prime motivation. Significantly, the outer "text" of Emma's plan and its execution remains unaltered, in spite of the different and conflicting strands embedded in it. Emma's account is believed to be true because in essence it was, but like a sacred text's, its essential truth is multilayered. So are its possibilities of interpretation, and among these I offer the seemingly remote comparison with a constantly reread sacred text as a salient example of Borges's brilliantly imaginative exploitation of a Kabbalah-inspired motif for fictional purposes. The Kabbalistic notion of God, or the Divine, as a Text, unfathomable and changeless, yet open to multiple, ever renewable interpretations, accords with Borges's personal concept of a literary text, and arguably characterizes the openness of his own palimpsestic fiction.

Christian themes

The presence of Christian themes is an under-researched topic in Borges studies, though, as any concordance will show, Borges writes within a marked Christian frame of reference, making prolific use of Christian allusions. However, his attitude to Christian orthodoxy is consistently conflictive, most stridently so in his vituperative disparagement of its central dogma, the doctrine of the Trinity: "a useless theological Cerberus," "a case of intellectual teratology, a distortion only the horror of a nightmare could engender" (*SNF* 130). This grotesque definition is often cited as evidence of Borges's animosity, but it should be noted that Borges's words are directed to the doctrine's offence against rationality and do not negate the mystical power of Trinitarian theology. As he admits in "A Defense of the Kabbalah," "the Trinity shines in full mystery" (*SNF* 85), and, as with the Kabbalah, there is an argument to be put forward that as a religious metaphor, the mystery of the Trinity accords with his own poetic sense of the unknowableness of the universe, and the Holy Spirit as a metaphor for poetic inspiration. In fact, in this essay Borges discusses the hermeneutical numerical considerations of Kabbalah mostly as an introduction to complexities of the numerically based concept of the Trinity.

Such theological considerations are the backbone of Borges's most famous detective story, "Death and the Compass," in which two hermeneutical approaches are adopted by opposing detectives for the solution of a mystery. Treviranus, as his name implies, is drawn to a solution based on the number "three," while Lönnrot is convinced that the solution is based on the number "four." The Trinity is not mentioned explicitly but is present throughout as a presupposed undergird; the Tetragrammaton, YHWH – the four letters of the secret, unpronounceable, Jewish Name of God – plays a more active role, each murder being linked to one of its letters.

Both detectives set out to investigate the murder of a Jewish scholar attending the Third Talmudic Congress. Treviranus immediately guesses that the intended target was the Tetrarch of Galilee and the emeralds in his possession, while Lönnrot is inspired by the Jewish and Christian Kabbalistic writings of the victim and sets out to find a more esoteric and metaphysically based solution. Two other crimes are committed at regular distances in terms of place and time, and Treviranus is content that the precise symmetrical triangle formed – a tacit reflection of the perfection of the Trinity – is an indication of the completion of the series. Not so Lönnrot, who learns that the Jewish day begins at sunset and takes this to be a cryptic indication that the crimes are being committed not on the *third* day of consecutive months, but on the *fourth*. He therefore believes he can anticipate the exact time and place of a fourth killing, and so extends the triangle into a rhombus. The revelation that the final letter of the Name of God brings is that of the expected secret, the fourth murder, but with an unexpected twist – the investigator himself being the intended victim. The search was set up by the master criminal as a perverse charade, an act of revenge for the imprisonment of his brother some years earlier.

"Death and the Compass" works brilliantly as a detective story, but clues to other levels of interpretation are strongly embedded in it. Numerical allusions feature prominently in the story, ranging from a passing reference to the Pentateuch, the five books of Moses, to the double-faced Janus, and ending with the single straight line of Zeno, but it is the numbers three and four that dominate: they are important at the structural as well as the thematic level. The persistent use of words such as Treviranus, third congress, three years, three thousand years, and the three false names given to the third (false) victim, all strongly suggest a triple configuration for the solution of the mystery. But this series is disrupted by other clues based on the equally mystical number four, namely, Tetrarch, the quadrilateral rhombus, and the Tetragrammaton. However, the numbers three and four are cryptically intermeshed in this story, for the Tetragrammaton belies its Name: it is made up not of four but of three letters, YHWH, since the H is repeated at the end. As for the notion of the murders occurring on the fourth day of the month, this is a totally esoteric construct built upon the start of the day according to the Jewish reckoning, but planted in the months of a Christian calendar.

The story would appear to suggest the Trinity and the Tetragrammaton as alternative roads to the secret of the Universe but this notion is undermined by the final revelation, showing them to have been false clues set up to entrap Lönnrot in a plot of calculated revenge. Borges's "creative misreading" of theology for its fictional potential will always inspire "creative misreading" of his fiction, and this is true particularly of this secular story of revenge, so full of religiously based allusions. My point is not to deny the validity of symbolic interpretations which these allusions clearly invite, but to highlight the realist framework that will always, insidiously, challenge them.

One aspect of Trinitarian theology that occupied Borges was what he saw as the irreconcilable opposition between the notions of the eternal Father and his Son, held to be equally divine yet conceived in time. He discusses this contradiction in "A History of Eternity," whose witty title encapsulates the dilemma of Jesus's passing trajectory on earth set against his eternal godliness. Borges touches on this topic frequently in his poetry, where, it is worth noting, Christian themes are not subjected to the same level of abhorrence as elsewhere. In two poems, both entitled "John I:14," Borges engages with the implications of the eponymous verse: "And the Word was made Flesh, and dwelt among us." One of his last poems, "Christ on the Cross," is a tender meditation on Christ's physical suffering, though ultimately his divinity is dismissed and his redemptive power denied. But not altogether, for "He has left us splendid metaphors."

The fiction presents a more complex picture. There are several stories which deal overtly or indirectly with the figure of Jesus, for example "The Gospel According to Mark," a chilling rewriting of the New Testament, and an ironic take on the Gospel's meaning of "good news." The story pivots around a literal reading of the Gospel and enacts the Passion, re-contextualized in time, place, and genre. Briefly, a young medical student from Buenos Aires called Baltasar Espinosa finds himself trapped in a ranch because of prolonged rain and, to while away the time, reads aloud *The Gospel according to St. Mark* to the Gutres, the name of the foreman and his family. His illiterate listeners fail to appreciate the difference between text and reality: they confuse the student with Jesus, assuming that he is talking about himself. Similarities between Espinosa and Christ are insinuated by a series of clues: his name is that of one of the Magi, his surname alludes to the crown of thorns ("*espinas*" is the Spanish for thorns), he is a thirty-three-year-old medical student with some healing powers – he cures a little lamb – and is a good orator of "almost unlimited goodness." The story is set toward the end of March. Other biblical allusions include a flooding river, wooden beams, the Ark, and, most tellingly, a goldfinch, symbol of Christ's Passion. The resident family is described in terms suggesting a trinity: "There were three members of the Gutre family: the father, the son (who was singularly unpolished) and a girl of uncertain paternity" (*CF* 398). This last comment can be taken as a veiled reference to the Holy Ghost and also to the debate that lies at the heart of the separation of the Eastern and Western Church regarding whether the Holy Ghost is derived specifically from the Father or "also the Son" (*filioque*). All three are involved in the fatal ending, deathly and by now unavoidable. The girl adopts a sacrificial role and offers herself to Espinosa on the eve of his own sacrifice; the father and son are "joined" in hammering and nailing some pieces of wood, and finally, in a replica of the Gospel's verses 19–20, they lead him to the Cross.

In re-contextualizing the Passion, the story plays with notions of its eternal and universal validity, positing the cyclical idea of time, with Christ's sacrifice appearing as a recurring miracle. On the other hand, the Passion's relocation to the Argentine plains could also be taken as a disparagement of the sacred text, its uniqueness compromised, even trivialized by an unholy repetition. I suggest another interpretation based on the re-awakening of the "harsh Calvinist fanaticism" (*CF* 400) of the Gutres' Scottish ancestors, the Guthries, whose forgotten Bible was being read. A final comment: the conflation of Espinosa and the Christ figure is extended to include biographical details relating to Borges himself. The choices of how to interpret this particular bravado of self-figuration are endless.

"Three Versions of Judas" offers a radical re-interpretation of Jesus from the vantage point of his relationship to Judas. The story is presented as if it were an essay, which lends an air of authority to its obviously tongue-in-cheek speculations. These are ideas developed progressively by one Nils Runeberg, a Swedish theologian, who, inspired by De Quincey's contention that "all the things which legend attributes to Judas Iscariot [are] false," sets out to find the meaning of this obscure sentence. In the first version which he puts forward he argues that Judas's betrayal was unnecessary since Jesus was sufficiently well known to thousands. He proposes, instead, a metaphysical explanation of the betrayal as an extreme sacrifice mirroring God's own sacrifice in becoming human. When this idea is declared anathema he reconsiders and puts forward his second version, based on moral considerations of his own unworthiness, and concludes that Judas chose a crime of unmitigated heinousness because he believed that goodness was a divine attribute and "should not be usurped by men" (*CF* 165). Finally, he arrives at a third version, declaring that God debased himself in order to redeem mankind, and did so completely, by becoming the most abject of men: "He was Judas" (*CF* 166). The blasphemy of this discovery, so redolent of Gnostic heresy, weighed so heavily upon Runeberg that he first lost his reason and then died.

Gnostic themes

It is not surprising, given Borges's mistrust of all orthodoxies, that he should have been particularly attracted to Gnosticism, a Christian sectarian movement dating from the second century and declared heretical by the Church Fathers. It took many forms, evolving into some seventy sects, but though there is no Gnostic canon, certain features are common to the movement as a whole. The name, derived from the Greek *gnosis* ("knowledge"), emphasizes its preoccupation with a direct knowledge of God and the secrets of salvation. Knowledge, for the Gnostics, meant not rational cognition but the means by which an individual could arrive at spiritual redemption.

In Gnostic dualistic thinking, God is "absolutely transmundane," a nameless, uncreated, changeless divinity, removed from the world which he has not created and does not govern. In "A Defense of Basilides the False" ("A Vindication" in the original Spanish), Borges discusses certain ideas attributed to Basilides, arguably the movement's principal teacher: "From [God's] repose emanated seven subordinate divinities" (*SNF* 66), and from these came further emanations, the last of which being the Demiurge, to whom the creation of the material world is ascribed. In this account of creation as "a chance act" we may find an explanation for the existence of evil in the world, and see, too, an argument for mankind's complete insignificance in the cosmos. Borges does not seek to promote or exonerate the doctrine, but like the similarly entitled essay on Kabbalah, he discusses it with an eye on its literary potential.

Basilides's main ideas are repeated and fictionalized in "Hakim, the Masked Dyer of Merv" in *A Universal History of Iniquity*. Hakim is not a prophet but an impostor claiming to have been "forced into heresy" (*CF* 43). His veiled face, a parody of an unknowable divinity, helps him to dupe his followers into thinking that he is God incarnate, but when he is eventually betrayed the secret of his ravaged face is revealed, and he loses his power and his life. Gnostic ideas, which set up a theological backdrop for Hakim's rise to fame, are highlighted in a sub-chapter entitled "Abominable Mirrors." There are parallels between the "false" theologian Basilides, who pretended to possess a secret tradition transmitted from St. Peter, and Hakim, the "false" prophet who duped his followers by claiming to be endowed with special powers by the Almighty. Both, moreover, are known only through mediated, uncertain sources. At the end, the unmasking of Hakim, the Masked Dyer, becomes a powerful metaphor mocking the mysteries of divine revelation.

The story of the Masked Dyer of Merv puts forward the dispiriting belief that the world we inhabit is an error, an incompetent parody: "Mirrors and paternity are abominable because they multiply and affirm it" (*CF* 43). One of Borges's most complex and ambitious stories, "Tlön, Uqbar, Orbis Tertius" repeats this gnomic pronouncement twice, with slight variations. It is positioned prominently on the first page and becomes the springboard for all that follows, starting with the land of Uqbar and the heresiarch to whom it is attributed. This provenance may be thought to compromise its trust-worthiness, insinuating that what follows is unorthodox and, by extension, a fanciful hoax. Such an assumption is supported by the narrator's suspicion that the mysterious unknown country and the anonymous heresiarch may have been an invention of his friend Bioy Casares.

In this Gnostic-driven reading of "Tlön," I would like to point out the concept of "emanations" as a structural motif supporting the series of pro-gressive creations of lands, world, and planets. This concept is also alluded to indirectly by the story's main conceit, the *hrön*, Borges's invented word referring to ideas willed into the world. These dreams and desires are meta-phorically projected onto the real world as solid, poetic objects, and they are said to derive from previous *hrönir*, and ultimately, from an *Ur*. The sequence of their evolution is unsmooth and unpredictable, in caricatural contrast to Basilides's account of celestial emanations. A number of ideas professed by some Tlönists strongly evoke other Gnostic beliefs concern-ing the universe, such as its creation by "the handwriting of a subordinate God trying to communicate with a demon," or its comparison to a crypto-gram, but one in which not every symbol is significant. I offer the forego-ing thoughts, not in a foolhardy attempt to define the meaning of "Tlön" (which will always surpass any interpretation), but to highlight the presence of Gnostic elements in the story and argue for their structural significance.

Gnosticism occupies a more central role in "The Theologians," a story set in an atmosphere of caricaturized theological debates and rivalries. Oppositional points of belief alternate between orthodoxy and heresy to the point where their differences become blurred and without meaning. Aurelian and John of Pannonia are ecclesiastical rivals who are in agreement in their opposition to the ideas of the heretical sects known as the Annulari, but are in fierce competition for the acclaim of being the first to denounce them. The heretics are put to death, though eventually their ideas regarding the cyclical nature of time are accepted as orthodox. A second heretical sect spreads from the East, known variously as Histrioni, Abysmals, or Speculari, names that reflect their wild behavior and their beliefs, which are based on hermetic ideas and distortions of biblical verses. They hold that evil here on earth is inversely reflected by good in heaven and that, since history never repeats itself, the commission of all possible horrendous acts today will preclude their occurrence in the future.[2] In his denunciation of the Speculari, Aurelian quotes John of Pannonia out of context, and the latter is accused and burnt at the stake. In time, Aurelian is struck by lightning and also burns to death. In heaven, he comes to the devastating realization of the irrelevance of these theological niceties: for God, he and his rival are as one.

"The Theologians" offers an excellent example of the consistently countercultural and subversive use of theological elements in Borges's fiction. In this particular story, the sheer density of erudite theological references emphasizes the pettiness of the society in which they flourish, and is an indication of shallowness rather than the opposite. While there is a historical basis to the easy interchange between orthodoxy and heterodoxy, this is parodied here by the zealotry and envy among theologians, and also illustrates their abuse of decontextualized biblical quotations. The two heresies that infuse the story are the cyclical repetition of time, and a dualistic specularity, a belief in the debased reflection of everything and every being. These heresies are woven into both the form and the content of "The Theologians." For example, the burning of the library of Alexandria at the beginning of the story, the deaths by burning first of the Annulari, then of John of Pannonia, and finally of Aurelian, dramatically re-enact the first heresy, while the various decontextualized misreadings in the story – of Plato, of a text by John of Pannonia, and of biblical verses by the Speculari – are textual deflections which illustrate the second. The skeptical ending ultimately undercuts both.[3] Gnosticism is clearly not an end in itself in this story but its strands serve as a metaphor to express the precariousness on which mankind's "certainties" are based.

I have divided this overview of theologically based elements into three religious classifications in the Borgesian spirit of mocking categories by setting them up and then dismantling them. The "three" embedded in the "four," the points of contact between Kabbalah, Gnosticism, and Neo-Platonism, the intermingling of orthodoxy and heresy with regard to both Jewish and Christian beliefs, the drawing together of the sacred and the secular (as in

"Emma Zunz"), the presence of Kabbalist ideas in the mind of a Mayan priest, all attest to the fluid interplay that Borges sets up in his use of theological allusions. His use of distilled metaphors for their poetic potential has been my primary concern, but, going one step further in the dismantling of categories, I suggest that it may also enrich our understanding of their original theological context: the irreverent in dialogue with the reverent.

NOTES

1 See Jaime Alazraki, *Borges and the Kabbalah and Other Essays on His Fiction and Poetry*, Cambridge, Cambridge University Press, 1988, 33.
2 Gene H. Bell-Villada, *Borges and his Fiction: A Guide to His Mind and Art*, Chapel Hill, University of Carolina Press, 1988, 159.
3 See Mercedes Blanco, "Fiction historique et conte fantastique. Une lecture de 'Los teólogos'," *Variaciones Borges* 4 (1997), 5–50.

6

LUCE LÓPEZ-BARALT

Islamic themes

In his essay "*The Thousand and One Nights*," Borges addresses his perplexity about the East with a quotation from Juvenal: all that seems mysterious and remote is located precisely "*ultra auroram et Gangem*" – "beyond the dawn and the Ganges" – that is to say, in the East. Although the East is inscrutable, the Argentine *maestro*, like Kipling, finds it also irresistible: "Once you have heard the call of the East, you will never hear anything else" (*SNF* 46). Borges mastered with uncanny ease the literature of both the West and the East, and set them, like shifting mirrors, into an unexpected dialogue. The Islamic literary canon is one of the most important in Borges's revision – and rewriting – of Western *belles lettres*, even though he did everything in his power to conceal his grasp of Islamic culture. In this chapter, however, I propose to decode some of Borges's fundamental Islamic enigmas.

How much did Borges really know about Arabic literature? More than he openly admitted, and certainly much more than his critics have so far presumed.[1] Borges read deeply in Islamic literature, theology, and mysticism, so deeply that we are still in the process of understanding the real implications of his artistic experiment. His passion for this forbidding Eastern world was such that he even ventured to learn the rudiments of the Arabic language. But even had Borges been innocent of Arabic, he must have had at least some notion of its grammar and vocabulary, especially the complexities of that language's triliteral root system. Throughout his life, he would quote the old quip which says that "every word in Arabic means itself, its opposite, and a kind of camel" and he used (ironically?) the concept of triliteral roots and the words that derive from them – individual verbs and nouns, verb conjugations, and forms of nouns – in "Tlön, Uqbar, Orbis Tertius," where the system of derivations of the *hrönir* roughly parallels those of the Arabic noun. Again, the mysterious Uqbar is another "crypto-Arabism," for it might point to 'Ukbara, an ancient city on the Tigris river surrounded by gardens but then destroyed in the twelfth century as the result of a change in the Tigris's course, or it might also suggest the root *q-b-r*, meaning "to bury." *Uqbar*, then, would literally mean "I am buried," and Uqbar was indeed a false country "interred" in a pirated encyclopedia.[2]

Borges never used Islamic literature for the purpose of local color, being by admission "a user of symbols"; instead he employs traditional Islamic motifs mostly for their aesthetic connotations and suggestive power. He began using Islamic symbols with expertise as early as 1935, in "Hakim, the Masked Dyer of Merv" in *A Universal History of Iniquity*, and he was still making good use of them in 1985, in the nostalgic poem "On the Diverse Andalusia," in *Los Conjurados*. Some of the most remarkable prose works containing Arabic *leitmotifs* are "The Zahir," "Averroës' Search," "Ibn-Hakam Al-Bokhari, Murdered in His Labyrinth," "The Approach to Al-Mu'tasim," "The Mirror of Ink," "Mahomed's Double," "The Translators of the *Thousand and One Nights*," "*The Thousand and One Nights*," "Someone," "The Simurgh and the Eagle," "H. G. Wells Against Muhammad," "(Antoine Galland's Selection of) *The Thousand and One Nights*," and "Robert Louis Stevenson – The New Arabic Nights – Markheim." As for his Islamic poems, there are "Ariosto and the Arabs," "The Unending Rose," "The Orient," "Rubaiyat," "An Oriental Poet," "Metaphors of the *Thousand and One Nights*," "Alhambra," and "Alexandria, 641 A.D.," to mention only a few. Even in works that are not directly related to Arabic literary matters, Borges manages to include Islamic *leitmotifs*. Let us briefly explore a few of these Oriental *topoi* and symbols.

Circular mirroring: searching for Averroës and for Scheherazade

Borges managed to transform the magical tales of the *Thousand and One Nights* into a literary symbol of the infinite: "The idea of infinity is consubstantial with *The Thousand and One Nights*," he declares in his passionate essay on the stories (*OC* 234). In another essay, "The Translators of the *Thousand and One Nights*" (*SNF* 92–109), he carefully collates the different versions of the Arabic tales rendered by Burton, Galland, the verbose Mardrus, and the chaste Lane, among other Arabists, in a book he appropriately titles *A History of Eternity*. The book into which Scheherazade's stories are collected is infinite for Borges because of its circular structure: in some editions of the *Nights* the copyists introduced a "disturbing" interpolation into Night 602, wherein the King unexpectedly hears his own story from Scheherazade's lips. He is therefore destined to hear the stories over and over again each time the ingenious storyteller reaches Night 602, "magical among the nights."[3] The infinite circularity of the *Thousand and One Nights* is even more dizzying, says Borges, than that of *Don Quixote* or

Hamlet, both of which also contain a story within a story. Borges celebrates his fascination with the *Nights'* concentric structure with a delicate verse by Tennyson: "Laborious orient ivory, sphere in sphere" (*SNF* 109).

This potentially infinite story of the *Thousand and One Nights* constitutes also a labyrinthine dream: "The dream divides into another dream / and that dream into others and still others, / all of which idly interweave an idle labyrinth" (*OC* 170; my translation).[4] Borges mirrors this labyrinthine dream-within-a-dream in his "Circular Ruins" from *Fictions* and in one of his best Islamic stories, "Averroës' Search." The famous philosopher Averroës (Ibn Rushd), writing a commentary on Aristotle's *Poetics*, finds himself unable to understand two words in the "monumental work" – "tragedy" and "comedy" – because Averroës' Islamic culture has no concept for, no conception of, "theater." The same happens with Borges, who searches in vain for Averroës, for Borges, in turn, lacks sufficient knowledge – both intellectual and cultural – to fully grasp Averroës' Muslim culture. Averroës vanishes from the Argentine writer's literary mirror at the end of the story, resisting Borges's search. Borges in turn is destined to be the object of his readers' search for the meaning of Borges's own intriguing text. This incessant, circular mirroring evokes the dizzying *regressus ad infinitum* that Borges learned so well in the unending *Thousand and One Nights*.

"Ibn-Hakam Al-Bokhari, Murdered in his Labyrinth"

The Oriental symbol of the infinite verbal labyrinth is central in "Ibn-Hakam Al-Bokhari, Murdered in his Labyrinth" from *The Aleph* (*CF* 255–62). The story opens with a verse from a Qur'anic sura (XXIX: 40) called *'Ankabut* or "The Spider," which alludes to those who, like the spider, patiently construct a complex labyrinthine web in which to trap their prey, only to see it destroyed by a gust of wind or a swipe of the hand. In the Qur'an the meaning is spiritual – human beings rely too much on the material, evanescent world – while in Borges the symbol of weaving a labyrinth seems to point to literature – Arabic literature.

The story is as follows. Two English friends, Dunraven (a poet) and Unwin (a mathematician), decide to explore a mysterious circular labyrinth constructed in Cornwall by Ibn-Hakam Al-Bokhari, who had arrived in England many years ago. On his arrival, Al-Bokhari built a Moorish "house" unheard of among Christians. Like the Qur'anic spider's web, it was circular and had only one central room. Dunraven remembers his surprise as a child when he first saw the Arab with a "saffron yellow beard," escorted by a negro slave and a lion, and in his astonishment he fancied this personage to be the "King of Babel" (*CF* 257). The whole scene is codified: the two Englishmen are lured by the symbolic Arab "spider" (Ibn-Hakam) to enter his labyrinthine web. Borges's discreet clues help us see that he is speaking symbolically of the Western fascination with Oriental literature: for Borges, the lion usually stands for the East, and the combination of colors – a yellow lion and a black slave – can be understood to represent, as Arturo Echavarría has argued, the act of writing: the traces of (black) ink on (yellow) paper or parchment.[5] Ibn-Hakam seems to be symbolically introducing Arabic literature into England and seducing readers toward its verbal labyrinth.

The name "Ibn-Hakam Al-Bokhari" also points to Arabic literature, since it evokes the Cordoban Al-Hakam II al-Mustansir (reigned 961–76), the finest scholar of all the Muslim caliphs, under whose rule the University of Cordoba came to house a library of the first magnitude. Some of the four hundred thousand texts it contained were read and annotated by Al-Hakam himself. Borges's Arab character is thus the symbolic "son" (*Ibn*) of this cosmopolitan Muslim scholar. To continue the allusions, "Al-Bokhari" refers cryptically to Muhammad b. Isma'il al-Bukhari (810–70), perhaps the most famous traditionalist of all Islam, the man who compiled the *Sahih*, a collection of ninety-seven books of sayings (*hadith*) attributed to Muhammad.

It seems that Ibn-Hakam, after ruling with cruelty the Arabic tribes of the desert, robbed them with the assistance of his cousin Sa'id, and fled with his plundered treasure. In "Ibn-Hakam Al-Bokhari," Borges seems to be alluding obliquely to *The Thousand and One Nights*, whose Arabic original, written in a colloquial, unornamented prose, is not valued as much in the Eastern world as it is in Europe, thanks to the numerous European (mostly English) translations it has had. Is Ibn-Hakam, much like the historical Al-Hakam II, symbolically shipping this Oriental literary treasure from the East to the West, only this time not to Cordoba but to England, and thus to the hands of translators like Burton and Lane?

The name Sa'id or Zaid, furthermore, stands for Islam's foremost written tradition. Zayd ibn-Thabit of Madinah, formerly Muhammad's secretary, collected the scattered portions of the Qur'an, written on palm leaves and stone tablets or preserved in the memory of men, and from these fragments codified Islam's Holy Book. So far, all the Arabic names in Borges's tale are related to Islamic encyclopedic knowledge and to the written word, including the most sacred of all books – the Qur'an.

Ibn-Hakam, provoked by the metaphoric touch of a spider's web (again, a reference to Qur'an XXIX: 40), dreams of a nest of vipers and upon awakening fears that Sa'id might claim his share of the treasure that is about to be taken abroad. He kills Sa'id and destroys his face, but in a prophetic dream he hears Sa'id speak a curse: Sa'id will return from the dead to kill Ibn-Hakam, he says "as you slay me now." Ibn-Hakam then flees to England with his golden treasure, and constructs his strange rosy labyrinth to protect himself from the revenge of Sa'id's ghost.

In time, a sailing ship called the *Rose of Sharon* – again the pink color – arrives from the East before leaving again for the *Red* Sea. Distraught, Ibn-Hakam confesses that he found his lion and his slave dead, with their faces crushed, and he fears that Sa'id (or rather, Sa'id's ghost) was responsible for the horrible deed. Soon Ibn-Hakam himself will meet the same fate. His treasure, hidden in an ark with inlaid marquetry decorations, also disappears. Not a single coin remains.

The two English friends, Dunraven and Unwin, ponder the strange event, and Unwin declares Ibn-Hakam's story to be false. He proposes another version of the mystery: Sa'id was the one who stole part of the treasure before fleeing to England, and with his booty he constructed his labyrinth in order to attract and kill Ibn-Hakam. This he did, and so was able to crush Ibn-Hakam's face and those of his lion and his slave as well. Sa'id then continued in his impersonation of Ibn-Hakam. For Unwin, then, Sa'id was an impostor, but let us remember that for Borges, "all fiction is an imposture."[6]

The multiple effaced faces and erased identities in "Ibn-Hakam Al-Bokhari" all point, in true Borgesian fashion, to the act of writing and reading literature. Dunraven is somewhat convinced by Unwin's interpretation, which equates Ibn-Hakam with Sa'id, but he has a lingering doubt: Why would Ibn-Hakam come all the way to England to claim a "squandered treasure," a portion of which remained "interred" in the Orient? (*CF* 262). Unwin corrects his friend: not "squandered," but *invested*: "Invested in erecting upon the soil of infidels a great circular trap" (*CF* 262). My guess is that the Islamic treasure that ends up in Europe would be Borges's beloved *Arabian Nights*, a portion of which remained, indeed, in the East, but which became more famous in the West, thanks precisely to its multiple translations, which have "entrapped" readers with its magic and its mysterious charm. The enigmatic colophon of Borges's story – the tale entitled "The Two Kings and the Two Labyrinths" – tends to corroborate this conjecture.

The King of Babylonia built a brass labyrinth, and in it he imprisoned the King of Arabia, who had come on a visit to his kingdom. After wandering all day through the labyrinth, the King of Arabia managed at evening, with the aid of Allah, to escape, and he vowed to repay the King of Babylonia by ensnaring him in another labyrinth in his own kingdom. The King of Arabia then went home, gathered his troops, attacked Babylonia, devastated the kingdom, captured its king, and imprisoned this monarch in a most unusual labyrinth, "with no stairways to climb, nor doors to force, nor wearying galleries to wander through, nor walls to impede [one's] passage" – imprisoned him, that is, in the sands of the Arabian desert (*CF* 263). The colors "brass" and "sand" suggest that we are again in Borges's East, *ultra auroram*. The first king, of Babylonia, reminds us of Babel – the multiplicity of languages, the universe, the infinite labyrinth that Borges usually associates with literature. In this story's particular context, however, it seems to refer to the multiple European versions of the *Thousand and One Nights*, which blur and alter the original Arabic text they try to convey in English, French, or Spanish. (Borges, we should remember, explored in depth these versions, which varied greatly among themselves.) If the King of Babylonia points to Babel, or to the proliferation of languages, or to spurious "versions" of an original, unique language, the King of Arabia represents the original Arabic text conceived in the Arabian sands. The latter chastizes the King of Babylonia, the literary "squanderer," and brings him back to the original tales written in Arabic: that forbidding labyrinth of infinite sand that Borges was never able to really explore but was never able to escape from either. Thus, interpreters of this literary "treasure" – both Muslims and Europeans – enter the spider's web which the Arabic original, be it the original Qur'an or Scheherazade's original *Nights*, poses for them. The historical and literary tensions created by these different cultural and literary points of view, which had their good share of war and blood, are too complex to be dealt with here, and Borges sums up the situation at the end of his tale with a knowledgeable version of *wa Allahu 'allamu*: "Allah's knowledge is greater" (CF 263).

Unending roses and Sufi nightingales

In his delicate ode "To the Nightingale," Borges evokes the two different cultural traditions that celebrate the nightingale – "the nightingale [sung] by Virgil and by the Persians" – for he knows perfectly well that in Sufism the famous bird is associated with joyous mystical experience rather than with the Virgilian *miserabile carmen* or melancholic song: "The Muslim dreamed you / in the delirium of ecstasy" (*SP* 355). The erudite Borges, setting the mystical *bolbol* exalted by Rumi and 'Attar against Ovid's and Heine's and Keats's Philomela, succeeds again in contrasting – and merging – the Western and Islamic literary canons.

The rose, so charged with symbolism, so ubiquitous in mythology, belongs, like the nightingale, to two very different literary traditions, European and Islamic, and Borges is conversant not only with the European poets but also with Sufi poets who equate the Rose with the presence of the living, ineffable God. In the poem "The Unending Rose," one of his finest pieces incorporating Islamic literary motifs, Borges depicts 'Attar of Nishapur as an old man, against the backdrop of the Mongol invasion in Persia. The end is near. Alone in his garden, the poet, now blind, smells the fragrance of a rose he cannot see and that might therefore have any color or any shape. Here, under the literary mask of the Persian poet 'Attar, Borges is invoking the fragrant rose that language saves from oblivion, and that could take any shape or color in the reader's mind. Borges's *alter ego*, 'Attar, is blind in the poem, like Milton and like Borges, and cannot distinguish the flower's real color: "The whiteness of the sun may well be yours / or the moon's gold, or else the crimson stain / on the hard sword-edge in the victory" (*SP* 367).

The poet seems to be pondering the magical power of language to redeem the flower from time. But there is another rose at the end of the poem: the "profound Rose" that is "music, / rivers, firmaments, palaces, and angels" (*SP* 367). This flower, like the Aleph, contains the "inconceivable universe," and 'Attar expects the Lord to unveil it to his unseeing eyes once he dies. Borges is cunningly alluding to the Sufis' non-verbal Rose, a well-known symbol of the infinite Deity, which the nightingale celebrates in ecstasy. The historical 'Attar, ironically, was not blind like Borges, but he does refer to his symbolic blindness in the *Book of the Secrets*. The Sufi knew well that at the moment of ecstasy – or in death – God will lift the veil ("the rending of the Veil" or *kashf*) so the mystic can finally see the eternal Rose of God's epiphany. At that moment the mystic will leave behind corporeal vision – "the shadow of the rose" – that is to say, the ephemeral rose. He will even leave behind the literary rose preserved in language that momentarily saves the earthly flower from oblivion. 'Attar's mystical Rose, which contains music and angels, palaces and rivers, is a veritable Sufi "Aleph" beyond language.

The Simurgh

Erased faces or identities are a recurring theme in Borges. Language and literature efface identities, for "the moon of Bengal is not the same as the moon of Yemen," even though language is doomed to celebrate both with the same words (*CF* 238). In his "Arabic" texts, Borges ponders this linguistic truth through Islamic symbols such as the mystical Simurgh, in whose sacred essence all other birds' individuality is effaced. In texts such as "The Simurgh and the Eagle" from *Nine Dantesque Essays* (*SNF* 294–97) and "The Approach to Al-Mu'tasim" from *The Garden of Forking Paths* (*CF* 82–7), the author puts to good use the mystical symbol of the Simurgh, which Muslims would be quick to recognize. In the *Conference of the Birds*, Farid ud-din 'Attar depicts the Simurgh as the King of the Birds, who lives in the mountain Kaf. Birds from all over the world set out upon a long journey, flying over valleys and seas trying to find their King. Only thirty birds survive the perilous flight and, at the very instant that they reach the Simurgh's palace, they realize, with bewilderment, that they themselves are the Simurgh they were searching for. In Persian, Simurgh means both "the King of the Birds" and *Si-murgh*, "thirty birds." Borges was fascinated by this "inextricable" Sufi symbol and in "The Simurgh and the Eagle" considered it to be much more imaginative than the paradisiacal Eagle that Dante celebrates in his *Commedia*, Cantos XVIII, XIX, XX.

In "The Mirror of Ink," Yaqub the Afflicted discovers his own face and even his death (his ontological "death" as a literary character) reflected in a magic mirror of ink poured into his hand by a Muslim sorcerer (*CF* 60–62). The magical device is used in Islamic folk magic, but in Borges, again, it stands for literature's "magical" power to erase identities in the act of reading. "Hakim, the Masked Dyer of Merv" reaffirms this idea (*CF* 40–44). A veil covers Hakim's face, but when it is finally lifted, it reveals a horrible face eaten away ("erased") by leprosy. This Hakim of Merv, the "Veiled" or "Masked Prophet of Khorasan," called *Al-Moqana*, was a false prophet, for Muhammad is considered the *khatimi al-nabiyyin* or "the Seal of Prophecy": there will be no prophets after him. Muhammad's face radiates light, and Islamic painting, out of respect for the Prophet, usually covers his luminous face with a veil. Hakim is thus an impostor who covers his face in the fashion of Muhammad, but a doubly deceitful one, for he is also a dyer or "*tintorero*" – one who masters a "craft known to be a refuge for infidels and impostors" (*CF* 41). Hakim works with ink (*tinte* or, metaphorically, *tinta*) and is therefore a writer who falsifies reality. The whole scene is conceived against the backdrop of Islam, for the Qur'an (XXVIII: 88) states that "Everything (that exists) will perish, except [God's] own Face." This unspeakably radiant "Face" is *veiled* to us, and cannot be put into words. Our personal identity is annulled when we look upon the Face; personal identity has no true ontological meaning, for there is only the One True Self in God. In many of his texts, Borges applies to literature this Islamic spiritual notion of the effacement of identity and the Veiled Face of the Transcendent Deity.

"The Zahir"

Borges puts Islamic symbols to good use in "The Zahir," one of his most mysterious works. In Arabic the word *zahir*, from the triliteral root *z–h–r*, means "visible" or "manifest." The fictionalized "Borges," who is the narrator and protagonist of the story, describes the Zahir, which is for him an Argentine coin worth 20 *centavos*. The night before the Zahir came into the possession of the narrator, he had attended the wake for Teodelina Villar, whom he had loved when she was twenty (again, the monetary value of the coin). The narrator gives us a clue to the significance of the coin: in other times, the Zahir has been many other things: in Gujarat, it was a tiger; in Java, a blind man in the Surakarta mosque; in Persia, an astrolabe; in the synagogue of Cordoba, a vein in the marble. The drunkenness of "Borges," the protagonist, is another clue to its meaning, for in Islamic mysticism, inebriation is related symbolically to the mystical experience, which is beyond reason and language. The coin obsesses the narrator, and he thinks of burying it in the garden – Teodelina was also buried, but Borges could be referring again to a "verbal" garden – or of hiding it in a corner of the library (thus hiding it in literature). To get rid of the coin, the narrator pays for another brandy with it, but the Zahir returns to haunt his memory. A book by Julius Barlach, *Urkunden zur Geschichte der Zahirsage* (*Documentation Regarding the History of the Zahir's Representations*), gives our fictional "Borges" some pseudo-erudite information regarding the ominous disk. He reads that the myth of the Zahir – which he now learns means "visible" or "manifest" – dates, apparently, to the eighteenth century. But there is nothing farther from the truth, since the founder of the Dhahiriyya (Zahirite) sect, Dawud ibn Jalaf al-Isbahani, known as Al-Zahiri because he defended the literal sense of the Qur'an and prophetic tradition, lived in the *ninth* century. The fictitious study adds that the Islamic Zahir has had many faces or manifestations and that obsession with it could lead to madness: in other times it was a copper astrolabe; a magic, infinite tiger; a prophet from Khorasan. There is always a Zahir, although it presents itself under different guises. "God is inscrutable," concludes the study, and here, Borges is again loosely translating the respectful phrase that usually closes metaphysical or religious treatises in Islam: *wa Allahu 'alamu* ("Only God is wise" or "Only God knows").

Barlach's book consoles our protagonist, for in it he learns that others have also come under the spell of the Zahir. But the book also quotes a verse from 'Attar's *Asrar Nama* (*The Book of Things Unknown*): "The Zahir is the shadow of the Rose and the rending of the Veil" (*CF* 248). I have already mentioned these famous Sufi symbols, which point to the mystic's experience of the material, shadow rose giving way to the Infinite Rose the instant God rends His Veil (*kashf*). Now "Borges" wants to see the face and the reverse of the coin all at once, imagining it to be like the crystal, translucent sphere of the Aleph – a symbolic mirror of mystical plenitude, and of the infinite universe.[7] Both of these small orbs – the Aleph and the Zahir – seem to be symbols of the mystic's "eye of the soul," through which vision finally becomes self-vision. Lost in thought in the Plaza Garay, "Borges" thinks about the mystical passages of the *Asrar Nama* and remembers that contemplative Sufis recite their names or the ninety-nine names of God until the words lose their meaning: until language is annulled. Borges is describing the technique of the *dhikr*, by which, in a melodic mantra, Sufis recite the Divine Names to induce a contemplative state. Anyone who could pronounce the Highest name – the hundredth name, which remains hidden – would unveil the Deity, that is, would have the mystical experience beyond language. "I long to travel that path," he says, referring to the Sufi repetition of the verbal Names to finally efface language – because "perhaps behind the coin is God" (*CF* 249).

Borges is again showing his expertise in Islamic mysticism. The orthodox Zahiri or literalist Islamic school of thought, which accepted only the literal ("visible") interpretation of the Qur'an and which was, therefore, attached to exterior language and theology, had its counterpart in the sect of the Batinniyya, those who found under the letter of the Qur'an a hidden, esoteric meaning. *Batin* means precisely that: the hidden, the non-verbal, the unutterable. Any expert in Islamic mysticism knows that the terms *Zahir/ Batin* are inseparable: the two sides of the coin of two opposite approaches to the Deity: the theological and exterior versus the mystical and interior. The esoteric teaching of the Batiniyya was aimed at a spiritually select group, while the others were given the *Zahir*, or external doctrine. Borges is here dealing with a theological-mystical coin: on one side we have the *Zahir* of the literalists who follow the superficial meaning of the word, that is to say, who are satisfied with physical reality and with the rational language that depicts it. On the other side we have the *Batin*, the incomprehensible, infinite Deity beyond language. We are again confronted with "the shadow of the rose," which is identified with the *Zahir*, versus the longed-for "unveiling" or "rending of the Veil," which leads to the unending Rose or *Batin*, and which Borges leaves unspoken.

The silent void that lies behind the symbolic coin of the Zahir is one of Borges's most successful Islamic symbols, and here the arcane story merges with a more prosaic one: "The Zahir" is a binary narration, like the dual 20-*centavo* coin. Teodelina Villar had been a model whose photographs (or "attributes") had littered the pages of worldly magazines, thus becoming "common currency" for all those who superficially "possessed" her in the commercial advertisements. But her inner being would forever escape her admirers, as her name suggests, for "Teodelina" points, in fact, to the Zahir: *Teo* refers to God, and *delina*, from the Greek *delo*, means "to clarify," to make visible or manifest: thus, the visible or manifest God. Her occult reverse is also like the unreachable other side of the Zahir: *a-delo* (the occult and inscrutable) gives way in Spanish to a common name – *Adela* – which would be the secret and "mystical" name of the woman with whom "Borges" was in love. Yet he never mentions this secret "reverse" name of Teodelina; he leaves her secret name, "Adela," unsaid, as a true Sufi would have done with the unspeakable *Batin*. And with good reason: he will keep to himself forever what lies on the other side of the coin: what lies beyond the reach of language.

Curiously enough, the Islamic undertones of the short story do not end here. Borges is also conversant with Islamic numismatics, and seems to know that there are Islamic coins with the Zahir inscribed on one side and God on the other. This type of coin was minted by the Mameluke sultans – Al-Malik al-Zahir (the Victorious), for instance, a thirteenth-century sultan, who minted his name on one side of the coin and, on the other, respectfully evoked the name of God (*La illaha ila Allah*: "There is no god but God").[8] Without a reasonable grasp of Islamic culture this story remains inscrutable and may even seem a failure, as is the case with many of Borges's "Islamic" texts.

Approaching – and finding – Al-Mu'tasim

It is evident that Borges has engaged in a momentous literary pilgrimage *ultra auroram*, whose consequences we are just beginning to understand. In undertaking this cultural journey, he has been as courageous as the protagonist of "The Approach to Al-Mu'tasim" (*CF* 82–88), Mir Bahadur Ali of Bombay, who sought to approach the distant, evanescent Muslim sage Al-Mu'tasim. *Bahadur* means precisely "the brave," while *al-mu'tasim*, from the Arabic *i'tasama*, means "he who goes in quest of [refuge]" (*CF* 86). Let us remember also that the sage Al-Mu'tasim irradiates light ("a glowing light" or "*claridad*"), and that the student in Bahadur's story searches for him "by means of the delicate glimmerings or reflections his soul has left in others" (*CF* 84). The successive seekers after the great master share an ever-increasing portion of his light, even though they might be his mere "mirrors." In any case, it remains clear that the student has been "illuminated" by Al-Mu'tasim, and to such a degree that the reader suspects that the student was himself Al-Mu'tasim all the time, much like the Simurgh that Bahadur evokes in his stories was in the end all the birds that flew in search of him. The name of the author, Mir Bahadur Ali, tends to confirm this, for "Mir" is a title given to Muhammad's descendants, and Muhammad is depicted in Islam as a figure of light who literally passed on his radiance to others, and, like Al-Mu'tasim, he is "an emblem of God," the pure Light (*CF* 83). The "enlightened" reader, in turn, reconstructs or "reflects" the text he is reading, which momentarily, in the very act of reading, includes both him and the author's written word. We come so close to Al-Mu'tasim that finally we *are* Al-Mu'tasim.

Bahadur's fiction offers an interesting parallel to Borges's penchant for reading Eastern (specifically Arabic) literature. Like Bahadur, Borges seems to "courageously" seek literary "refuge" in the rich Oriental tradition. What is more, he seems to have experienced the same curious "*ibbûr*," or metempsychosis, alluded to at the end of "The Approach to Al-Mu'tasim": "the soul of an ancestor or teacher may enter into the soul of an unhappy or unfortunate man to comfort or instruct him" (*CF* 86). "Unhappy" or "unfortunate" ("*desdichado*") is an adjective Borges often applies to himself, so we can deduce that he himself has been "comforted" and "instructed" by the opportune revisiting of Islamic authors who have been cyclically "reincarnated" in his literature. Borges may have known that in Arabic, *ishraq* means both "illuminated" and "Oriental," because the first light of dawn comes from the East. The Sufi *illuminati* or *ishraqiyyun* were, simultaneously, the "illuminated" *and* the "Orientalized." The Argentine master managed to "mirror" the Eastern literature which he read with such scholarly passion that the mysterious "Oriental" world *ultra auroram* finally became his own. We might go still further: Borges, truly "enlightened," became one with the Orient.

NOTES

1 See the following: Ian Almond, "Borges the Post-Orientalist: Images of Islam from the Edge of the West, " *Modern Fiction Studies*, 50 (2004), 435–59; J. E. Bencheikh, "À propos des sources arabes d'un texte de J. L. Borges: 'Le teinturier masqué: Hakim de Merv'," *Cahiers Algériens de Littérature Comparée*, I (1966), 3–10; Vicente Cantarino, "Notas sobre las influencias árabes en Borges," *Hispania*, 52 (1969), 53–55; Mohammed Habib (ed.), "Jorge Luis Borges et l'héritage littéraire Arabo-Musulman," *Horizons Maghrébins: Le Droit à la Mémoire*, 41 (1999), 3–120; Julia Kushigian, *Orientalism in the Hispanic Literary Tradition: In Dialogue with Borges, Paz and Sarduy*, University of New Mexico Press, Albuquerque, New Mexico, 1991; Erika Spivakosky, "In Search of Arabic Influences on Borges," *Hispania*, 51 (1968), 223–30, and "A Further Word Regarding Arabic Influences on Borges," *Hispania*, 52 (1969), 417–19.

2 George Wingerter, "Arabismo y criptoarabismo de Borges," *Sin Nombre* V (1983), 34–35.

3 "Partial Enchantments of the *Quixote*," in *Borges: A Reader*, Emir Rodríguez Monegal and Alastair Reid (eds.), New York, E. P. Dutton, 1981, 232–35.

4 "Metáforas de las *Mil y una noches*," in *Historia de la noche* (OC III, 170).

5 Echavarría, *El arte de la jardinería china en Borges y otros ensayos*, Madrid, Iberoamericana 2006, 40–41.

6 "Toda ficción es una impostura," "Arthur Machen: Los tres impostores," in *Biblioteca personal. Prólogos* (OC IV, 474).

7 It is interesting to note that even the famous "Aleph" was destined for a time to have an Islamic name, for in Borges's manuscript the mystical orb was to be named "*mihrab*," which is the sacred niche in the mosque from which the *imam* directs the prayers of the congregation. See Julio Ortega, "'El Aleph' y el lenguaje epifánico," in *Jorge Luis Borges: Intervenciones sobre pensamiento y literatura*,

A. Kaufman (ed.), W. Rowe, C. Canaparo and A. Louis (compilers), Buenos Aires/Barcelona/México, Paidós, 1999, 95.

8 Luce López-Baralt, "Lo que había del otro lado del *zahir* de Jorge Luis Borges," in *Conjurados. Anuario Borgeano*, Centro de Estudios Jorge Luis Borges, Alcalá de Henares, Franco Maria Ricci, 1 (1996), 90–109, and Luce López-Baralt, "Borges o la mística del silencio," in *Jorge Luis Borges. Pensamiento y saber en el siglo XX*, Alfonso and Fernando de Toro (eds.), Frankfurt, Vervuert/Madrid, Iberoamericana, 1999, 29–70.

7

PHILIP SWANSON

Borges and popular culture

Despite his reputation as an erudite weaver of philosophical puzzles, the focus of much of Borges's life and work is the popular or even the vulgar: the gaucho code; the exploits of Buenos Aires hoodlums; pirates, cowboys, and gangsters; detective stories and other genre works; classical Hollywood movies; tangos; and so forth. However, Borges's engagement with what is nowadays called popular culture is very selective. There is, for example, little about soccer or other sports in his work, the disdain for mass movements is palpable (often in the form of a virulent anti-Peronism), and the attitudes to the folkloric or displays of earthy sexuality are distinctly ambiguous. Yet this ambiguity is crucial. The distinction between "high" and "popular" culture is really a false one, and the categories are increasingly seen as porous. Indeed, it is my view that it is precisely in this undecidability that the appeal of Borges as a writer of literature lies. He is tantalizingly and provocatively "in-between," or, as Beatriz Sarlo would put it, "on the edge," in the shady yet unspeakably alluring territory of the *orillas*.

The *orillas* of Buenos Aires

The *orillas* is both a literal and an imagined or conceptual space in Borges. It refers to the edge of Buenos Aires in the early twentieth century, the frontier between the city and the *pampa*, the open countryside. By the 1920s Buenos Aires had been and was still being transformed by modernization, fueled to a large extent by immigration (especially from Europe). The sometimes romanticized rural past of nomadic gauchos and vast open spaces was being overtaken by the reality of modernity – a kind of complex and uncertain culmination of Domingo Faustino Sarmiento's postulation of the clash between "civilization" and "barbarism" in which modernity is both a triumph of progress and a loss of tradition.[1] The city limits or *suburbios* were characterized by Borges as streets without pavements or sidewalks on the other side (the famous "*calle sin vereda de enfrente*"), that is, facing the grasslands of the interior. Instead of the gaucho, here one would find his urban successor, the figure of the *compadrito*,[2] a sort of flashy wiseguy whose toughness and prowess with a knife became the stuff of legend.

Legend is both an appropriate and an inappropriate term. Base, tawdry creatures were to some degree glorified in tangos and in Borges's own works. Moreover, they were figures of the imagination as much as reality, if not quite vanished then probably largely subsumed into everyday urban life by the time they were being written about. On top of this, Borges's fascination with these men lies alongside his tendency toward *criollismo*, an admiration for the values associated with a line of longstanding Argentine families untainted by immigrant blood. The identity of the *compadrito* is in reality fractured along these lines of purity and contamination, while the supposedly *criollo* rural past is as threatening as it is seductive. And the chubbyish sedentary man of letters, Borges, is about as far away from both as it is possible for an admirer to get. This mixedness is equally reflected in the cultural conflicts of the 1920s and 1930s in Buenos Aires. The key fault line in these culture wars is often presented synecdochically in terms of a clash between the literary posh old Argentines of the *Martín Fierro* group (to which Borges technically belonged) and the immigrant-tainted leftist orientation of the "Boedo" group, this rivalry usually grafted onto a version of the tension between the artistic avant-garde or *vanguardia* and a species of social realism. Again, the true picture is much more diffuse. The cultural history of 1920s and 1930s Buenos Aires is really about the intersections or hybridities between these seeming opposites. Indeed, Borges's own affected *criollismo* was tempered by his attraction to the underworld of the slums and their lurid inhabitants, while his championing (initially at least) of literary experimentation and, later and more dilutedly, literariness was matched by a fascination with tradition, the popular, and economy or simplicity of expression. As the writer of the *orillas*, Borges did invent a sort of new cultural nationalist myth for Argentina, but one which was far from straightforward, combining as it did a kind of deep populism with a sort of nervous patrician distance.

Two important early manifestations of Borges's fascination with the Buenos Aires subculture are his "biography" of Evaristo Carriego (1930) and his first book of "stories," *A Universal History of Iniquity* (1935). Carriego, a minor figure who would probably be largely forgotten were it not for the Borges connection, was a dissolute poet who fancied himself a pal of the *compadritos* and the toughest of them, the *guapos*; he even got somewhat close to the notorious Palermo godfather Don Nicolás Paredes (whom Borges would later get to know himself while researching his book). A very young Borges was initially attracted to Carriego because of his flamboyant recital of poetry (cultural mixture once more), but soon became taken by his association with the shady local underworld.[3] Indeed the first chapter of *Evaristo Carriego* is a rather romanticized contextualization of the poet, concentrating on the history of the old neighborhood of Palermo and the tales of *compadritos* and *cuchilleros* (knife-fighters). Yet Borges's prologue to the 1955 edition of the biography brings out the imaginary dimension of this history:

> For years I believed I had grown up in a suburb of Buenos Aires, a suburb of dangerous streets and showy sunsets. The truth is that I grew up in a garden, behind a fence of iron palings, and in a library of endless English books … What was going on, meanwhile, on the other side of the iron palings? What everyday lives were fulfilling their violent destinies only a few steps away from me in some unsavoury saloon or ominous vacant lot? What was Palermo like then …?[4]

The biography, then, even in the chapter on Carriego's own life, is something of a fantasy. The author in fact characterizes the book as "less documentary than imaginative" (34). Two chapters focus on Carriego's collections of poems, *Heretic Masses* (*Las misas herejes*) and the *The Neighborhood's Song* (*La canción del barrio*), the titles of which suggest extolling the pleasures of a sinful excursion into the *arrabales* or suburbs on the fringes of the city. These sections are hazy reflections rather than analyses, and often descend into a species of imagined memories of the pseudo-legendary deeds of a group of men whose exploits can really only be known second hand. Carriego is lionized as "the first observer of our poorer neighborhoods," but as such is both "the discoverer" and "the inventor" (105). The implication is that he (and Borges) are creating a myth as much as recreating a reality. But this myth has meaning. Borges's embracing of Carriego also has much to do with his and his group's rejection of *modernismo*, particularly as embodied in Argentina's once fabled late *modernista* poet Leopoldo Lugones.[5] Though Lugones was a right-wing polemicist, *modernismo* was associated in the minds of many with empty aestheticism. Thus Carriego comes to embody a strain of earthy authenticity, yet one still channeled via poetic imagination. What Borges seemed to see in him was the chance to renovate *criollismo* by creating a new poetics of the city rather than one of rural tradition, a modern myth for the new Argentina based not just on the land and its lost gaucho inhabitants but in the concept of the *orillas*. Though Borges sees himself and Carriego as breaking with a conventional fad for picturesque *costumbrismo* or local color, he seeks to use the myth of the *barrio* or neighborhood to fabricate a new kind of cultural nationalism which is not backward-looking but open to modernity. The project is impossibly flawed, but poetically quite compelling.

A Universal History of Iniquity

Borges's own seminal contribution to the legend of the *compadrito* would be his first real short story published in a book, "Man on Pink Corner" (see below), from *A Universal History of Iniquity*. However, the bulk of the stories in this collection are not centered principally on Argentina and are not really stories in the usual sense. They are basically a series of short riffs on established biographical accounts (the sources are given in the text) of a series of lowlifes: hoodlums, conmen, cowboys, pirates, and so forth. The link to the Palermo *guapos*, though, is most definitely there. Even in the stories about North American rogues, the narrative voice keeps situating events in relation to Latin America.

The first piece, about the Mississippi horse-thief and trafficker in falsely emancipated negro slaves, Lazarus Morell, begins with a digression on Bartolomé de las Casas, the sixteenth-century Dominican priest, Bishop of Chiapas, and champion of the indigenous natives of the Spanish Crown's so-called "New World." The second entry, on the famous nineteenth-century legal case of the Tichborne claimant, begins with an allusion to his assumed name on the streets of Santiago de Chile and Valparaíso, Tom Castro. Most strikingly, the account of New York gang leader Monk Eastman starts with a direct anticipatory comparison with a duel to the death between two knife-wielding *compadritos*, a scenario that is said to encapsulate "the story of the Argentine underworld" (CF 25). Yet Eastman, like some of the other rogues featured in the book, is ultimately diminished. After a staggeringly violent career in which he once led a gang of twelve hundred men, he is caught by the police, packed off to Sing Sing for ten years, and dies anonymously and unexplainedly (here at least) in a downtown street, his inert body being sniffed over by an uncaring cat. Lazarus Morell, meantime, "contrary to all poetic justice," is not swallowed up by "the river of his crimes" but dies, prosaically, "of pulmonary congestion in the hospital at Natchez" (CF 12). And Billy the Kid, in the story "The Disinterested Killer Bill Harrigan," after a slow and undignified death, is said to have "that unimportant sort of look that dead men generally have" – the degradation completed by the dressing and making-up of his corpse to be "exhibited to horror and mockery" in a shop window (CF 34). There is a definite uneasiness, then, about the aggrandizement of scoundrels and even a strong hint of the extreme epistemological and ontological skepticism of some of Borges's fiction of later decades. For example, in reference to a series of Monk Eastman's multiple aliases, the comment is made: "Those shifting 'dodges' … fail to include the man's true name – if we allow ourselves to believe that there is such a thing as 'a man's true name'" (CF 26).

Knife-fighters: *guapos*, *gauchos*, and *compadritos*

Though more of an obviously Argentine atmosphere piece about *guapos* and the *esquinas* or street-corner bars they used to frequent, there are similar existential undertones in "Man on Pink Corner" as well as a similarly deflationary technique. While the story does not really recreate the local slang, *lunfardo*, it does capture the cadences of *barrio* speech and is told by a young narrator purportedly directly to a gentleman called "Borges." A Northside tough, Francisco Real, known as the Yardmaster, bursts into a bar outside his territory and challenges the *guapo* Rosendo Juárez (alias the Sticker and described as one of Don Nicolás Paredes's men) to a knife fight. Juárez refuses to fight and his disgusted moll, La Lujanera, goes off instead with the interloper. Later that night Real is stabbed to death by a stranger. The trick ending of this clever little tale implies that the apparently green narrator is not just an onlooker but the probable killer, and the story ends with him heading to the bed of La Lujanera. (By all accounts, Borges was sexually timid and there may be an element of compensatory sexual fantasy here, linking masculinity to virility.)

The celebration of courage is clearly not as straightforward as some proponents of Borges as admirer of tough guys might like to think. The story is a reworking of two earlier versions ("Men Fought" and "Legend of a Crime"), but, as Donald L. Shaw has pointed out, the revisions actually replace a duel for the sake of it with a refusal to indulge a violent whim – or could it be mere cowardice? – and a rather sordid killing motivated by petty jealousy (an equally downbeat account is offered from the Sticker's perspective in "The Story from Rosendo Juárez" in a much later story from *Brodie's Report* [1970]).[6] And, as with some of the cases from *A Universal History of Iniquity*, the macho fighter is much deflated in death. As a bystander comments: "Man thought so highly of himself, and all he's good for now is to draw flies" (*CF* 51).

That the tension between heroic fantasy and grubby reality is so enmeshed in this tale is perhaps explained by its roots. Though he did meet people like Paredes, Borges's experience of the underworld is largely through other sources, often cultural products like stories, poems, or songs. Behind much of Borges's mythology of the *arrabales* lies a fascination with gauchos and tango. The *compadrito* or *guapo* is really a semi-urban version of the rural cowboy or gaucho, a figure equally famed for his manliness and his prowess with a knife. Yet by the 1930s, the gaucho was most definitely a phenomenon of the past, now only truly alive in any pure sense in literature and the public imagination (and Borges's fictional *compadritos* were often also a dying or even dead breed by the time he was writing about them – certainly no longer a part of an essentially Argentine identity but increasingly characterized by immigrant Italian blood).

Many of Borges's stories from the 1940s onward feature gauchos and references to (and even characters and episodes from) the great national literary epic on this theme, *The Gaucho Martín Fierro* (by José Hernández, 1872 and 1879). The point is that the sources are literary rather than real. Juan Dahlmann, the protagonist of Borges's most famous story on this theme, "The South," from *Fictions*, is a clear echo of the author: a bookish, sedentary city-dweller with a heroic Argentine family line and a penchant for a cultivated *criollismo*. His journey to the south is presented as a journey deep into Argentina's rural past, but Dahlmann is compelled to recognize that "his direct knowledge of the country was considerably inferior to his nostalgic, literary knowledge" (*CF* 177). Indeed when he enters the dangerous store-cum-bar where he is challenged to a duel to the death by a local and egged on by an old gaucho who "seemed to be outside time" (*CF* 178), he is rather affectedly struck by its resemblance to an engraving from an old edition of a popular French novel. His romanticized (fundamentally literary) vision of the past, then, in which he appears to imagine in his mind a dramatic and deeply "Argentine" death in a knife fight, is really masking a crude history of mindless violence.

Borges himself was clearly something of a fantasist about the ideal of gaucho heroism and dedicated himself on occasion to co-editing anthologies of "gauchesque" poetry (poetry celebrating the gaucho tradition but not written by gauchos themselves). Yet his *criollista* impulses often suggest a sense of the feared barbarism of the countryside and its role in the nation's past, sometimes linked to more contemporary concerns about the direction of a modern urbanized Argentine society. A brief glance at one of his more renowned poems illustrates this tension. "Conjectural Poem," from *The Self and the Other* (1964), speculates on the final thoughts of Borges's ancestor Francisco Narciso de Laprida, a major figure in the Independence movement who died violently in 1829 at the hands of a band of gauchos operating under a traditional *caudillo* (a kind of rural boss or mob leader), José Félix Aldao. Laprida, "who studied law and the civil canon," sees himself as a force for civilization, but:

> ... victory goes to the others,
> to the barbarians. The gauchos win.

Nonetheless, as the enemy dagger slides into his throat, he realizes that:

> ... At last I come face to face
> with my destiny as a South American. (*SP* 159)

In other words, Laprida realizes that his life's achievement actually lies in the exemplary sacrifice of dying at the hands of Latin American barbarism and the lesson this teaches to future generations. What is perhaps most interesting, though, is that the poem, at its end, is very specifically dated 1943.[7] This was the year in which power was seized in Argentina by a fascistic nationalist military junta, which modeled itself on the regime of Juan Manuel de Rosas, the embodiment of barbarism for liberal thinkers from Sarmiento onward. It was a prelude to the rise to power of Juan Perón and the rise of Peronism as a popular urban mass movement. Borges had "Conjectural Poem" read out in Montevideo, where he was lecturing at the university, just days after orchestrated demonstrations by the unions and Eva Duarte's (later Perón) *descamisados* or "shirtless ones" (the urban poor of the capital) in October 1945, events that formed the platform for Perón's election to President in February 1946.[8] Far from celebrating the culture of the masses, Borges here seems to see the popular classes as a decidedly menacing rabble prone to manipulation and mobilization. By implication too, the now fading *criollo* class, to which he sees himself as belonging, is the last bastion of European-influenced and Enlightenment-driven liberalism – a value system based on the taming of the near innate barbarism of the ordinary people by a process of civic education from a privileged, civilized elite.

Tangos and *milongas*

Borges's liminal world of the *orillas*, then, contains all the inevitable contradictions of what is essentially a fabrication of the human imagination. When the young narrator swaggers out of the bar on "Pink Corner" in the story from the 1930s, he sees what look like hardwood trees (*ñandubay*) on a hill, though they are really posts tied together by wire. The rural gaucho past and the urban present are merging here in a landscape that is both real and imaginary. He had also earlier seen lying outside some cheap guitars that had been strummed near the start of the story. This may evoke memories of the fireside songs of the gauchos, but inside the bar the customers are dancing to the tunes of tangos and their prototypes, *milongas* – a relatively new hybrid form of song and music of the *suburbios* danced suggestively in and on *esquinas* (street corners or taverns).

The tango is just as much a source of Borges's versions of popular culture as is gauchesque literature, and is generally associated by him with the evocation of the exploits of the *guapos*. Borges is really interested in *milongas* or early, traditional forms of tango, not the sophisticated dance or jazz-influenced musical style into which it would later morph. Indeed, Borges's biographers often point out his lack of any musical sensibility, which suggests that what matters to him is what the tango represents as much as what it is. Some of his own *milongas* (actually poems to which the reader is asked to imagine the musical accompaniment) are collected in *For Six Strings* (1965). Robert Folger has described these *milongas* as evoking "a Homeric past from the point of view of a lyric subject that glorifies *gauchos*, soldiers and *compadritos*."⁹ The title of the opening poem, "Where Can They Have Gone?," sums up this cod nostalgic tone and echoes a much better poem from *The Self and the Other*, entitled "The Tango."¹⁰ This poem presents itself as "an elegy" that asks "of those who are no more": "Where can they be?" Recalling the motiveless machismo of *guapo* knife-fighters, the poem complains that "a mythology of daggers" has today been replaced by the sordid realities of crime reports. Yet these distant "heroes" somehow survive:

> Today, beyond time and fateful
> death, those dead men live on in the tango.
>
> They are in the music, in the strings
> of the obstinate, laboring guitar,
> which insinuates into a spirited *milonga*
> the celebration of innocence and courage.

The tango transcends time and allows the reader the sensation of effectively experiencing the heroics of the *compadrito*:

> ... The tango creates a hazy
> unreal past which is in some sense true,
> the impossible memory of having died
> fighting on a street corner in the slums.

This perhaps gets close to the crux of Borges's relationship with the popular. His tales of the *compadritos* are the compensatory fantasies of an everyday modern man: the pleasure, as in an adventure film, lies in the momentary identification of the reader or viewer with a dramatic or exciting life that he (or maybe she) will never live in reality. The irony is that, in one of his supplementary essays on the tango included in the 1955 edition of *Evaristo Carriego*, he had already complained that the myths fostered by certain tangos (and his own earlier readings of them) were already revealing "a clear symptom of certain nationalistic heresies that later swept the world" (146). The myth was too strong for Borges, though, and he continued to rework tangos, even collaborating in 1965 with the very non-traditional modernist tango composer Astor Piazzola. The ensuing recording contained a suite called "Man on Pink Corner": Borges's work was beginning to exist as much "outside time," it seems, as the old gaucho from "The South."

The detective story

Gauchos and lowlife city slickers, however, are probably not what international readers of the cosmopolitan "Borges" promoted abroad from the 1960s would associate with the author. If such readers were to see a link with popular culture, it would probably be with the detective story and his rather cerebral reinvention of the genre. Borges is clearly an admirer of the genre *per se*. Detective fiction (imported and home-grown) has a very long (and continuing) tradition in Argentina. Borges himself reviewed vast numbers of detective novels and, together with his friend and collaborator Adolfo Bioy Casares, founded and directed a crime series called *El Séptimo Círculo* (*The Seventh Circle*) which published 366 titles between 1945 and 1983 (120 chosen by the friends during their stewardship of the collection between 1945 and 1955).[11] The pair defended such popular fare by claiming that "some critics deny the detective genre the status it deserves simply because it does not enjoy the prestige of being tedious."[12]

The appeal of the detective story for Borges is in part its classical construction, that "it is safeguarding order in an era of disorder" ("The Detective Story," *SNF* 499). Those readers who characterize Borges as a "difficult" high modernist might do well to remember this: his stories, while in many ways complex, are usually linguistically straightforward and formally very tightly constructed. Even so, Borges does seem to favor the analytic detective, distanced and detached, who eschews "physical risk"[13] and, in a distinctly non-realist way, prefers "the fact of a mystery that is solved by the intellect, by an intellectual operation" (*SNF* 495). The model for this detective is, of course, C. Auguste Dupin, the protagonist of what is widely regarded as the first ever detective story, Edgar Allan Poe's "The Murders in the Rue Morgue" (1841).[14] Borges's "Death and the Compass" features the ace gentleman-amateur sleuth Erik Lönnrot, "who thought of himself as a reasoning machine, an Auguste Dupin." However, the sentence continues: "but there was something of the adventurer in him, even something of the gambler" (*CF* 147). Borges's detective or spy stories do not, of course, always avoid the threat of physical risk and, in any case, the analytic detective usually gets his comeuppance. This is the case here, where Lönnrot's Sherlock Holmes-like rationality actually leads him into an elaborately laid trap plotted by his arch-enemy Red Scharlach. The story ends with the undermining of the analytical explanation of the mystery and the murder of the detective. It is not the intention here to add to the leagues of print already expended on this story. Suffice it to mention once more the extreme ambiguity of Borges's fiction, his utterances on literature and culture and, of course, his relationship to the popular.

Borges also produced crime stories that were presented more directly as collections of detective fiction rather than being smuggled, like "Death and the Compass," into a series of metaphysical *ficciones* – though ambiguity is still rife in such tales. Together with Bioy Casares, he created the detective Isidro Parodi, who appeared most famously in *Six Problems for Don Isidro Parodi* (1942) written under the pseudonym of H. (Honorio) Bustos Domecq.[15] The detective figure, unsurprisingly, is not straightforward at all. As his surname, Parodi, implies, he is a parody, and his character and adventures grew out of Borges's and Bioy's regular evenings of chatting and joking in the latter's home.

Parodi, a former barber from Barracas in the Southside of Buenos Aires, languishes in the city penitentiary, having been framed for the gang murder of an Italian butcher felled by a blow from a seltzer bottle. "Now in his forties, sententious and fat,"[16] he sits in his prison room and solves, with thought alone, the absurd mysteries told to him by a cavalcade of eccentric visitors to the now celebrated Cell Number 273. In a sense, as the spoof introduction to the *Six Problems* suggests, "Parodi's lack of mobility is the symbol and epitome of intellectuality" (12), though his circumstances are rather less salubrious than those of his prototype, Auguste Dupin, who cracks his cases from his gentleman's quarters armchair in the comfort of Paris's Faubourg St. Germain. Nods to the classic detective genre abound. For example, the stolen letters in "The God of the Bulls," or the location of the missing precious stone right before everyone's eyes in "the one place … beyond suspicion" (157) in "Tai An's Long Search," are clear allusions to "The Purloined Letter," while the revelation in "The Nights of Goliadkin" that the crime on the train was masterminded by a whole group of travelers using false identities is an unambiguous echo of Agatha Christie's *Murder on the Orient Express* (1934). Yet the idea of a jailbird hairdresser detective is surely a joke, and the book's (again, spoof) afterword actually states that, in these stories, Bustos Domecq "attempts to combat the cold intellectualism in which Sir Arthur Conan Doyle, Ottolenghi etc., have immersed this genre" (160). The stories are, in fact, exaggeratedly colorful and linguistically playful, offering the reader a gallery of rogues who unintentionally effect a pretty wide-ranging satire on contemporary Argentina.

The resolution of the mysteries is really at the service of this humorous social satire, the apparently elaborate riddles all being reduced in the end to rather mundane examples of venal motivation. In the opening story, for instance, the baffling tale of a secret "Druse" sect and their obsession with the signs of the zodiac turns out to be a prosaic case of embezzlement and arson (one red herring is an overheard discussion about books: rather than a literary debate, it transpires that it is an argument over a firm's fiddled accounts books!). And the comic style used to tell the mysteries is often largely a means of satire too: one randomly chosen example, from "Free Will and the Commendatore," is the description of a meeting set up with murder victim Pumita as "more rigged than a Rioja election" (104–5) (La Rioja is an Argentine province). The satire is fairly good-humored, however, and not much punishment or retribution is usually meted out to the perpetrators (such an outcome is specifically repudiated by Parodi, e.g., 108, 158). Indeed Parodi's power as a character possibly lies in his unreal nature. Though his name and some other references might suggest immigrant roots, his values and comments (not to mention, in one of a number of echoes of Evaristo Carriego, his berating of Italians) link him, despite his humble background, to a species of Argentine tradition. It is through time in prison that Parodi "had become an old established Argentine" (109), we are told in "Tadeo Limardo's Victim." The implication may be that the sleuth – confined to his cell – lives outside of time and inhabits another kind of *orilla*, therefore embodying a kind of ideal Borgesian Argentine identity, aware of but relatively uncontaminated by the onward march of urban modernity.[17]

The cinema

One aspect of modernity and, indeed, popular culture that Borges does seem to embrace from early on is the cinema (a feature of *Six Problems for Don Isidro Parodi* is that it is replete with references to the so-called seventh art). Borges and Bioy Casares collaborated on a number of screenplays, their first being about the Buenos Aires underworld, *Los orilleros* (*The Hoodlums*, 1955). The detective genre also made its way into their films, most notably in Hugo Santiago's *Invasion* (1969), though the format disintegrates into a fantastic fable in which a Buenos Aires-like city is taken over completely by a powerful outside force. However, Santiago and Bioy himself would later complain of Borges's over-literary style and his penchant for monologues.[18] This is an interesting position, given that Borges's career as a prolific film reviewer suggests a preference for westerns, gangster movies, and classical Hollywood cinema rather than the art-house variety. Borges appears to appreciate the formal simplicity of such movies and the very generic nature of studio system productions. This is reflected in his own writing of fiction, which, albeit often subversively, uses genres, employs strict narrative forms, and even imitates the technique of cinematic montage.[19]

In his 1931 essay "The Postulation of Reality," Borges emphasizes the importance of selectivity in reading, "the conceptual simplification of complex states," and expresses his admiration for what he calls "the cinematographic novels" of director Josef von Sternberg, which are "made up of significant moments" (*SNF* 61, 63). This cinematic style is probably most transparent in the early stories of *A Universal History of Iniquity*. What feels like a cut to the cat next to the protagonist's dead body in the final scene of "Monk Eastman, Purveyor of Iniquities" is like a piece of classical editing for effect, while the opening of "The Disinterested Killer Bill Harrigan" offers the reader-cum-viewer a pair of "image(s)" (*CF* 31), in which the narrative cuts from an establishing shot of the arid Arizona landscape to one of Billy the Kid, the rider seated on his horse. But the technique is also present in the more technically complex mature stories: one has but to think, for instance, of the cuts, as in a montage sequence, that characterize the more dramatic moments of a tale like "The Garden of Forking Paths" from *Fictions*, or "Emma Zunz" from *The Aleph*.

However, perhaps the most interesting aspect of Borges's relation to cinema, particularly for an author so repeatedly associated with ideas like "the death of the author" and intertextuality, or with the function of the reader in recreating new versions of prior texts, is the question of his role in it, his "influence" on it. There have been a number of Argentine and other Latin American adaptations of Borges's stories, though none of them especially notable. The best-received high-cultural translation to the screen is Bernardo Bertolucci's self-conscious political meditation on the fluidity of identity, *The Spider's Stratagem* (1970), based on "The Theme of the Traitor and the Hero" from *Fictions*. However, the most satisfying adaptation is, without doubt, Alex Cox's garish punk fantasy from 1996, *Death and the Compass*. Steeped in the imagery of 1980s pop culture (reinforced by a synthetic soundtrack by Pray for Rain), the movie, nonetheless, does not shirk complexity and shows considerable familiarity with Borges's literary universe. There are a series of clever embedded allusions to other stories (like "The Garden of Forking Paths," "Emma Zunz," "The House of Asterion," and "The Aleph"), and a cameo featuring a blind detective called Comandante Borges (played by Cox himself in a witty auteurist nod), whose actions are said to set in train events that would come to envelop everyone – a fairly clear reference to Borges's concepts of interlinked destinies and intertextuality *avant la lettre*. The latter link is reinforced by the knowing use of the popular film motif of a spinning newspaper front page, coming to a halt to reveal a dramatic headline: in one case, the paper's title happens to be *The Postmoderna*.

There are also plenty of examples of non-postmodern movies based on the life of Borges in which he appears as a character. None is particularly distinguished, though it is perhaps worth mentioning in passing, for its curiosity value, Javier Torre's *Un amor de Borges* (*A Love of Borges's*, 2000), inspired in part by the penetrating if uncomfortable memoirs of Estela Canto, the

object of Borges's largely unrequited desire in the mid 1940s.²⁰ More significant in cultural terms, though, are the less mimetic representations of Borges
in film, such as Cox's tribute mentioned above. The most notorious homage is, perhaps, Nicolas Roeg and Donald Cammell's dark, labyrinthine,
swinging-sixties romp through identity crisis, *Performance* (made in 1968,
but released in 1970), starring Mick Jagger and featuring various allusions
to Borges, including a more-than-subliminal on-screen shot of him during
a peculiar montage sequence. A cheekier insertion comes in Jean-Jacques
Annaud's 1986 film *The Name of the Rose* (after, of course, Umberto Eco's
splendid 1980 novel) in which the key to a very Borgesian murder mystery is
revealed to lie with the blind old librarian, the venerable Jorge de Burgos!

While the adjectives "Borgesian" or "Borgean" have not yet become
as decoupled from their original referent as terms like "quixotic" or
"Kafkaesque," there can be little doubt that there is a chain of metonymic
influence or association linking Borges or the Borgesian to anterior and pos-
terior texts. Without necessarily wishing to suggest direct or consciously
transferred influence, one can surely identify traces of Borges in a whole
host of mainstream Hollywood movies. Could films like David Fincher's
Seven (1995) or Bryan Singer's *The Usual Suspects* from the same year, with
their twist-endings revealing the villain's secret scheme, really exist without
"Death and the Compass"? Could even a TV movie (albeit one celebrated
by film buffs) like Steven Spielberg's first feature *Duel* (1971), with its story
of a city man imperiled in an alluring yet terrifying landscape of the interior,
complete with tense scene involving urban visitor and rural folk in a road-
side diner, exist without "The South"?

Two more recent examples of Borgesian allusions in film and televi-
sion serve to illustrate the ongoing and potentially infinite nature of such
borrowings or interconnections. Tom McCarthy's screenplay for Johan
Grimonprez's movie *Double Take* (2010) is based on "August 25, 1983"
from *Shakespeare's Memory*: it echoes Borges's fantasy of an encounter with
his death-bed self in a story of Alfred Hitchcock's visitation by his double
on the set of *The Birds* in 1962. This hint of different possible temporal
outcomes is also taken up in Episode 17 of Series 1 of the popular ABC
TV show *Flashforward*, first broadcast also in 2010. The episode is entitled
"The Garden of Forking Paths." In its account of an elaborate trap laid
for ethnically Chinese FBI agent Demetri Noh by his arch-enemy, supreme
trickster and time-twister Dyson Frost, it calls to mind both the Borges story
of the same name and, in the debate on possible future killings, the final
encounter of Lönnrot and Scharlach in "Death and the Compass."

Such an intertextual understanding of cultural production would actually
chime perfectly with Borges's own poetic creed. In his "Ars Poetica," from

The Maker (1960), he casts a poem in the light of, presumably, Heraclitus's river (always the same yet always different) and observes that poetry is "immortal and poor" (*SP* 137). Originality is a form of reproduction, then, and identities and images repeat themselves endlessly throughout time and culture. "Borges" continues to exist in culture in all sorts of seen and unseen ways and has even penetrated the everyday life of the popular. At the end of "Death and the Compass," Lönnrot asks Scharlach to employ an alternative labyrinth with which to snare him "when you hunt me down in another avatar of our lives" (*CF* 156). One suspects that, in another incarnation, Borges might not be just the purveyor of puzzling literary-philosophical abstractions, but perhaps a man of popular pleasures and actions, that Borges might be not just one of an elite, but a man of the people, one of the boys. In another life, Borges would be a *compadre*.

NOTES

1 See Domingo F. Sarmiento's seminal 1845 text, *Facundo, Or Civilization and Barbarism*, Penguin Classics, New York, Penguin, 1998. For more on the civilization-versus-barbarism ethic, see Philip Swanson (ed.), *The Companion to Latin American Studies*, London, Arnold, 2003, 69–85.
2 *Compadrito* is the diminutive form of *compadre*, the latter meaning something like "buddy" or "one of the lads."
3 See Edwin Williamson, *Borges: A Life*, New York, Viking, 2004, e.g. 42–44.
4 *Evaristo Carriego*, New York, E. P. Dutton, 1984, 33. In all works cited, where there is no ambiguity, subsequent page references will be incorporated into the main text.
5 *Modernismo* was a finesecular literary movement whose poetry had its roots in French Symbolism and Parnassianism, and was commonly connected with the notion of "art for art's sake."
6 Donald L. Shaw, *Borges' Narrative Strategy*, Liverpool, Francis Cairns, 1992, 22–28.
7 This date is not included in the edition cited here.
8 See Williamson, *Borges: A Life*, 286.
9 Robert Folger, "Notes on a Critical Edition of *Para las seis cuerdas* by Jorge Luis Borges," *Neophilologus*, 85 (2001), 411–14 (414).
10 The translations of this poem are my own. For the original, see *Obra poética 1923–1976*, Madrid, Alianza, 1979, 209–11.
11 Pablo A. J. Brescia, "De policías y ladrones: Abenjacán, Borges y la teoría del cuento," *Variaciones Borges*, 10 (2000), 145–66 (146).
12 Jorge Lafforgue and Jorge B. Rivera, *Asesinos de papel: ensayos sobre narrativa policial*, Buenos Aires, Colihue, 1996, 250 (my translation).
13 "The Labyrinths of the Detective Story and Chesterton" (*SNF* 112).
14 See John T. Irwin, *The Mystery to a Solution: Poe, Borges and the Analytic Detective Story*, Baltimore, Johns Hopkins University Press, 1994.
15 The characters from these stories would reappear in 1946 in the novella *Un modelo para la muerte* (*A Model for Death*), written by the pair under the

nom de plume of B. [Benito] Suárez Lynch. The double-barrelled pseudonyms – Bustos Domecq and Suárez Lynch – are taken from the names of ancestors of Borges and Bioy Casares.

16 Jorge Luis Borges and Adolfo Bioy Casares, *Six Problems for Don Isidro Parodi*, Penguin, London, 1981, 18–19.

17 See Cristina Parodi, "Una Argentina virtual: El universo intelectual de Honorio Bustos Domecq," *Variaciones Borges*, 6 (1998), 53–143. The critic calculates that the barber was imprisoned in 1919 and that the first mystery must be set in 1933.

18 David Oubiña, "El espectador corto de vista: Borges y el cine," *Variaciones Borges*, 24 (2007), 132–52 (141–42).

19 José Eduardo González has an excellent chapter on Borges and the cinema in *Borges and the Politics of Form*, New York, Garland, 1998, 98–141, in which he explores, among many other things, the relationship between cinema and Borges's own narrative style in terms echoed here.

20 Estela Canto, *Borges a contraluz*, Madrid, Espasa-Calpe, 1989.

8

ROBIN FIDDIAN

Post-colonial Borges

In his poem "The Other Tiger," Borges invites his readers to imagine him writing "from this house in a far-off seaport in South America" (*SP* 117). The adjectival phrase "far-off" sits at the very heart of Borges's invitation and conveys ideas of relative remoteness and peripherality which critics have stressed in their accounts of Borges and his place in the contexts of world literature, Latin American writing, and the specific national context of Argentina. Alfonso de Toro and Edna Aizenberg have expressly re-interpreted a number of stories and essays by Borges as evidence of his concern with a range of political issues originating in the colonial and post-colonial history of South America.[1] In this context, the term "post-colonial" references not only the immediate post-Independence period (starting, in the case of Argentina, in 1810) but also the enduring legacy of colonialism in terms of the nation-building project, differentiation from the former imperial metropolis, the critique of Eurocentric thinking, and personal and collective identity.[2]

Borges's "The Argentine Writer and Tradition" is an emblematic text inasmuch as it challenges parochially conceived myths of cultural identity put forward by the nationalist intelligentsia of mid-twentieth-century Argentina and argues instead for a less restrictive, differential model of cultural relations. In this essay, Borges asks, "What is the Argentine tradition?" and answers: "I believe that our tradition is the whole of Western culture, and I also believe that we have a right to this tradition, a greater right than that which the inhabitants of one Western nation or another may have" (*SNF* 426).

Borges cites the case of Jewish contributions to Western culture as evaluated by North American sociologist Thorstein Veblen, who attributed the "preeminence" of Jewish figures to the fact that "they act within that culture and at the same time do not feel bound to it by any special devotion" (*SNF* 426). Borges posits a similar relationship between Irish thinkers and the British establishment, which allowed them to "make innovations" in

English culture. He then concludes: "I believe that Argentines, and South Americans in general, are in an analogous situation; we can take on all the European subjects, take them on without superstition and with an irreverence that can have, and already has had, fortunate consequences" (*SNF* 426). As Borges acknowledges, his blueprint is valid for the cultural production not only of Argentina but of the entire sub-continent of South America. Nevertheless, as far as writers living in Argentina are concerned, the thrust of his argument is that they are free to exploit their peripheral position vis-á-vis the European (including the Spanish) canon and to realize the potential for "irreverence" that is their prerogative. Writing from the periphery, they will be able to imitate, parody, and ultimately to subvert the intellectual and linguistic authority of a center that is neither fixed nor essential, but rather historically determined and therefore liable to change.

As regards Borges's post-colonial sensibility, I will consider four key aspects of his work. They are the problematical question of foundations; the relation between place and identity; attitudes to Western hegemony; and Borges and the Orient. Jointly and separately, these themes constitute a litmus test of Borges's correspondence with post-colonial studies as they have developed since approximately 1975. At the same time, they help to cast the uniqueness of Borges's position into relief.

Foundations

The modern republics of South America gained their independence through the military campaigns that were conducted under the leadership of generals Bolívar, Sucre, and San Martín, between 1814 and 1824. The battle of Junín, fought high up in the Andes on August 6, 1824, was a landmark event that contributed crucially to the outcome of the Wars of Independence in the continent. In a felicitous confluence of family and political history, Jorge Luis Borges's great-grandfather, Colonel Isidoro Suárez, actually fought at Junín alongside Bolívar, who commended him for his bravery and the part he played in the liberation of a significant area of South America.[3] This is something that Borges would proudly celebrate on a number of occasions, for example in "A Page to Commemorate Colonel Suárez, Victor at Junín" (1953), where the poetic voice records his distant relative's thirteen years' service in "the Wars of America" and imagines him experiencing "fulfillment [and] ecstasy" in the epic of a single afternoon (*SP* 169); thirteen years later, in "Junín" (1966), the same voice addresses "Grandfather Borges" and wonders "what you were like and who you were."[4]

In prose, Borges touches on the subject of Junín elliptically in "Theme of the Traitor and the Hero." There, he intertwines family romance with

97

considerations of metafiction, historiography, and a discourse of archetypes and paradox. According to the narrator, "The Theme of the Traitor and the Hero" is little more than an "*argumento*," or outline of a possible story, which he will perhaps flesh out some day. For the time being, he volunteers a narration that is incomplete and dates it January 3, 1944, which coincides with the year of publication of "Theme …," in *Fictions*.

He is teasingly imprecise about the geographical location of the events of the story, which, he says, "takes place in an oppressed yet stubborn country – Poland, Ireland, the republic of Venice, some South American or Balkan state …" (*CF* 143). Or rather, he elaborates, "it has taken place, since, although the narrator is contemporary, the story he tells happened in the middle or at the beginning of the nineteenth century." Narrowing down the choice of country, he decides on Ireland, "for narrative convenience," and suggests that the year of events is 1824. He then embarks on the convoluted tale of an Irishman, Ryan, who over a century after the events, seeks to find out the truth about his great-grandfather, Fergus Kilpatrick, who fought for the freedom of Ireland and was assassinated in mysterious circumstances. As Ryan delves deeper and deeper into the matter, he uncovers a series of clues and improbable coincidences with the plots of Shakespeare's *Julius Caesar* and *Macbeth*; he finally cracks the enigma of his forebear's death, which nestles inside a larger story of betrayal and retribution culminating in Kilpatrick's assassination on August 6, 1824, in Dublin.

Critics have understandably been dazzled by the layers of playful allusion and contrivance in this particular fiction by Borges. It is nonetheless surprising that they have generally failed to notice the coincidence between the date of Kilpatrick's death in Dublin and the Battle of Junín, or to spot the match between Ryan and his great-grandfather and Borges's own family romance. Yet the dates and the correspondences are there for all to see, on the surface of "The Theme of the Traitor and the Hero." What is more, Borges's narrative contains a second date, which can help with grounding the story. I refer to the year 1944. Remembering the narrator's self-reflexive comment, that the story of which he has imagined the outline has a narrator who "is contemporary," we intuit another probable clue in the geographical reference to "an oppressed and tenacious country" at the time of writing. In the European arena, Poland would seem to fit such a description, given its occupation by German troops from the start of World War II. On the other hand, Ireland in 1944 definitely does not: the Black and Tans of the early to mid 1920s would have long since returned to England.

If we consider the South American context, a primary candidate and match with the 1944 location of "The Theme of the Traitor and Hero" is Argentina: for that is the year in which Juan Domingo Perón became Minister of War and then formed the first of many governments over which he would subsequently preside. Functioning partly as a *roman à clef*, therefore, "Theme …" references the Argentine political situation under the "oppressive" rule of Perón. At the same time, it loses none of its force as a historical narrative, hinting at elements of mystery and betrayal surrounding the foundation of Peru and other independent nations of South America around 1824. Unlike the 1953 and 1966 poems, which visualized Borges's great-grandfather's epic feat in Junín, the story uses the trappings of family romance to expose vain fictions of glory and valor, calling into question myths of national foundation and the claims of legitimacy that follow from them.

The motifs considered here come together once more in "Guayaquil," where a contemporary narrative again runs parallel with a famous historical event – in this case, the meeting, in the Ecuadorian city of the story's title, between Generals Bolívar and San Martín, in August 1822; shrouded in enigma ever since, the meeting would determine the post-colonial fate of the South American republics. On a personal note, the narrator of "Guayaquil" corresponds closely with Borges: "On the wall in my office hangs an oval portrait of my great-grandfather, who fought in the wars of independence, and there are one or two glass cases around the room containing swords, medals, and flags" (*CF* 392). In an echo of the earlier story's questioning of the protocols of history, the narrator of "Guayaquil" identifies himself as a "professor of Latin American history" living in Buenos Aires. He intimates how he was recently visited by one Dr. Eduardo Zimmerman, a "foreign-born historian driven from his homeland by the Third Reich and now an Argentine citizen"; at the end of a tense and short-lived meeting, the narrator consents to signing a document which authorizes Zimmerman to travel in his stead to a Latin American republic in the Caribbean and fulfill the mission of a lifetime: he will collect a letter written by none other than Bolívar, "dated from Cartagena on August 13, 1822" (*CF* 391), and only recently discovered, which the two historians believe will throw light on the details of Bolívar's meeting with San Martín. By signing the sheet of paper prepared by Zimmerman, the narrator does more than make a professional concession: he also capitulates in an intimate battle of wills that causes him deep and lasting humiliation. His story suggests that San Martín probably made the same concession and experienced the same humiliating defeat some hundred and forty years earlier.

In its imaginative reconstruction of national foundations and the birth of an independent South America, "Guayaquil" exudes the same sense of malaise and anxiety as "Theme of the Traitor and the Hero." Doubts about what "really" happened at Junín are pushed two years further back into the past, to Guayaquil in 1822. In the process, the narrative destabilizes even further the truth claims of competing nationalistic narratives that would privilege now Bolívar, now San Martín, in the creation of the republics of South America. For Borges, elements of fiction and deceit complicate any search for foundations – a point that he illustrates through the contamination of the world of the narrative (the world of the narrator and of Zimmerman) with details of the (completely fictional) topography of *Nostromo* by Joseph Conrad, which are reproduced in the first pages of "Guayaquil." Finally, this story of two historians locking horns in an unedifying battle of wills recalls Borges's pronouncement in the 1953 poem that "Junín is two civilians cursing a tyrant on a street corner, / or an unknown man somewhere, dying in prison" (*SP* 171). Here we have two historians fighting over the legacy of Bolívar and San Martín in contemporary Argentina or Costaguana.

Place and identity

The ironic treatment of geography in "The Theme of the Traitor and the Hero" highlights a peculiar set of relations between place and identity in Borges's work. As well as the parallel with Ireland, a number of poems and stories by Borges link Argentina with other countries, of which India seems to have been a favorite. Crucially, the analogy with these countries hinges around their colonial status: this is the case of "Theme …," where the main action "has already taken place" during a time of supposed colonial unrest and utopian dreaming in Ireland. In connection with India, Borges often evoked the name of Benares, the ancient center of many faiths that stands on the banks of the Ganges, doing so as early as 1921 in a short prose piece and then again in a poem dated 1923. Beyond the mere mention of that city, what is most significant is the context in which Borges twice evoked its name: for in the first instance, Benares is linked with Madrid in a three-way description of modern-day Buenos Aires; and in the second, it is the subject of a poem, only apparently misplaced, which Borges incorporated into his inaugural collection of verse, *Fervor de Buenos Aires*. Unnoticed by critics until recently, Benares serves in both texts as a spatial analogue for the Argentine capital and even nestles within the name, "BuENosAiRES." Written when India was still part of the British Empire, prose piece and poem alike fuse post-colonial Buenos Aires with a colonial city in India, and mischievously attribute a persistent colonial identity to Argentina, a full century after Independence. This unflattering implication recurs in *Moon Across the Way*, which includes a poem dedicated to Dakar, in the modern-day Republic of Senegal: another "foreign body" in an Argentine-themed collection, which this time compares Buenos Aires with a coastal city in West Africa, still culturally and politically dependent on France at the end of the first quarter of the twentieth century. In these elusive (and allusive) works, Argentine identity is constructed as a hall of mirrors, refracted and overlaid with images of others whose location may be elsewhere but whose situation reflects that of the Argentine Republic.

Themes of nation and identity come to the fore, and obsessively so, in the stories of *Brodie's Report*. In the Foreword to the collection, Borges describes all but one of the eleven stories as "realistic" and studded with "circumstantial details" that are a prerequisite of the genre (*CF* 346). The opening sentences of "The Story from Rosendo Juárez" and "The Gospel According to Mark" can be taken as typical of this alleged "realist" discourse:

> It was about eleven o'clock one night; I had gone into the old-fashioned general-store-and-bar, which is now simply a bar, on the corner of Bolívar and Venezuela. (*CF* 358)

> The incident took place on the Los Alamos ranch, south of the small town of Junín, in late March of 1928. (*CF* 397)

Details of time and place abound, as Borges claims, and his stories invite superficial interpretation as tableaux of Argentine life, both rural and urban, at specific moments in the nineteenth and twentieth centuries. In line with this approach, the nation depicted in *Brodie's Report* is a horrendous place peopled by murderers, cowards, and duelists, its citizens susceptible to envy, violence, and degeneration. "We all come to resemble the image others have of us," says Santiago Fischbein of "Unworthy" (*CF* 354), lamenting his personal inability to throw off perceptions of him as a coward, but also glossing the dilemmas of other characters in the collection, no less the prisoners of reputations which characterize them as essentially barbaric. How ironic, then, that the same Fischbein should boast, "I'm a good Argentine and a good Jew. I am respected and respectable" (*CF* 354).

The picture of Argentina that is drawn in *Brodie's Report* evidently tends toward caricature; in order to avoid falling headlong into an interpretative trap, the reader should be aware of the tongue in Borges's cheek in his comment about his stories' realism, and in the various narrative scenarios that follow thereafter. That said, there is no denying that, beneath the layers of caricature that adorn its surface, the collection projects a vision of Argentina which contains elements of a certain truth – centering around national pride, authoritarianism, and machismo, among other things.

The supposed realist logic of *Brodie's Report* is subject to qualifications in other areas, too. As interpreted by Sylvia Molloy and Donna Fitzgerald, stories including "The Gospel According to Mark" and "The Interloper" masquerade as parables about the classic Argentine theme of civilization against barbarism, whilst "problemati[zing] clean-cut divisions, univocal formulations of difference."[5] Molloy shows how Baltasar Espinosa, in "The Gospel …," is denied the stable subject position of the white, Christian, urban *criollo* in his confrontation with the Gutres, a family of barbaric peasants. In her reading of the story, Borges compromises and contaminates both of the terms that make up an all-too-familiar binary: to Baltasar, he gives "an Anglophile free-thinking father, a devout Catholic mother, and a name unerringly pointing to a Sephardic heritage"; for their part, the Gutres "are not the indigenous inhabitants, or the Spanish-Amerindian *mestizos* that have been routinely reified as 'other' in Latin America. Instead they are the product of Scots 'gone native,' a combination of Inverness and the Argentine pampa."[6] Thus, the story confounds the European reader's preconceptions of the ethnic categories of "*criollo*," "*mestizo*," and indigenes in Borges's Argentina.

Fitzgerald's study of "The Interloper" yields similar conclusions about the author's narrative strategies and the story of post-colonial Argentina that is related in its pages. Taking issue with prevalent "masculinist" interpretations of the story which center on Cristián and Eduardo Nilsen as misogynistic gauchos, Fitzgerald focuses on the role of the interloper, Juliana, who drives a wedge between the brothers before she is eventually murdered. What in the domestic sphere is a crude *ménage à trois*, symbolizes, in the outer realm, a "territorial *agon*," or conflict, between two representatives of the repressive, *criollo*, Catholic, and patriarchal order, over a third party who is repressed and "other" in the crucial respects of gender, culture, and race (Fitzgerald reads Juliana as "crypto-Jewish").[7] What is more, the Nilsen brothers are of tantalizingly uncertain origin, being *criollos*, certainly, but of Danish or Irish stock. Relayed to the narrator many years after it was originally told by Eduardo at the wake held for his elder brother "in eighteen-ninety-some-thing … in the district of Morón" (*CF* 348), the story remains etched on the popular psyche: a testimony to the monstrous failings of a national project which worked on the basis of the narrowest and most exclusive definitions of manhood and nationhood, continuing down to the time of writing and perhaps to the present day.

I believe there is a final, added complication to the construction of Argentine identity in *Brodie's Report*: this centers on the meanings and implications of the title story, which have a retrospective knock-on effect on the entire collection.[8] "Brodie's Report" is a pseudo-ethnography of a tribe called the Mlch, who are visited by a Scottish Presbyterian missionary in their tribal homeland somewhere in central Africa or, possibly, Brazil. Dr. Brodie announces that he will call the Mlch "Yahoos," after one of the peoples encountered by Lemuel Gulliver in the famous novel by Jonathan Swift, "lest my readers should forget the bestial nature of this people" (*CF*

402); what follows are several pages of evidence of the Mlch's cruelty, backwardness, and barbarism. At the end of his report, which we discover is addressed to Queen Victoria, Dr. Brodie expresses the earnest wish that the Mlch/Yahoos be given the same consideration as other subjects of the British Empire, since he believes that, although they are "a barbarous people … they represent, in a word, culture, just as we do, in spite of our many sins" (CF 407–8).

The ambiguity surrounding the geographical location of Dr. Brodie's "Yahoos" is a matter of some critical debate. William Luis has identified the Mlch with the Bush people of South Africa,[9] but I maintain that the story's geographical ambiguity is essential in enabling the story to function as a wide-ranging critique of nineteenth-century Western imperialism around the globe. Within those broad parameters, the barbarous customs of the Yahoos are also easily assimilated to the Argentine scenarios depicted in the remainder of *Brodie's Report*, where images of self and others – be they lands, peoples, or cultures – interrelate in a systematic way, in "Unworthy," "The Gospel According to Mark," and elsewhere.

Critiquing Western hegemony: "Brodie's Report" and "The Stranger"

The narrative climax of "Brodie's Report" is made up of two components. First, there is the revelation that the report is addressed to no less an authority than "Your Majesty's Government." It is important that the reader should appreciate the force of interpellation of Dr. Brodie's appeal to the Monarch, which may be likened to the representations made by the celebrated Dominican missionary, Bartolomé de las Casas, to Emperor Charles V on behalf of the American Indians, whom he wished to protect from continuing abuse by the Spanish colonizers. The second component consists in a reversal of perspective that effectively turns the tables on the recipients of Brodie's report. Having allied themselves with Brodie's white, European, and Christian assumptions throughout, his readers are suddenly required to recognize a mirror image of themselves in the concluding descriptions of the Mlch, who Brodie now insists are "redeemed" by practices and conventions including institutions, a monarch, and "a language based on abstract concepts" (CF 407–8). These properties align the readers inescapably with the Mlch and effectively pull the rug of complacency from under our feet.

A major casualty of the turning of the tables at the end of "Brodie's Report" is the reputation of Christianity and Christian ethics. Several years later in a prose piece entitled "Istanbul," Borges will denounce the Crusades as "the cruelest undertaking registered in the history books and the least denounced of all."[10] Though not directly besmirched by a history of cruelty, the Scottish missionary of "Brodie's Report" nevertheless joins the Mlch in fighting like a good Christian soldier against their warring neighbours, the ape-men. He is also tainted by sins of pride and condescension, which make him the embodiment of a set of values that are compromised at root. Borges dramatizes this problem brilliantly in a poem which expands on both the themes and the narrative design of "Brodie's Report."

"The Stranger" ("El forastero") was published in *The Limit* and is one of a small number of imaginative excursions made by Borges into territory concerning Japan.[11] The title of the poem recalls an earlier one, published in *The Self and the Other*, but "The Stranger" breaks completely with the themes and setting of its homonym. Its subject is a Shinto priest, whom Borges impersonates in direct speech, beginning with a vivid evocation of setting. The poem then advocates Shintoism as "the lightest of religious practices, the lightest and the most ancient." In relation to other belief systems, including Buddhism and Christianity, Shinto is distinguished by a lack of dogmatism and heavy-handedness: the priest explains, "It tells us that we should do good, but it has no fixed ethical code"; "it does not say that man fashions his own karma"; and it does not blackmail its followers with a system of rewards and punishments. The remainder of his description conveys a sense of wonder and piety that contrasts with his implicit put-down of Christian doctrine.

Ten lines from the end, Borges's poem undergoes an unexpected transformation in form and style. Ceasing to function as the pious exposition of a cosmology, it takes on the more familiar rhythms of narrative, as the priest relates how, "This morning we were visited by an old Peruvian poet. He was blind … Through an interpreter I tried to explain our religion to him. I don't know if he understood me." With this, the thrust of the poem is re-directed toward the subjects of inter-cultural understanding and the unstable, shifting grounds of people's perceptions of one another. Referring to his visitor, the priest remarks that "Western faces are masks that cannot be deciphered," which patently reverses the commonplace that Eastern faces are inscrutable and indistinguishable to the Western observer. Through his comment, "The Stranger" acquires a sting in the tail that is all the more piquant given the priest's identification of the blind man who visits his temple as "Peruvian": a characterization that almost certainly involves a misrecognition and misrepresentation of Borges himself, on the grounds that, to a Japanese observer, all South Americans look (and probably are) alike.

This clever articulation in Borges's poem produces several meanings and effects that are germane to the present study. Within the thought process that unfolds in "The Stranger," the initial identification of the Shinto priest as the referent of the title is turned inside out and replaced by the realization that it is the Peruvian (Western) poet, and not the Shinto priest, who is "foreign." Through the dialectical structure of his poem, Borges enacts the injunction to "see ourselves as others see us" and submits to the imaginative experience of being "other." In addition to personal considerations,[12] "The Stranger" showcases values, especially ethical values, that are surely to be preferred to the heavy-handed codes of Christianity. In ideological terms, the poem goes beyond a mere defense of the relative merits of another culture and instead adopts the perspective of an ancient and venerable Eastern civilization, in order openly to critique historic assumptions of Christian Europe and the political and spiritual hegemony of the West.

The Orient and Orientalism(s)

The Shinto priest of "The Stranger" is the latest in a long line of Oriental subjects in Borges's work which stretch back at least as far as *Universal History of Iniquity* (1935). That collection took its subjects from a broad spectrum including China, Japan, Turkestan, and Equatorial Africa, also featuring characters and locations found in that indispensable archive of images of the Orient, *The Thousand and One Nights*, translated first by Edward W. Lane and then by Sir Richard Burton. Sandwiched between "The Uncivil Master of Ceremonies, Kotsuké no Suké" and "Man on Pink Hakim, the Corner" in Borges's collection of infamous characters, "Masked Dyer, of Merv" is an example drawn from the world of Islam, or more precisely, from a heresy in Islam identified with a prophet of gloom, called Al Muqanna' or Hakim, who was born in Turkestan and preached "a life of penitence and a death steeped in opprobrium" (*CF* 42; translation modified). As part of his creed, Hakim believed: "The earth we inhabit is an error, an incompetent parody. Mirrors and paternity are abominable because they multiply and affirm it. Revulsion, disgust, is the fundamental virtue" (*CF* 43). In spite of the overlap with Borges's oft-professed terror of mirrors and paternity, Hakim is no *alter ego* but rather a deterrent example of killjoy asceticism, which does not hold for the mainstream of Islam. At the end of the story, he is summarily exposed, dismissed as a liar, and "run through with spears," a fate consistent with his inclusion in Borges's rogues' gallery and anthology of monstrous human beings.

Ian Almond discusses "Hakim of Merv," along with several other stories on Islamic themes that Borges produced between 1933 and 1956.[13] Almond acknowledges considerable variety in Borges's interest in Islam at the time, also linking him to different figures and strands in the Western discipline of Orientalism. In the case of "Hakim of Merv," Borges draws on the nineteenth-century Irish Romantic, Thomas Moore, and produces a much pared-down version of a poem that was 20,000 lines long; other stories rework material from the likes of Edward FitzGerald, and Miguel Asín Palacios; Percy Sykes's *A History of Persia* is another source. This diversity of influence suggests that Borges's relationship to the Orient was as complex as his relationship to Orientalism – or to a variety of Orientalisms developed, from the eighteenth century on, in England, France, and Spain, to mention only three countries in Europe with a history of Orientalism. Whether Almond is right to see in Borges's output "a slightly simplistic model for the progression of Western responses to Islam and Islamic cultures" remains open to debate, especially in the light of later developments in his life and career.[14]

In this regard, there are three essays included in *Siete noches* (*Seven Nights*, 1980) which are plainly relevant.[15] "*The Thousand and One Nights*," "Buddhism," and "The Kabbalah" encapsulate much of the mature Borges's attitude to that congeries of cultural, historical, and geographical phenomena that go under the labels of "the Orient" or "the East"; the first essay, in particular, is worth considering in some detail here. Apart from an encyclopedic range of knowledge of things Oriental, the most noticeable characteristic of the essay on "*The Thousand and One Nights*" is its meandering structure and heterogeneity of argument. The main thread is the story of the entry of the East into Western consciousness, starting with Alexander the Great's military campaigns that led to his "discovery" of the Orient in Persia and India, in the fourth century BC. Virgil, Pliny, and Juvenal constitute further landmarks in the process, which reached a crossroads with the publication, in 1704, of the first European version of *The Thousand and One Nights*, by Antoine Galland: an event which, Borges asserts, thoroughly changed the European mindset. At the same time, as he consolidates the linear structure of his essay, Borges weaves another pattern which works against the conventional assumptions of chronology. That pattern imitates the embedded structure of many tales in the *Nights* and insinuates that Borges's essay is itself an interpolation into the larger story of the *Nights*.

At crucial moments in his essay, Borges makes a number of significant observations. Three of these are of particular interest here. First, East and West, the Orient and the Occident, are political and cultural constructs that do not correspond to any fixed geographical coordinates. Borges observes that, historically, "part of the Orient was in fact the Occident, at least from the standpoint of the ancient Greeks and the Romans," and he gives the example of North Africa as an area of shifting cultural and geographical identifications. He also makes the controversial but logical claim that "Western culture is impure inasmuch as it is only half Western" – he privileges the Greek over the Christian stratum of Western civilization, on the grounds that the latter was of Middle Eastern origin. Second, the relation between East and West is not hierarchical but built on interdependence and reciprocity. The lexicon that Borges uses to describe this relation includes the words "encounter," "dialogue," "gift," and "*comercio*" or exchange. The point about reciprocity is nicely illustrated by the remark: "There is a book by a French writer entitled *The Discovery of Europe by the Chinese*." Third, abstracted from the flow of time, "the Orient" acquires connotations of fancy and mystery that merge into an aesthetic of "fascination," "beauty," "nostalgia," and a "presence" that is "felt."

In schematic terms, these three aperçus focus respectively on geo-politics, ethics, and aesthetics, and can be illustrated in numerous works that Borges wrote in the 1970s and early 1980s. The issue of geo-politics and identity is present throughout *The Limit*, starting with "Ronda" and culminating in the Japanese-themed poems at the end of the collection. One short item, "The Act of the Book," insists paradoxically on the Oriental origins of Spain's national literary classic, *Don Quixote*, which Borges's narrator maintains was based on a book written in Arabic and unknown to the Orientalists, except via the version in Castilian Spanish.[16] Iberian and Argentine nationalists alike are challenged to accept the idea of a legacy that was hybrid (or "impure") even before it was transported to the Americas at the dawn of the modern age.

The preoccupation with ethics and reciprocity is dramatized in "The Stranger," as seen above, and in the self-deprecating portrait of "a minor poet from the southern hemisphere" penned in "That Man" ("Aquél"), where Borges admits his embarrassment at having indulged "a fondness for the Orient, which peoples of the miscellaneous Orient do not share" (*SP* 431). His attitude of humility and respect sets him worlds apart from the typical Orientalist characterized by Edward Said as an arrogant imperialist, intent on subduing the inferior Other and denying him or her the subject-position granted without reservation to the citizens of Europe.[17]

Finally, Borges's poetics of the East finds a quintessential expression in "The East" ("El Oriente"), published in *La rosa profunda* (1975).[18] This impressive poem builds up a composite sense of the Orient through a series of motifs including the silk-road from China, the Crucifixion at Golgotha, the sixty-four hexagrams of I Ching, the haiku, and several other motifs. The Orient that is evoked is manifestly stylized and dependent on a tradition of topoi and images that Borges could have drawn from any number of Orientalist sources. In so much, "The East" is open to the accusation that it remains unquestioningly within the bounds of Orientalist discourse. However, besides that, the poem also tells two significant stories, the first of which reformulates in poetic language the history of Europe's encounter with the Orient as told in the essay, "*The Thousand and One Nights*." Early references to Virgil and Juvenal establish a narrative sequence that accommodates the Holy Bible, Prester John, and Camões, and continues down to

Kipling, whose canonical novel *Kim* was published in 1901, two years after Borges was born. The inference that the reader can be expected to draw is that the Orient is a concept thoroughly mediated by the Western tradition, which Borges has inherited and which he reconstructs and embroiders in his own work. The other story that is told in "The East" is one of loss and sadness, centering almost certainly on the poet's mother, Leonor, who died shortly before Borges wrote the poem. Desolate, he found in the topoi and frame of reference of the Orient a means to navigate a tumultuous inner world and a language for expressing intimate feelings of loss and emptiness that could only be rendered in the diction of poetry.

Conclusion

"*The Thousand and One Nights*" and "The East" bear witness to the complexity inherent in Borges's overall relationship both to the Orientalist tradition and to the broader frame of post-colonialism. In his handling of Orientalist materials, we have seen how Borges could use them as a source of lyrical inspiration but also as a framework for geo-political and ethical considerations. The critique of Western hegemony that we have observed in the third section of this essay is without doubt a crucial element in Borges's ideological make-up and one that links him to intellectuals in Africa, Asia, and other parts of the post-colonial world around the midpoint of the twentieth century. Decades before that, however, Borges's ideas about place and identity, center and margins, were already seminal, as has been noted by several critics. One of them, Edna Aizenberg, has claimed for Borges the role of "post-colonial precursor."[19] From a comparative and metropolitan perspective, this is a valid assessment. Yet, in my opinion, it is incomplete without an acknowledgment of Borges's unique interrogation of the post-colonial history of Argentina and South America. As shown in the first section of this chapter, anxiety about the foundations of the sub-continent's modern nation states in the first half of the nineteenth century suffuses both the prose and the poetry of Borges and constitutes a troubling legacy that endures. As important as his sense of place within the geo-political order of things, Borges's preoccupation with history is integral to his post-colonial sensibility and is a facet of his intellectual profile that distinguishes him from post-colonial authors in other settings.

NOTES

1   Alfonso de Toro, "Post-Coloniality and Post-Modernity: Jorge Luis Borges: The Periphery in the Centre, the Periphery as the Centre, the Centre of the Periphery," in F. de Toro and A. de Toro (eds.), *Borders and Margins: Post-Colonialism and*

Post-Modernism, Frankfurt, Vervuert; Madrid, Iberoamericana, 1995, 11–43; E. Aizenberg, "Borges, precursor poscolonial," in *Borges, el tejedor del Aleph y otros ensayos*, Frankfurt, Vervuert; Madrid, Iberoamericana, 1997, 158–69.

2 For a fuller outline, see Ania Loomba, *Colonialism/Postcolonialism*. London, Routledge, 1998; Robert J. C. Young, *Postcolonialism: An Historical Introduction*, Oxford, Blackwell, 2001; and Robin Fiddian (ed.), *Postcolonial Perspectives on the Cultures of Latin America and Lusophone Africa*, Liverpool University Press, 2000, Introduction, 1–26.

3 See Edwin Williamson, *Borges: A Life*, New York, Viking, 2004, 3–4.

4 "Quién me dirá cómo eras y quién fuiste," in *El otro el mismo*, OC II, 319. All translations from the *Obras completas* are my own.

5 Silvia Molloy, "Lost in Translation: Borges, the Western Tradition and Fictions of Latin America," in *Borges and Europe Revisited*, ed. Evelyn Fishburn, London, Institute of Latin American Studies, 1998, 8–20; and Donna Fitzgerald, "Borges, Woman, and Postcolonial History," *Romance Studies*, 24 (2006), 227–39.

6 Molloy, "Lost in Translation," 11.

7 Fitzgerald, "Borges, Woman, and Postcolonial History," 233, 235.

8 In Robin Fiddian, "What's in a Title? Political Critique and Intertextuality in *El informe de Brodie*," *Variaciones Borges*, 28 (2009), 67–86, I argue that the geographical, political, and moral aspects of the title story also hold for the preceding stories.

9 William Luis, "Borges, the Encounter, and the Other: Blacks and Monstrous Races," in F. de Toro and A. de Toro (eds.), *Borders and Margins: Post-Colonialism and Post-Modernism*, 61–78 (71).

10 "Estambul," *Atlas*, OC III, 408.

11 "El forastero," in *La cifra*, OC III, 332.

12 Williamson interprets this poem from a biographical perspective, in *Borges: A Life*, 444–45.

13 Ian Almond, "Borges and the Finitude of Islam," in *The New Orientalists: Postmodern Representations of Islam from Foucault to Baudrillard*, London and New York, I. B. Tauris, 2007, 65–93.

14 Ibid., 89.

15 *Siete noches*, in OC III: "*Las mil y una noches*" (232–41), "El budismo" (242–53), and "La cábala" (267–75).

16 "El acto del libro," in *La cifra*, OC III, 292.

17 See Edward Said, *Orientalism: Western Representations of the Orient* [1978], Harmondsworth, Penguin, 1985.

18 The collection *La rosa profunda* is translated as *The Unending Rose* in Penguin's *Selected Poems* but "El Oriente" is not included in the latter. See OC III, 114.

19 Aizenberg, "Borges, precursor poscolonial," in *Borges, el tejedor del Aleph y otros ensayos*, 158–69.

9

DANIEL BALDERSTON

Fictions

Ficciones (*Fictions*) was the name used from 1944 on to designate Borges's most influential collection of short stories, one that includes such famous stories as "Tlön, Uqbar, Orbis Tertius," "Pierre Menard, Author of the *Quixote*," and "The Garden of Forking Paths." This was not the original title of the collection, and the contents of the book varied later when it was included in the (incomplete and chaotic) *Obras completas*, but it is the title most commonly used for that collection, and a highly influential title, as we shall see. (It was even preserved as the title for the English translation of the book that Anthony Kerrigan made for Grove Press in 1962.)

In the late 1930s Borges was working as a cataloguer at a small branch library in the Boedo neighborhood of Buenos Aires. His knowledge of library classification systems comes up a number of times in his subsequent writings, most notably in "John Wilkins' Analytical Language" (1942) in *Other Inquisitions*. His library work no doubt focused his attention on one of the basic classification schemes, the division of printed work between "fiction" and "non-fiction." "*Ficción*" was not a common classification category in Spanish at the time (*cuento, novela, narrativa* were all more common), but in the English-speaking world, school and public librarians were in the habit of dividing their books that way, even though one of the most common classification systems used in such libraries, the Dewey Decimal System (developed by Melvil Dewey in 1878), did have a decimal classification for fiction (within the 800 numerals used for literature). Public libraries in the United States, however, frequently did not follow this aspect of the Dewey classification system. These small, non-academic libraries usually contained a high percentage of novels, a fact that counseled for a pragmatic separation of works of fiction from other works in the library collection. The distinction between fiction and non-fiction, of course, has ancient roots in literary criticism, since the concept of *fiction* or *invention* was contrasted with truth. Plato's and Aristotle's concept of *mimesis* was informed by a distinction between truth and verisimilitude, between the thing itself and representations of it, and Borges refers numerous times in his literary criticism of the 1930s to this distinction.

In Borges's career, the switch from mostly non-fiction to significant fiction writing was notable. His early writings (from 1919 to 1930, roughly) were mostly poetry and poetry criticism, though already by the middle of the 1920s he had become an important book reviewer, and more generally a cultural critic (with writings on art and film, as well as occasionally on popular music and other aspects of popular culture). What are usually considered his first short stories were written in 1933 and 1934 for a literary supplement, and were collected in the volume *A Universal History of Iniquity* in 1935; they were, however, not original stories (except for one), but recast versions based on published sources that were listed in a bibliography at the end of the volume. Critics have noted the important ways in which Borges rewrote these "twice-told tales," but there is no dispute that they are not "fiction" in the fullest sense, since they were rewritten from earlier ("non-fictional") sources. The first full *ficción* is "The Approach to Al-Mu'tasim," but that too was not cast fully as a short story, masquerading instead as a book review, and for good measure was first published in *A History of Eternity* (1936), a book of essays. (It would later be included in *The Garden of Forking Paths* and *Fictions*, and omitted from some later editions of *A History of Eternity*.) The cluster of stories written between 1939 and 1941 and then collected as *The Garden of Forking Paths* (issued the last day of 1941 but circulated beginning in 1942) were notable, then, within the context of Borges's career at the time, since he was mostly considered a book reviewer and essayist, and was characterized as such in early editions of *Quién es quién en la Argentina* (*Who's Who in Argentina*).

A bit more than two years after the initial publication of *The Garden of Forking Paths*, Borges published *Fictions*. The first section, entitled *The Garden of Forking Paths*, reproduced the earlier book (including the earlier mock book review "The Approach to Al-Mu'tasim"); a second section entitled *Artifices* added six stories. Editions of *Fictions* that appeared from 1956 on included three additional stories, "The South," "The Cult of the Phoenix," and "The End," which were written after the publication of *The Aleph* (Borges's other path-breaking book of stories) in 1949. The history of the book, then, is quite complex, with the majority of the stories written between 1940 and 1944, but with a few that were written earlier and (quite a bit) later. The Spanish title, *Ficciones*, was a bold one at the time, since most other collections of stories in Spanish would have been called "*relatos*" or "*cuentos*."

If Borges is known as the master of *ficciones*, though, this has not so much to do with the choice of one word over another as for the fact that the stories collected in the volume were radically different from anything that anyone had written up to that time (in any language). The success of the title, then, has to do with its distilling in a single word something of the anomalous nature of those texts. In what remains of this chapter, I would like to discuss the stories collected there, one by one in the order in which they appear in the book (which is not the order in which they were written or published in periodicals), then return to the question of what *ficciones* means here.

The opening story has the rather daunting title "Tlön, Uqbar, Orbis Tertius." Published originally in *Sur* in May 1940 (and reprinted a few months later in the *Antología de la literatura fantástica* edited by Borges with Adolfo Bioy Casares and Silvina Ocampo, and translated into English as *The Book of Fantasy*), it tells the story of three anomalous objects that appear in the narrator's world: a four-page article on an imaginary region (Uqbar), the eleventh volume of the *First Encyclopedia of Tlön*, the rest of that encyclopedia, and some mysterious metallic objects that are not of this world. The temporal setting is 1935 to 1947 (the latter being the date of a postscript that appeared in the original 1940 publications of the story); the spatial setting is various small towns on the outskirts of Buenos Aires. The story narrates the detective work done by Borges and several of his friends to understand the origin of these anomalous objects, which eventually leads them to uncover an international conspiracy that would overthrow the ways we think about the world. This conspiracy is metaphysical, but by the end of the story it has political effects, and they seem atrocious to the narrator. Subtly, then, Borges writes about imaginary encyclopedias but he is also writing about the crisis shaking the world as he writes (at the beginning of the Second World War).

"Tlön" was one of several stories that Borges would describe in the Foreword to the volume as "notes on *imaginary* books" that would have the advantage over other apocryphal books on books (he mentions Carlyle's *Sartor Resartus*) of being much shorter (*CF* 67). They are reviews in the sense that they sum up and critique a work, showing with carefully chosen examples and an occasional flare of polemics, the contours of an intellectual project. In a parallel sense, the narrator of "Tlön" notes that the article on Uqbar (and then the encyclopedia of Tlön) has the dry tone of writing in encyclopedias: "quite plausible, very much in keeping with the general tone of the work, even (naturally) somewhat boring" (*CF* 69). This contrasts with the tone of the story itself: if the narrator can say that his father and Herbert Ashe had "one of those close English friendships (the first adjective is perhaps excessive) that begin by excluding confidences and soon eliminate conversation" (*CF* 71), he himself is anything but reticent about the impact of the discoveries on himself, his circle of friends, and eventually the wider world. A passionate text that plays off the idea of dispassion, "Tlön" hovers, then, over the very distinction between ideas and reality, or perhaps between fiction and non-fiction.

In many editions of *Fictions*, "The Approach to Al-Mu'tasim" appears next. As already explained, it had been published initially in the essay collection *A History of Eternity* in 1936; it was subsequently included in *The Garden of Forking Paths* and *Fictions*, but has now been moved back to *A History of Eternity* in the latest editions of the *Obras completas*. (In individual editions of *A History of Eternity* and *Fictions* it often appears in both.) The first of the fictive book reviews, it opens with invocations of Dorothy Sayers and other figures in the British intellectual world of the time, and masks as a review of the first Indian crime novel. The "reviewer" has at hand only the second edition of the novel, published in London and with a strong allegorizing (or Orientalizing) tendency that he hypothesizes was not as strong in the original Bombay edition. The story came out at a time when Borges was especially active as a book reviewer, and the touches of verisimilitude are so strong that his best friend Adolfo Bioy Casares is said to have tried to order the book from London. Like the later "The Man on the Threshold" (in *The Aleph*) it is a story that plays on Kipling, and evinces a strong interest in British India. At the same time, it seems to be at least partly a mock review of *El enigma de la calle Arcos* (*The Mystery of Arcos Street*), an anonymous Argentine crime novel (at least no one has deciphered in a convincing way the identity of the author hidden behind the pseudonym of Sauli Lostal), first published serially in 1932 in the newspaper *Crítica* (whose literary supplement Borges would direct with Ulises Petit de Murat in 1933–34) and in book form in 1934; the dates, and the physical description of the book, are very close to those in "The Approach to Al-Mu'tasim."

Another of the famously challenging stories, "Pierre Menard, Author of the *Quixote*," predates "Tlön," since it was published in *Sur* in May 1939. If "The Approach to Al-Mu'tasim," the only story in *Fictions* written before "Pierre Menard," masquerades as a book review, "Pierre Menard" masquerades as an obituary, written by some obscure provincial French man of letters in Nîmes in 1939 (as the colophon of the story informs us). The narrator writes to defend the reputation of his late friend against others, whom he considers opportunistic and treacherous, most notably a local lady named Madame Henri Bachelier. The story begins with Menard's funeral, but most of the middle consists of an annotated bibliography of Menard's "visible work," and a discussion of his unfinished version of *Don Quixote*. Of the latter, he finished only two and a half chapters (chapters 9, 22, and 38 of Part One of the Cervantes novel), but from a single phrase that he quotes we know that his version is identical (down to the punctuation) to the Cervantes text and yet "almost infinitely richer" (*CF* 94), or so he insists. The "previous" writing of Menard is so strong that, as in a palimpsest where the original text can be recovered from the marks on the parchment (*CF* 95), Cervantes's text in its entirety seems to the narrator to have been written by his friend, more than three hundred years (and in a different country) from the original.

One of the many intriguing features of the story is the fact that there was a French intellectual named Dr. Pierre Menard (without an accent, as in the Borges story) in Nîmes in the decades when Borges's fictional character lived there, and that he wrote a series of books on the contributions of graphology to psychoanalysis, most notably *L'Écriture et le subconscient: psychanalyse et graphologie* (*Writing and the Subconscious: Psychoanalysis and Graphology*).[1] Dr. Menard hypothesized that handwriting analysis would provide a scientific basis for psychoanalysis, and provides his reader with a detailed course whereby to analyze the writer through the inclination, size, width, speed, and shape of his or her letters. Something of this comes through in the final footnote of the story, which refers to Menard's "insect-like handwriting" and use of graph paper for his manuscripts (as was the case for Borges during this period), but more importantly the book focuses on analyzing through copying or tracing the letters of the original, so that the analyst can fully identify with the analysand. This is the very idea of the Novalis fragment mentioned in the story (fragment 2005 of the Dresden edition reads: "I demonstrate that I have really understood a writer only when I am able to act in the spirit of his thoughts, and when I can translate his works and alter them in various ways without detracting from his individuality"). This idea of "total identification," as the narrator terms it in the story, effaces and yet heightens the distance between Menard and Cervantes, or perhaps (as critics have argued) between any reader and any author.

The fact that the fictional author's name is that of a medical doctor interested in psychoanalysis is suggestive, since it plays with Freud's and others' speculations at the time (and Freud died in London only a few months after the publication of the story) on the relations between literature and the psyche, between imagined and lived experience. The story, then, plays with a theme just developed in "Tlön," of the fascination and difficulty of a rigorous imagining of a world in which nothing is outside of perception, and in which psychology is the master discipline. (That Borges was skeptical of the claims of psychoanalysis, and had devastating things to say about "psychological fiction," makes his underlining of psychological processes the more interesting here.) "Fiction," then, can express a complex truth about its author, just as handwriting can betray the secret impulses of the person who puts pen to paper.

"The Circular Ruins" was first published in *Sur* in December 1940. Once again, the relation of "fiction" to "reality" is the thing at stake, this time as a magician (in some ancient time, and unspecified place) tries to imagine a "son" and introduce him into reality. The time and place of the story are not, however, anywhere so vague as it would seem, and Mac Williams has established that the story makes clear use of Zoroastrian beliefs (a fact that Borges hinted at with his mention in the story of the Zend language), particularly those at stake in the so-called Zurvanite heresy.[2] The purification rituals, the totem animals, the use of ruined temples, the sacred nature of fire all point toward ancient rituals of renewal and creation. At the same time, Borges's interest in mathematics (expressed eloquently in his review of Kasner and Newman's *Mathematics and the Imagination*, SNF 249–50) subtends the mathematical structure of the story, concerned with ruins n and $n+1$ in an infinite series. The dreamer dreamed: the Baroque conceit at the heart of the story points toward the idea developed a few years later in the essay "Partial Magic in the *Quixote*," that the presence of a *mise en abyme* in a text like this one calls attention to the "fictional" or "literary" nature of that text, but also contaminates with unreality the "real" status of the reader.

"The Lottery in Babylon," first published in *Sur* in January 1941, has often been read as political allegory, though there is little consensus about whether it refers to all human societies or to particular varieties of totalitarianism. The narrator, who like his fellow citizens has been allotted very different destinies at different moments of his life, is missing a finger (an indication of one of the whims to which he was subject) and informs us near the end that his ship is about to sail. The world around him is radically unstable, with everything being determined by lot – with negative as well as positive consequences. The story, written at a particularly fierce moment in the Second World War, seems to anticipate later existentialist writing (though Borges would be unsympathetic to that movement when it emerged after the war), with its portrayal of a radically alienated individual in a chaotic universe. The affiliation with (later) existentialism could have as its symbol the sacred latrine named Qaphqa – Borges was of course a devoted reader of Kafka throughout this period, as Sartre and Camus would be later – and by the slightly creepy use made of it, as a place where denunciations can be left. The world of Kafka's trial and castle, and of his strange parables, is very much the world of this story.

"A Survey of the Works of Herbert Quain" appeared in *Sur* in April 1941. It is mentioned in the prologue to *The Garden of Forking Paths* as another one of the notes on imaginary books, in this case the several novels of the imaginary author mentioned here. These include a Freudian novel, a detective novel, and a novel that plays with temporal regression (a mirroring of the motif developed in the title story of the volume a few months later). A Herbert Quain novel is what Ricardo Reis reads in José Saramago's novel *The Year of the Death of Ricardo Reis*, in which the eponymous Reis (one of the heteronyms adopted by the Portuguese poet Fernando Pessoa) returns to Lisbon after the death of his author, confirming in a strange way that Quain's fiction is inserted (by Borges, then by Saramago) into a different kind of fictive reality. Quain's motto in the story, "I belong not to art but to the history of art" (*CF* 107), is ironic, since the narrator quickly informs us that Quain regarded history as an inferior discipline; of course, it is hard to see how a novel could *only* belong to a history of the novel or a painting *only* to the history of painting. "History" is inflected as an accumulation of absences here: a negative capability, in Keats's famous phrase, where he refers to Shakespeare's, and then to Coleridge's, "fine isolated verisimilitude caught from the Penetralium of mystery, from being incapable of remaining content with half-knowledge." Again, the question of verisimilitude: the fictional construct sneaks into the history of such constructs, as the world of Tlön sneaks into our world.

"The Library of Babel" was previously unpublished when it first appeared in *The Garden of Forking Paths* at the end of 1941, but it is closely related to an earlier essay, "The Total Library," that had appeared in *Sur* in August 1939. The society of librarians described in the story, alienated from their own task by the nonsensical nature of the volumes that surround them (apparently generated by some sort of random number generator, though it generates letters instead of numbers) and the uncertain nature of the size of the library that surrounds them (is it finite or infinite?) lend the story a tone of quiet desperation: some librarians commit suicide, others go blind or go mad. The narrator never explains how the (apparently all male) society reproduces itself, though there are two references (one masked by a famous typographical error that has been perpetuated in decades of editions, which speaks of "final necessities" instead of the "fecal necessities" mentioned in the first edition, and clearly visible in the first page of the manuscript) to another of the lower bodily functions.

"The Garden of Forking Paths" was also unpublished when it appeared as the final and title story in the 1941 volume. Chosen as title story perhaps because of the way in which its title is at once the text itself, the novel described in the text, and the garden described in biographies of the writer of the novel, the story is also (as I have argued in *Out of Context*) a representation of the chaotic world of 1916, the year of the ghastly Battle of the Somme, to which explicit reference is made in the opening of the story. Borges plays in this story with a series of fractured colonial histories – the bitter end of English colonialism in Ireland, the brief German colonial adventure in Tsingtao, China – to suggest that the characters cannot find solutions to the mysteries in their lives because those solutions are open secrets that others can see but that they cannot.³ (As John Irwin argues, the similarities to Poe's "The Purloined Letter" are no doubt intentional.⁴)

"The Garden of Forking Paths," whose very title ("El jardín de senderos que se bifurcan") sounds in Spanish as if translated from English (and perhaps from Chinese to English) and is often misremembered as "El jardín de los senderos que se bifurcan" (which would sound less strange or "foreignizing," to use the term from translation studies), involves a philosophical excursus into alternate notions of time, but a rigid historical time is the one that actually takes precedence at a crucial moment at the end of the story. Yu Tsun, stimulated by Stephen Albert's theory of proliferating times, feels surrounded by himself and Albert in other "dimensions" of time, and says that in every one of them he is Albert's friend; Albert responds that in at least one of those other times they are enemies, and at that very moment Yu Tsun sees the Irish detective, Richard Madden, arriving at the garden and is forced to shoot Stephen Albert. The historical context is clear: as the reference to the Liddell Hart book clarifies, the Battle of the Somme is about to be joined in swampy terrain of northern France (the "Serre-Montauban line" mentioned in the story), and a map in Liddell Hart shows the position of the town of Albert behind the British lines. Borges was fond enough of the Liddell Hart book to mention it a couple of times as one of the books that he had most reread and annotated (the others are Mauthner's dictionary of philosophy, Spiller's *The Mind of Man*, Lewes's *Biographical Dictionary of Philosophy*, and Kasner and Newman's *Mathematics and the Imagination*, a fascinating and strange little library). His Irish detective is suspected of disloyalty so soon after the Easter Rising in Dublin, and his Chinese spy taught English at the Deutsche-Chinesische Hochschule of Tsingtao (which really existed, and where English was in fact taught in the years before the First World War): Borges has interpolated his fiction into a dense web of historical references. The title story is indeed a memorable one, and one that provides insight into what Todorov calls the "poetics of prose" (though not specifically apropos of Borges). "Fiction" works in tandem with "non-fiction," and the responsible reader will necessarily want to follow up the many references.⁵ Only then will the complexity of Borges's achievement come into focus.

The second half of *Fictions* is called *Artifices*, and as already noted it contains stories published between 1942 and 1944 (when *Fictions* was first published under that title), with three additions that date from after the publication of *The Aleph*. The title of the second section highlights the "artificial" nature of the stories, the fact that their very essence is "artifice," though again there is a complex interplay between the artificial and the natural (or between the fictional and the non-fictional). Many of the stories again work from references to extra-textual realities, and their "artifice" calls attention to their complex genesis.

"Funes, His Memory," one of the most famous of these stories, first appeared in the newspaper *La Nación* on June 7, 1942. Like "Pierre Menard" it is masked as a memorial text, though unlike the former it is not written soon after the character's death but decades later, when a group of Uruguayan intellectuals were bringing together a group of essays on their extraordinary late fellow countryman and decided to invite the narrator (despite his being Argentine, and as such something of a rival) to contribute his reminiscences of Funes. The memoir of Funes begins with an emphatic use of the ways in which the narrator remembers the young man, and the ways in which he is unworthy of using the verb "remember": there is no competing, even decades later, with Funes's extraordinary memory. The story is famous for its touching, almost funny description of the terrible thing that it would be to be endowed with a total memory. Reality crowds in on Funes after the accident that leaves him paralyzed; in order to sleep he thinks of blank surfaces (the dark bottom of a swift river, the other side of a shed built since his accident) since only these are not tense with detail and particularity. The numbering system Funes invents, which the narrator finds chaotic in the extreme, is idiosyncratic and only available to him; it is what Wittgenstein called a private language. Many of his "numbers" refer to Uruguayan culture, and we know from the narrator that he disdains that of neighboring Argentina (particularly the snobbish culture of its capital city); the memoir is also troubled by the tension between the two countries, since the narrator (inhabitant of the larger and more powerful one) feels superior to his country cousin, but then comes to realize the extraordinary intellect of the cousin's young peon.

"The Shape of the Sword" also first appeared in *La Nación* (this story on July 26, 1942). A memoir of the Irish civil war of two decades earlier, it (like "Funes") is set in rural Uruguay, this time by an Irish fugitive who addresses his listener at the end as "Borges." The retelling of the story of John Vincent Moon hinges on a lie, and the fact that the listener ("Borges") does not catch on turns the story into something like a challenge (perhaps like the knife fights associated so strongly by Borges with rural settings, as well as with marginal urban ones). Taking up again the question of the Irish struggle for independence (which was in the deep background of "The Garden of Forking Paths," and will be the central theme of the following story), Borges tells a story of a heroic sacrifice, but waits until the very end to have Moon reveal himself as the coward. This narrative trick forces the reader to reread the whole of the previous text, and on this rereading a whole series of details, beginning with the ironic nickname given Moon in Uruguay, where he is called "the Englishman at La Colorada" (*CF* 138), come to the fore. "The Shape of the Sword" is told by a character who, like the "traitor and hero" in the following story, calls attention to his duplicity, and thus forces the question of responsibility onto his listener (and, by extension, onto us as readers). And like the following story, as well as the later "The South," it is a story that calls attention to its own artifice. Strikingly, that artifice turns on the unresolved dilemmas of colonialism, explicitly through the Irish setting, but also as present in the scimitar, a trophy of British colonial adventures in the Orient. The fight between Moon and his unnamed comrade takes place in the house of a General Berkeley, and the name suggests (as in "Tlön") that philosophical controversies about matter and perception have real-world consequences. This is a point also hinted at when Moon claims that his young revolutionary (apparently the other, but ultimately shown to be his younger self) subscribed to a vulgar Marxism, the reduction of "universal history to a sordid economic conflict." Marx and Berkeley, then: being is perception, but also the task of the philosopher residing not only in the understanding but also in the transformation of the world.

"The Theme of the Traitor and the Hero," first published in *Sur* in February 1944, is clearly a continuation of the same issue, though this is set not in the Ireland of 1922 but in the Ireland of 1824 (though the story is reconstructed a hundred years later by the protagonist's great-grandson). The epigraph from one of Yeats's great poems on the Irish revolution makes clear that the story is centrally about the intellectual's responsibilities, though this is treated ironically when Ryan discovers that Nolan has plagiarized from the English enemy Shakespeare: "The idea that history might have copied history is mind-boggling enough; that history should copy *literature* is inconceivable ..." (*CF* 144). The complexity of the story hinges not only on the double nature of its protagonist, but also on the fact that the process of the invention of a national tradition (in which literature is centrally important to the shaping of history) can be ascribed not only to Ireland in 1824 but also to Poland, the republic of Venice, or some Balkan or South American state. The story tells what Borges had earlier called a "universal history of iniquity" (as Andrew Hurley translates the title of the 1935 collection of stories); notions of "universal history" are invoked quite specifically with the allusions to Condorcet, Hegel, Spengler, and Vico. This is to say, the story zeroes in on the ways in which history depends on fables, yet recasts these patterns in specific ways depending on time and place: the story could be retold in Poland or in Peru, or in Bulgaria, but that would depend on a similar attention to the interplay between local history and local literature, on the ways in which language is a party to political and historical conflict.

"Death and the Compass" appeared initially in *Sur* in May 1942. Like the previous stories, this one is about the ways in which reading shapes the interpretation of reality: Lönnrot is a better reader of detective stories than he is a detective, Scharlach reads the popular press (and the texts mentioned in it) to spin his web. Here the philosopher invoked is not Berkeley or Marx (or Hegel or Condorcet, or the others just mentioned) but Spinoza, whose *"more geometrico"* (in his commentary on Descartes, and in subsequent writings) inspires the imposition of equilateral triangles and rhombuses on a city that turns out to be more Buenos Aires than somewhere in France. A detective story turned inside out, "Death and the Compass" poses the question of the limits of rationality (hence the invocation of Spinoza and implicitly of Descartes). Lönnrot's name invokes Elias Lönnrot, the compiler of folk poems into the *Kalevala*, who became thereby the creator of the idea of Finland (as a future state invented with a deep national past); this process of an "invention of tradition" is also at stake in Lönnrot's tardy (and misguided) attempts to understand Jewish mysticism, a field where his antagonist (a Jewish gangster figure like Monk Eastman in *A Universal History of Iniquity*) is way ahead of him. In keeping with the theme of *Fictions* as a whole, this is clearly a story about the ways in which reading fiction shapes the experience of reality, but also the ways in which the real world can give the fictive one a slip.

"The Secret Miracle," published in *Sur* in February 1943, is a story that clearly relates to the historical time in which it was written and published. Set during the Nazi invasion of Prague in March 1939, it is (like "The Garden of Forking Paths") a story in which games with time are played out against a historical background, and in which the prison house of chronology closes in on the subject. Jaromir Hladík's unfinished project, the verse drama "The Enemies," plays on psychoanalytic ideas of dream-life and traumatic return; the secret year which he is granted, that separates the firing of the bullets by the firing squad from the moment of his death, allows him to return again and again to his poem, to express the dilemma of the relations between reality and *"irrealidad,"* between experience and fiction.

"Three Versions of Judas" was published in *Sur* in August 1944 and shortly thereafter in *Fictions*. As Edna Aizenberg has shown, it anticipates by more than sixty years the publication of the lost *Gospel of Judas*, though Borges seems to have known the central idea of that book (that Judas was the true redeemer, since he abased himself to treachery and infamy for the sake of divine design) from medieval refutations of it.[6] The story plays off a wide variety of theological debates, and it is obvious that Borges takes pleasure in the absurdity of this mode of inquiry (at the same time that he obviously is knowledgeable about it, and perhaps even fascinated).

"The End," the first of the three stories added to the second edition of *Fictions* in 1956, was first published in *La Nación* on October 11, 1953 (and as such was the last story that Borges wrote before his blindness impeded his reading and writing: this story is also an "end" of an important stage of his literary career). It follows on the 1944 publication of "A Biography of Tadeo Isidoro Cruz," a story that rewrites a crucial episode in Argentina's most famous poem, José Hernández's *The Gaucho Martín Fierro* (1872). "The End" rewrites the ending of the second part of that poem, *The Return of Martín Fierro* (1879), suggesting that the rhetoric of national reconciliation that dominates the second Hernández poem (written at the time of a national accord that brought an end to sixty years of civil war) was just a sham, and that the poem's hero dies in a knife fight with the brother of a man he had slain some years before (in the first part of the poem). The story about Cruz was written in the decisive year of the rise to power of Juan Domingo Perón, an event that horrified Borges, and glorifies defiance of the state; the story about Fierro's death was written two years before the "Liberating Revolution" (of which Borges was an enthusiastic supporter) which ended the Perón regime, and which resulted in the muffling of dissent by members of Argentina's largest political party. Interestingly, "The End" is told through the voice of Recabarren, the paralyzed owner of a country general store (there are strong echoes of "Funes" here), who hears (but does not see) the events that are told through him: as if there were an impartial witness to history.

"The Cult of the Phoenix" first appeared in *Sur* in a double issue in September–October 1952; like "The End" and "The South," it was added to the second edition of *Fictions*. Like "Three Versions of Judas," this story plays with theology, though the "secret" suggested here does not seem to have to do with the true nature of divinity. Borges suggests that the secret that is at the core of his sect is mundane and all around us, and that all sorts of people initiate others into it. Many critics have suggested that the secret here is the sexual act, and Borges confirmed this on at least one occasion.

"The South," the final story in the second edition of *Fictions* (and in subsequent ones), was first published in *La Nación* on February 8, 1953. Dahlmann's life story is in many ways parallel to Borges's: both are products of families that descend from European men of letters as well as from *criollo* military figures, both work as librarians and are fond of similar books (and share a reverence for the Argentine politician Hipólito Yrigoyen), and both suffer accidents with a window frame that result in septicemia and delirium. Borges's accident occurred on Christmas Eve 1938, and he would write "Pierre Menard, Author of the *Quixote*" when recovering from it; Dahlmann's accident results either in his death in a hospital after surgery or in his death in a knife fight somewhere in the southern part of the province of Buenos Aires. The story is told in such a way as to justify both readings, and Borges mentions in his 1956 postscript to the preface to *Artifices* that the story (which he considers his best) can be read "both as a forthright narration of novelistic events and in quite another way, as well" (*CF* 129). The issue that is at stake throughout *Fictions* is highlighted in this last story, which harks back to the first stories in the book.

The whole of *Fictions*, then, though not written as a book (and interrupted in its second part by the stories that were collected in *The Aleph*), turn on the complex relations between fiction and non-fiction. The first page of "Tlön," the first story in the book, says that the narrator and his friend Bioy Casares were discussing the possibility of writing a first-person novel in which certain discordant details would suggest to a select group of readers that the fiction masked an "atrocious or banal reality"; the last story (which was in fact the next-to-last story that Borges would write before going blind) suggests that the reader must be willing to read a story in two antithetical ways. The games that Borges plays here with both reality and fiction are highly complex. His interest in techniques of verisimilitude, developed in the early 1930s in two crucial essays, "The Postulation of Reality" and "Narrative Art and Magic," provided him with a way of writing fiction that inserts itself into gaps in the discourses of reality (most notably that of history), while at the same time calling attention to the narrative conventions that are used to talk about reality. Radical stories like "Tlön," "Pierre Menard," "The Garden of Forking Paths," "Funes," and "The South" are all written about these gaps: between language and its referents, between text and reader, between the thing and the idea. *Fictions* is one of the most important books of twentieth-century literature precisely because it is so provocative in the ways in which its "fiction" tells of what is considered not to be fiction.

NOTES

1 Pierre Menard, *L'Écriture et le subconscient: psychanalyse et graphologie*, Paris, Librairie Félix Alcan, 1931.
2 Mac Williams, "Zoroastrian and Zurvanite Symbolism in 'Las ruinas circulares'," *Variaciones Borges*, 25 (2008), 115–35.
3 Daniel Balderston, *Out of Context: Historical Reference and the Representation of Reality in Borges*, Durham, NC, Duke University Press, 1993.
4 John T. Irwin, *The Mystery to a Solution: Poe, Borges and the Analytic Detective Story*, Baltimore, Johns Hopkins University Press, 1994.
5 Perhaps using as tools the Fishburn and Hughes, *Dictionary of Borges*, and the index to Borges on the Borges Center website, www.borges.pitt.edu/
6 Edna Aizenberg, "Three Versions of Judas Found in Buenos Aires: Discovery Challenges Biblical Betrayal," *Variaciones Borges*, 22 (2005), 1–13.

10

ROBERTO GONZÁLEZ ECHEVARRÍA

The Aleph

More than in other literatures, short-story collections have been of foremost importance in the modern literature of Latin America. The tradition seems to have been started, as so much else, by the Nicaraguan poet Rubén Darío, whose epoch-making *Azul* ... (1888), a volume of poems, stories, and other sundry texts, was the first continent-wide bestseller. Every book of poems or stories published since then owes its existence to *Azul* ..., and Borges's collections were no exception.[1] However, the writer who initiated, or at least popularized, the short-story collection in Latin America was Edgar Allan Poe. Poe perfected the artistic short story, the finely wrought plot cast in a poetic language that displays an astonishing coalescence of content and form. His stories contained germs of the uncanny, sometimes outright instances of the fantastic, and teased the reader with challenging enigmas. Poe's influence is evident in Darío, but even more clearly in Borges, whose collections of stories are deeply indebted to Poe, even as they surpass him.

When Borges published *The Aleph* in 1949, he did so following the success of *Fictions*, which had appeared in 1944, and adhering to the same principle of composition: to gather in one volume texts published in journals during the previous years. The collection would presumably display a technical and thematic unity, the development of an œuvre by a well-known author. Borges was fifty when *The Aleph* appeared, the respected author not just of *Fictions* but of other collections of stories, poems, and essays. He was also one of the more prominent members of the association of writers and intellectuals who published *Sur* which, with the Spanish *Revista de Occidente*, was one of the most influential journals to have appeared in the Spanish-speaking world. There were other literary magazines in Buenos Aires then, not to mention the powerful newspaper *La Nación* with its important literary pages. In the 1940s, the Argentine capital was a thriving cultural center in which, in spite of its geographical remoteness, groups of intellectuals and artists from Spain and Latin America gathered, bonded, and quarreled. High on the list of these groups was the one formed by Spanish exiles, fresh from the defeat of the Republic, who coexisted precariously with diplomats sent by Franco's regime to foster its own cultural program of "Hispanidad," which had begun much earlier in the thirties, and which Borges liked to mock. Perón's accession to power in 1946 drove a wedge into the Argentine artistic and literary world. Though not a political activist, Borges held strong positions against Peronism, Fascism, Communism, and anti-Semitism, all of which had a considerable following in Argentina. His opposition to Perón would cost him dearly, and for years Borges endured the scorn of the Latin American Left for his antagonism toward Communist regimes such as Castro's Cuba. This may have cost him the Nobel Prize. In contrast to the more generic title *Fictions,* a book which was a kind of manifesto in favor of pure fiction, *The Aleph* promised with its own more specific title a focused thematic content. In the earlier collection Borges was setting out what he considered to be the essence of storytelling and display-ing various ways in which it could come into being. Fiction for Borges is a world unto itself, which feeds on previous fictions rather than on real-ity, plays with its own literary conventions and techniques to boast of its being the product of invention, and which, by assuming a radically ironic tone, forecloses the promotion of any one philosophical position, except a Socratic self-deprecatory one that shows once and again how foolish we are in seeking satisfactory knowledge, particularly through language. In all that playfulness there is an agonistic "I" who struggles vainly to understand the world and itself, but that "I," to which Borges often gives his own name (as in "The Zahir"), systematically eschews pathos, preferring a stoic attitude best articulated through sophisticated humor. Though blind for much of his adult life and not endowed with physical strength, Borges adhered to a code of courage, which he chronicles often through characters who are soldiers, gauchos, criminals, or other men of action, of which this stance before the helplessness of the human condition is a most vivid example. In *The Aleph* this attitude will be the central concern of the book, rather than the for-malistic pronouncements implicit in *Fictions*. The title story, which would become one of his most famous, encapsulates this dogged but resigned quest for absolute knowledge in a tale of love. "The Aleph" contains the core of Borges's fictional world – its plots, topics, characters – like the device in that story through which the whole universe may be glimpsed simultaneously at a single glance.

It seems safe to assume, then, that Borges gave the collection the title *The Aleph* because he thought that particular story was the most signifi-cant in the group, the one that best reflected the book's main themes and, of course, that it was the best of the lot. Like the enigmatic gadget that presumably allows the narrator-protagonist of "The Aleph" to enjoy an all-encompassing vision of the universe and human history, the story sums up the other stories in the collection, and, indeed, the entirety of Borges's poetics. It could be imagined that with Borges being such a systematic writer, one could construct a story that is a synthesis of all his stories by using his well-known topics, stock characters, settings, objects, and even words, and that such an exercise would be very much in keeping with his own poetics. While "The Aleph" does not quite qualify as such a fabrication, it does contain the essence of the collection. The story's main concern is the desire to attain a totalizing vision of space and time, and the climax comes when the narrator-protagonist reports having such an experience while gazing at an "*Aleph*" – Aleph is, of course, the first letter of the Hebrew alphabet, but here it is a mysterious object possessing the magical power to produce such a vision, which an epilogue to the story attributes to Kabbalistic interpretations. He has been led to the Aleph by Carlos Argentino Daneri, in the basement of what was Beatriz Viterbo's house. Argentino is an eager, diligent, and ridiculously ambitious poet, who is the cousin of the diseased Beatriz, a beautiful, enigmatic woman with whom the protagonist was deeply, if discreetly, in love. In the end the reader cannot be sure if the narrator-protagonist, who is also a poet, has indeed had the vision he recounts, or if he suffered a hallucination provoked by the trauma left by the death of his beloved Beatriz. A typical Borgesian predicament involving ungraspable totalities and the desire to apprehend them, is linked here to a love story involving individuals of the Argentine bourgeoisie, mostly of Italian origin, whose very proper and measured behavior conceals burning passions.

A skeptical reader, a Borgesian reader, would have to adhere to the more mundane interpretation. In a state of emotional agitation, led by the mad Argentino to a dark and dank cellar and told to expect seeing an Aleph, the protagonist experiences a vision that he relates in the traditional rhetoric of visions, using the anaphoric "I saw," "I saw," "I saw." What he "saw" was an inchoate assemblage of things, events, peoples from different eras, lumped together following the poetic device known as "chaotic enumeration." This means that elements that are not linked to one another except by apposition, with no logic, sequence, or overarching principle or shape, are listed as if they cohered in some fashion and meant something. While this practice has been studied by literary scholars and theoreticians and obviously has much in common with Surrealism and its promotion of "automatic writing" (putting down whatever comes into one's head), it is also akin to the well-known psychoanalytic test known as "free association." Free association involves uttering words as they come to our minds without plan or deliberation, unconnected by syntax. The analyst, however, can pick up by the frequency and proximity of certain words the outline of a subtext, an underlying, repressed story that reveals the patient's neuroses. Borges was not fond of psychoanalysis, but the narrator's tirade contains elements that suggest a psychological interpretation; besides, literature preceded and inspired psychoanalysis.

In the jumbled listing of things the narrator saw there are two items that serve as clues to the meaning of the whole ensemble, to the drives behind his interest in the Aleph, as well as to Borges's own conception of storytelling. The first is the obscene letters from Beatriz to Argentino that he purports to have seen: "In a desk drawer (and the handwriting made me tremble) obscene, incredible, detailed letters that Beatriz had sent Carlos Argentino" (*CF* 283).[2] This is a shocking revelation in the context of the proper middle-class setting in which the story takes place, and more so given Beatriz's elegant demeanor and the narrator's idealization of her. Obviously the descendant of Italian immigrants, Beatriz had managed to mix and mingle with the upper crust, and to acquire their style. She is, moreover, a modern woman; she has married and been divorced, a startling detail because divorce was forbidden in Argentina until the end of the twentieth century, by the way. The protagonist, who adored Beatriz and pored over pictures of her in the house, is in the grips of jealous paranoia. He imagines a depraved relationship between the beautiful, chic Beatriz and her ridiculous cousin, who is not only lacking in physical attractiveness but is devoted to the preposterous task of writing an epic poem encompassing the entire world. That Beatriz would surrender to such a hack, her own cousin, and *write* such letters is like the correlative opposite of his idealization of her, the most abject image of her imaginable. How could she be seduced by such vulgarity?

The other horrendous discovery the narrator makes is Beatriz's rotting cadaver, listed among innocuous items in the list: "[I] saw the horrendous remains of what had once, deliciously, been Beatriz Viterbo" (*CF* 283). This disgusting image, together with the dirty letters, undermines the chaotic element from the enumeration. The image of Beatriz's body comes next to the view of his own blood, and is followed by a vision of the sexual act in relation to death: "[I] saw the coils and springs of love and the alterations of death" (*CF* 283) (*"vi el engranaje del amor y la modificación de la muerte"* [*OC* I 625]). The narrator's hallucination is sparked by his desire for Beatriz, tinged with guilt because of its physical dimension, and the trauma of her death, but it is also mediated by the presence of Argentino, the contemptible cousin. To begin with, there is his name. Argentino appears as a nearly allegorical figure of the Argentine – he would be the quintessential one – hence and inevitably a reflection of the narrator and of Borges himself. Then there is the fact that Argentino is a poet and that his obsession is the production of an epic poem of universal reach. That poem is the correlative opposite of the narrator's vision, which is also universal in scope, but shunning sequential development. There is a fear of self-reflection in the fantasy, a fear on the part of the narrator-protagonist of being like the cousin; yet at the same time a desire to be like the cousin, whom he imagines is desired by the desirable Beatriz. Lurking behind this sordid triangle, cast in the social context of immigrant Italian families in Buenos Aires, is a more portentous background: Dante's *Divine Comedy*. What poem could have a broader range than Dante's? Beatriz's name, her Italian background, her death and appearance in a vision, are all allusions to Dante, as is the commingling of erotic desire and aesthetic ambition. Borges's text is to the *Divine Comedy* what Argentino's poem is to the narrator's vision. Borges is a diminished follower of the great Florentine, a very minor poet whose Beatriz turns out to be whorish and a putrid body, not the beatific vision that appears in *Paradiso*, an Aleph if ever there was one.

"The Aleph" reveals that Borges's poetics cannot be reduced to negations, perplexities, dismissive witticisms, and aporias, that they obey a creative will that, in spite of apparent radical skepticism and threatening disorder, tells stories, imagines coherent sequences, invents characters, and faces its own horrific origins in very human dreads. (It is in this aspect that Borges shows his kinship with Schopenhauer, whom he often praised.) These are willful acts of courage, like those of the protagonist in "The Circular Ruins," the well-known story in *Fictions*. The basic plot in the stories of *The Aleph* is the overcoming of doubt and dread and their acceptance as part of the human condition. The stories are like a dance of phantoms, of radical incoherencies and meaninglessness and the willful struggle against them. The sand slips out of the clenched fist that does all it can to hold it. Those phantoms take the form of labyrinths, deserts, alphabets, coins, broken words, philosophical systems, religious doctrines, crimes, women who die, and courageous men who face violence and death unflinchingly. Many of those elements are in "The Aleph" as well as other recurrent commonplaces in Borges's works, even in a larval stage. For instance, Beatriz's house and the cellar in which the Aleph appears is a kind of labyrinth. Labyrinths in Borges naturally take an architectural form and allude to Daedalus, the prototypical architect. In their *arche* they conceal their mystery and the hint of an origin. But they are ultimately representations of the self. The infinite – another Borgesian topic – is present in the chaotic enumeration, as is also his obsession with sequences and their logic, be it of words, letters, or of tokens such as coins. There are also enigmatic objects, of a solid and stolid materiality, like the very heavy conical piece in "Tlön, Uqbar, Orbis Tertius," or more conventional artifacts like coins, astrolabes, and compasses. The Aleph is such an object.

The story that is closest to "The Aleph" is "The Zahir," another tale in which love and death intermingle to generate the plot. It is the story of a man, named Borges, who loses his mind progressively after the death of his beloved, Teodelina Villar. Narrated in the first person, the story is told by the insane narrator, who begins by calmly declaring that a Zahir is a common, twenty-cent Argentine coin, and then goes on to tell how many other disparate things are named Zahir – it is another chaotic enumeration. No such Argentine coin exists, of course, so this is a clue to the reader that the narrator is mentally unstable. Typical of Borges, a dramatic situation that in Faulkner, for instance, would have led to a great deal of sound and fury, is here muffled by the smooth, apparently reasonable discourse with which we are told about Teodelina's death, wake, and the obsession these events provoke in the narrator. Another hint of the narrator's madness, and of his passion, is his description of Teodelina's face at her wake:

> At wakes, the progress of corruption allows the dead person's body to recover its former faces. At some point on the confused night of June 6 [the night of the wake], Teodelina Villar magically became what she had been twenty years before; her features recovered the air of authority that comes from arrogance, money, youth, the awareness of being at the top, as well as limitations such as a lack of imagination, and a certain obtuseness. My thoughts were more or less these: No version of that face that had so disturbed me shall ever be as memorable as this one; better that it be the last one, because it could have been the first. I left her lying stiff among the flowers, refining her contempt for death. (CF 243; translation considerably modified)

In that simultaneous presence of Teodelina's multiple faces, the subsequent fixation with the Zahir is announced, because it is as if her profiles were all going toward the perfect one that could be engraved on a coin. Stasis, perfection, and multiplicity are written on Teodelina's final countenance, qualities that ironically she always sought, and the narrator admired – it adds to her allure that God is written into her name. The Zahir is given to him in the change after he leaves the wake and stops for a drink, clearly to calm down. This is the beginning of his madness because from now on he will not be able to think of anything else but the coin, or of its names, a constant thought that eventually leads to a meditation on his own insanity at the end of the story.

Borges is desperately in love with Teodelina, who is very much like Beatriz Viterbo. She is elegant, stylish, and famous for her good looks, clothes, and hairdos to the point that her picture appears in advertisements for beauty creams and automobiles – this, after her family suffers a socioeconomic collapse barely hinted at in the story. Teodelina is the slave of fashion, but more than anything she seeks perfection, the absolute, like Flaubert (CF 243). It is that pursuit of the absolute that makes her irresistible to Borges. This quest to be *au courant* shows fashion's superficiality, its fickleness, and vulgar struggle against time, but at the same time exposes how it ruthlessly determines matters of taste. This is evident in how Teodelina's death is reported: she commits the gaffe of dying in the middle of the Barrio Sur ("committed the breach of decorum of dying in the middle of Barrio Sur," CF 243). In other words, she allowed herself the vulgarity of dying in a popular neighborhood, not in a classy one. The irony here is that Teodelina's sense of elegance would not have allowed her to die in such an unsuitable place, that her stubborn pursuit of perfection would have led her to want to control even the location of her death.

The Zahir is like an Aleph to the narrator because it allows him to ponder and obsess on the infinite. Coins are parts of sequences, like letters, symbolizing value. Each is an indivisible object, complete unto itself, yet repeatable *ad infinitum*. It is the threatening presence of infinity and the shifting value and meaning of the coin, in the case of the Zahir multiplied by the many variants of its name, that drives the narrator insane. He tries several remedies to take his mind away from the Zahir, without success. Like the protagonist of "The Aleph," he is a writer and so he attempts to write a fantastic story, which describes a metamorphosis in which an ascetic dreams that he turns into a snake. This story turns out to be like an episode in the *Nibelungenlied* – again, the fear that all stories have already been told, as with the presence of Dante in "The Aleph." The narrator, who thinks that he was drunk the night that he was given the Zahir, following Teodelina's wake, has to take sleeping pills, and becomes increasingly aware of his deteriorating mental condition. He goes to a psychiatrist, to whom he only reveals that he suffers from insomnia, and that the image of any object would pursue him, "any random object, a token, coin, say …" (CF 246; translation modified). It does not seem to work. A book he reads, *Confessions of a Thug*, by one Meadows Taylor, about India, becomes a story about tigers that blend into each other and repeat or erase each other, some painted on the walls of the cell of a convict. He learns a few months later that Teodelina's younger sister, Julita, was interned in an insane asylum because she was rambling continually about some coin, the same as someone's chauffeur. The hallucination is becoming collective. By then his own delusions have led him to see the Zahir simultaneously from the back and the front, as if it were in a timeless void, and to discover that everything that is not the Zahir comes to his mind as if it were distant and having been filtered. This suggests – if psychoanalysis may be again invoked – that the whole thing is like a defense mechanism to ward off the pain he has suffered with Teodelina's death. He has also come to the disturbing realization that the contemplation of any one thing can lead to the knowledge of the universe, of the Absolute, so that it does not matter if all he can see is the Zahir. It does not matter either if he is, as he knows, insane, because living and dreaming are one, and the difference between sanity and insanity, irrelevant. When everyone thinks day and night on the Zahir no one will be able to tell the difference between dreams and reality, or between the earth and the Zahir. This radically skeptical conclusion, it is good to remember, is that of a madman, the madman who has just told the story.

Borges created several remarkable characters that have become part of the general literary memory. The best known are Pierre Menard and Funes "the memorious," but these are renowned because they were involved in abstract experiments: the first, the question of authorship; and the second, the limits of human memory. Otto Dietrich zur Linde, the protagonist of "*Deutsches Requiem*," confronts a very concrete historical situation: the transformation of Germany by the Third Reich, and whether to join the Nazi party and participate in the atrocities being committed as part of its program of "renewal." Narrated in the first person on the eve of his execution – the War has just been concluded – Otto's dramatic story is a deep probe into the dangers of political commitment in the twentieth century. Like the protagonists of "The Aleph" and "The Zahir," Otto falls victim to an obsession to which he devotes, literally in his case, his life. He is Borges's best-developed character in a conventional sense; the reader learns about his past, both remote and recent, details of his various decisions, and a good deal about his psychological make-up. "*Deutsches Requiem*" is very much embedded in its time and place – the post-war years, Argentina, the beginning of the Cold War – as well as in Borges's life.

Borges was fascinated by warfare. In "The Garden of Forking Paths" the story centers on an act of espionage during World War I and its unforeseen consequences. "The Secret Miracle" is the confession of a Jewish playwright, Jaromir Hladík, about to be executed by the Nazis. Many are the Borges texts – stories, poems, and essays – dealing with the Argentine wars of independence and the subsequent campaigns against its neighbors and against the Indians. In many of these texts he boasts that his ancestors were involved in these wars, and he longs for a military life that would have done honor to their memory. Courage, on the part of gauchos, criminals, soldiers, and adventurers, is a prevalent theme in all of Borges's fictions. In an Argentina convulsed with patriotic fervor under Perón, and in which much saber rattling took place in the form of military parades and other similar displays, Borges was faced with the unwanted result of certain variations of nationalism and militarism. He was, moreover, appalled by the substantial following that the fascist Italian and German regimes had in Argentina before, during, and after the war. Borges was also moved to denounce the anti-Semitism that accompanied manifestations of support for the Axis powers, and he came under attack as a result by partisans of the Third Reich, who "accused" him of being a Jew. In 1949, just after the end of World War II and Germany's defeat, "*Deutsches Requiem*" chafed against not a few raw nerves in Argentina and laid bare some of Borges's own personal anxieties and preoccupations.

To complicate matters, Borges, who had been partially raised in Switzerland and learned German in his youth, was enthralled by German culture, particularly philosophy and literature. It would not be inaccurate to say that he was a Germanophile. Borges was an admirer of Schopenhauer, as already mentioned, and a reader both of Nietzsche and Spengler, not to mention Goethe and the other great German poets, Schiller and Hölderlin. He often alluded to the *Nibelungenlied*. So to him it was particularly painful to see Germany turn to Nazism, and, as he says in the epilogue to *The Aleph*, "*Deutsches Requiem*" was the result: "During the last war, no one could have wished more earnestly than I for Germany's defeat; no one could have felt more strongly than I the tragedy of Germany's fate, which our own 'Germanophiles' (who know nothing of Germany) neither wept over nor even suspected" (*CF* 287). His answer was to create in Otto the quintessential Nazi and lay bare the intellectual and psychological fundamentals of evil.

Otto's is a case study of Nazism and of evil in its purest state. He is an intellectual, a lover of German philosophers like Schopenhauer, Nietzsche, and Spengler, and a devotee of Brahms's music. He joins the Nazi party because he has come to the conclusion, following Nazi doctrine based on misreadings of those philosophers, that the time for an apocalyptic historical change is near, and that Germany will emerge from it victorious and the leader of a new era. Though personally averse to violence, he participates in street actions prior to the war in which he is wounded, remaining a cripple for the duration. Because of his impeccable record and strict adherence to Nazi doctrine, he is made director of a concentration camp. There he not only arranges for the mass murder of Jews, but particularly of David Jerusalem, an old Sephardic poet of note, who has been assigned to his camp. Otto rationalizes his cruelty as being part of a general movement toward regeneration into which no pity can enter. With logical arguments he quells his moral scruples and forges ahead, carried forth by the triumphant atmosphere. Germany was then in the midst of a series of victories that would culminate with the capitulation of France. The second part of the War, however, led to defeat, which he justifies with the thought that, in the end, it does not matter who is victorious in this feast of destruction. Anticipating the Cold

War, he proclaims that Germany's defeat will lead to an even greater conflict among the winners, which will bring about an even more implacable time, perhaps a larger holocaust: "Now an implacable age looms over the world. We forged that age, we who are now its victim. What does it matter that England is the hammer and we the anvil?" (*CF* 234). Otto's flawless reasoning excludes his feelings, because he has managed to withdraw from his self any sense of individual responsibility or sentimentality. He is only a cog in history's relentless evolution. Otto finishes his confession stating that he does not fear death: "My flesh may feel fear; I myself do not" (*CF* 234).

Otto is not the only Borgesian narrator who tells his story on the eve of his execution: Ts'ui Pên in "The Garden of Forking Paths" and the poet in "The Secret Miracle" find themselves in the same predicament. On the one hand, being aware of impending death puts these characters in a privileged position to express the truth about themselves: they have nothing more to lose, and they have their entire life experience from which to draw a balance. Ultimately, however, like Otto's sense that he lives at the end of a historical era, his totalizing, Hegelian view is just as deceptive as any other contingent one. Otto's and the Nazis' interpretation of history is the best example of this massive error. "*Deutsches Requiem*" dramatizes the futility, and potential harm, of subjecting time, history, and one's life to an intellectual straitjacket, to "the exacting laws" of Borges's well-known aporia: "vague chance or the strict laws / that rule this dream, the universe" ("In memoriam A.R." [Alfonso Reyes], *OC* II 207, my translation). Those laws justify evil.

But evil is not an abstract force in "*Deutsches Requiem*." Otto is not a one-dimensional character painted entirely in black. He has one positive quality, even if misguided: his courage, which he draws from devotion to his ancestors, some of whom had given their lives in the field of battle, though for better causes. Moreover, by making Otto a cripple, Borges has hinted at a psychological motivation for his sustained resentment. "*Requiem*" in the title also suggests a moving farewell, not to mention a musical one (Mozart), to Germany. There is grief in the passing of this fanatic who took one version of what it was to be German to its ultimate consequences. In other words, there is grandeur even in evil, as readers of Milton know. Besides, Otto's demise spells that of Germany, with all of its admirable qualities. Borges must have followed with great interest the Nuremberg trials, in which issues about the individual and/or collective guilt of members of the Third Reich were amply and dramatically discussed, and many of them ultimately executed as a result.

Otto's crimes are of what Hegel would call world-historical dimensions. But evil in Borges also follows a more domestic pattern. This is the case in "Emma Zunz," a story that unfolds within the Jewish-Argentine community in Buenos Aires. Emma's father, Manuel Maier, she learns, was wronged by an unscrupulous business partner, Aaron Loewenthal, which led to his bankruptcy, exile, and suicide. Borges is better at drawing the economic foibles of his characters than one might suspect, and though he was no Balzac, there are often well-drawn socioeconomic motivations to his stories – the fate of Teodelina's family in "The Zahir," already mentioned, is a good example. Emma conceives an elaborate plan to take revenge. She sets up a meeting with the guilty partner, but goes beforehand to the docks and has intercourse with a foreign sailor, posing as a prostitute. Then she confronts the corrupt Lowenthal in his office, shoots him dead, and calls the police to tell them that she has killed him because he raped her. (Today, with DNA testing, Emma would have been convicted.) Her plot is like that of a well-wrought story, with the police acting as the reader expected to gauge its plausibility. The confluence of crime and storytelling, a recurrent theme in Borges, as seen in "*Deutsches Requiem*," is yet another theory about the origin of literary creation, parallel to those adduced in "The Aleph" and "The Zahir." Both in crime and in storytelling there is an effort to conceal the mechanisms of lying, and lying, with all the attendant moral connotations, is the incentive. Emma executes what she believes to be a perfect crime, just as a writer aspires to write a perfect story. Like Otto, Emma is courageous and acts out of a desire for revenge, which is what sustains the link between the present and actions that occurred in the past. That link is the plot of the story.

So far I have discussed stories in *The Aleph* dealing with contemporary themes and historical settings, and that have for the most part invented plots, even in cases like the title story in which a portentous previous work, *The Divine Comedy*, lurks in the background as a decisive source. There are several other stories in the book that purport to have been drawn, or at least to be a part of, remote or classical sources, by their themes, plots, settings, and characters, or all four of them. These pieces, though thematically akin to all the others, have, as Borges says of "The Man on the Threshold," "an antique, simple flavor … that it would be a shame to lose – something of the *1001 Nights*" (CF 269). This archaic flavor, which is that of the earliest collection of stories, emanates both from the features mentioned above, and from their structure as parables, perhaps the oldest form of storytelling. The idea behind this archaism is a well-known Borges axiom or conceit: that all stories have already been told, and that a writer can only aspire to produce a slightly modified new version, not necessarily better and perhaps even worse. These stories have been told not just in the *Thousand and One Nights*, but in classical mythology, the Bible, the Kabbalah, the Qur'an, Roman history, and other ancient sources.

In their presentation, as he also does in the "modern" stories, Borges occasionally adds a device that frames the texts, as if someone other than the writer or teller had intervened in the telling: an editor who, in footnotes or epilogues, clarifies certain points or actually disputes others. Sometimes the device takes the form of a frame tale in which the discovery of the text and the circumstances of its reproduction are given, as if the text to which the reader has access has been prepared by others. In doing this, Borges is presumably highlighting the "classical" status of the tales, which have already deserved an editor or commentator, but also has withdrawn from the text at hand any pretence of reliability or truthfulness. This is also an old Borges saw, the plural text, which really means that Borges assumes the roles both of writer and reader, enclosing, as in a tightly sealed vacuum chamber, the acts of writing and reading. The whole thing is also a typical Borgesian ploy to envelop his tales in a bookish atmosphere and to play with the reader, teasing him with his self-effacing persona, but also to underline the primordial or archetypal cast of his stories.

Two of these "archaic" stories stand out: "The Immortal" and "The House of Asterion." The first is the most ambitious story in the volume, which is perhaps the reason why Borges has it open the collection. It is also the longest. It is the story that contains all possible stories and the story that denies all stories. It begins, in very Borgesian fashion, with a manuscript found in the last volume of Alexander Pope's translation of the *Iliad*. The manuscript has been written by an antiquarian named Joseph Cartaphilus (lover of paper), from Smyrna, and it is the first-person account, by a Roman soldier, Marcus Flaminius Rufus, of a hallucinatory journey in search of the "City of Immortals." After a quest that takes him through the desert, accompanied by a few soldiers who eventually quarrel and leave him, he reaches the city. It is on a plateau and it is inhabited by troglodytes, incapable of speech. In the center of the city there is a palace that turns out to be an intricate labyrinth, or worse:

> A maze is a house built purposely to confuse men; its architecture, prodigal in symmetries, is made to serve that purpose. In the palace I imperfectly explored, the architecture had *no* purpose. There were corridors that led nowhere, unreachably high windows, grandly dramatic doors that opened onto monastery-style cells or empty shafts, incredible upside-down staircases with upside-down treads and balustrades. Other staircases, clinging airily to the side of a monumental wall, petered out after two or three landings, in the high gloom of the cupolas, arriving nowhere. (*CF* 188; translation slightly modified)

Marcus manages to escape, followed by a troglodyte to whom he tries to teach language. He fears that the troglodytes live in a world without time, hence without memory; but once he manages to have his mate articulate a few words, it turns out that he is Homer! The latter manages to remember that many years before he had composed *The Odyssey*. For a century he had lived in the troglodyte city, and when they destroyed it, he advised the survivors that they should build another. Marcus concludes that Homer was like a god who created both the cosmos and chaos, and that the world is a system of exact compensations in which everything has its correlative opposite, therefore everything is the same as everything else, a game of mirrors. He bids Homer goodbye.

Marcus then tells the rest of his story, in which he is supposed to have been present at the Battle of Hastings and other remarkable moments in history, which he enumerates until he reaches the present, where the blood of a slight wound tells him that he has again become mortal. There follow two commentaries on the story. In the first it is said that it is really the story of two characters. The first is the Roman warrior, the second is Homer himself, who is narrating and discovers himself as the teller because of the penchant for literary devices in the tale which he recognizes as his own. He declares that soon, like Ulysses, he will be nobody and everybody, and that he will be dead. The second commentary is a postscript dated "1950," a year in the future. It says that in a certain 1948 publication by one Nahum Cordovero the story by the antiquarian is mentioned in a list of works made up of quotations stitched together from various sources. Cordovero cites several examples of texts from which Cartaphilus has plagiarized and determines that the manuscript is apocryphal. But the narrator dismisses the charge, saying that the antiquarian himself had admitted that all that was left to him were words, and absolves him of literary treachery.

It is obvious that the "found manuscript" in "The Immortal" plays the role of an Aleph, only that it is more tightly confined to literature. In it are contained all possible stories since the time of Homer, as well as all possible authors. The quest for immortality is not original, of course. But the tale of the search through the desert for the City of Immortals, the anguish of the narrator caught in the labyrinth, the astonishment at finding that his dumb interlocutor is none other than Homer, are new and riveting, as is the tale-within-the-tale device, which here is particularly intricate and arresting. The City itself, and its inhabitants, the troglodytes, are fine inventions, in which readers of Borges will hear echoes of one of his most famous utopias, Tlön, found in his famous story from *Fictions*, "Tlön, Uqbar, Orbis Tertius." One could argue that "The Immortal," like "The Aleph," is a story that contains nearly all of Borges, and one criticism that could be leveled at it is that in it Borges writes too much in what one could call "the style of his style." For instance, there is perhaps one too many oxymora, and the presence of the infinite, which in regressions, in descriptions of the desert, and in the rooms of the palace-labyrinth is somewhat tiresome, even to the most devoted of Borges's admirers.

The briefest story in *The Aleph*, "The House of Asterion," is a real tour de force. The labyrinth again appears, but seen and described in the first person by its inhabitant, the Minotaur. With this device Borges indulges in what the Russian formalists called "defamiliarization." If, as in "The Immortal," the reader may be fatigued by the labyrinth, that familiar construction and the all-too-familiar myth of the Minotaur are given a twist that render them unfamiliar and new. It takes a while before the reader is shocked to learn that the narrator is the Minotaur, telling his story as it has never been told – from his point of view. The Minotaur, of course, is the monster born of the union of Pasiphae and a bull. He is a prisoner in the labyrinth, although here he protests that he is not. At the end, the awaited redeemer of the monster arrives: Theseus, who, with the clue provided by Ariadne, is able to escape from the labyrinth after slaying the monster. The last voice in the tale is that of Theseus, who reports to Ariadne that the Minotaur barely struggled, allowing himself to be killed as if resigned to a preordained fate. There are here again the topics of the story retold – since there are really no new stories – the labyrinth, and, briefly, a hero, Theseus. But the most compelling character is the monster himself, telling his life in a flat tone, as if it were the most normal of lives. By the end the reader feels sorry for the monster.

The Aleph was reissued several times, in expanded editions. It seems clear to me that Borges originally saw it as a unit, distinct from his other collections. But by the 1950s, and certainly the 1960s, when he became a universal figure, the stories in the collection joined the Borges canon, independently of the book. "The Aleph," "*Deutsches Requiem*," "The Zahir," "The House of Asterion," and a few others, became part of a core of Borges's fiction, and were variously anthologized and included in general collections of his texts. Because Borges was such a systematic writer, it is easy to forget the provenance of each piece, as they all seem to fit together comfortably in a complete works that were always already complete from start to finish. The title story is better remembered than the collection it named. Yet, when it appeared, *The Aleph* was a book unto its own, and a statement by its author of the richness of his literary imagination.

NOTES

1 For further details see the introduction to my *Oxford Book of Latin American Short Stories*, New York, Oxford University Press, 1997.
2 I have occasionally emended quotations from Andrew Hurley's translation in the Viking Penguin edition.

11

ALFRED MACADAM

The Maker

Throughout his career Borges used book publication to gather up the published and unpublished material he had on hand. While each collection expressed his poetic sensibility, his intellectual concerns, or his esthetic principles at a given moment, none ever focused on a single subject: this despite titles that announced a unified theme – *The Language of the Argentines* (1928), for example. Even his 1930 biography of Evaristo Carriego is a jumble of disparate elements and not a sustained study of the poet's life. All his books were, in effect, miscellanies.

This disregard for unity explains why he freely altered collections, adding new pieces and removing or rewriting (especially with regard to poetry) old ones. What the "correct" version of a given Borges text is – the first printing or the last to leave the author's hands – is a vexing issue, one that raises another: when (if ever) is a work of art finished? Like Borges's own musings on the infinite book or the infinite library, his perpetual meddling with collections and his constant reworking render every text potentially infinite.

The Maker is more a variation on that habit than a break with it, though it does mark a change in Borges's concept of the book as collection of disparate pieces:[1]

> Around 1954, I began to write short texts: sketches and parables. One day, my friend Carlos Frías, from Emecé, told me he needed a new book for the series of my so-called *Complete Works*. I told him I had nothing to give him, but he insisted, saying: "Every writer has a book if he'll look for it." Checking through drawers in my house one idle Sunday, I began to set aside poems and fragments of prose that hadn't been gathered up, some of which dated from my time at *Crítica*. That combination of pieces, selected, ordered and published in 1960, became *El hacedor* (*The Maker*). Surprisingly, this book, which I've accumulated more than written, seems to me to be my most personal book, and, to my taste, perhaps the best. The explanation is quite simple: There is no stuffing in the pages of *El hacedor*. Each text was written for its own sake, originating from an internal necessity. When I wrote the book, I'd come to

understand that artistic writing is an error, and an error born from vanity. Good writing – I firmly believe – should be done in a discreet manner.[2]

This declaration, like the autobiographical statement he published in the *New Yorker* in 1970, is fraught with inconsistencies and mystification. First, he posits a point of origin ("around 1954") without explaining why he began writing short pieces then, though a plausible reason is his severely hampered eyesight.[3] His definition of those texts is also curious: "sketches and parables." "Sketches" (in Spanish, *boceto*, the Hispanified Italian word *bozzetto*, sketch, preparatory drawing, project), and "parable," a short allegory usually, though not in Borges's case, containing a moral or religious message. The tentative, the unfinished, on one hand, on the other the allegorical, a shocking idea from a man who as late as 1949 declared allegory an esthetic error ("From Allegories to Novels," *SNF* 337–40), but not so shocking when we recall that Borges was a critic and translator of Kafka, who redefined the parable as a genre. In fact, the quotation Borges imputes to Carlos Frías looks like a banal truism that Borges literally enacts, rendering his statement about compiling *The Maker* a parable.

He begins writing these pieces some six or so years before publishing *The Maker* in 1960. His publisher, at some unspecified moment, intervenes because he needs another volume for the "series" of what Borges himself calls his "so-called *Complete Works*." A more accurate title would be "incomplete works" since complete implies totality and completion, impossible for Borges in 1960, first because he had deliberately excluded most of the essays he published between 1925 and 1932, and second because he was only sixty years old and likely to write a great deal more. Borges tells his publisher he has no book for him, but Frías insists, so the dutiful Borges spends an "idle Sunday" rummaging through drawers and picking out unpublished "poems and fragments of prose." The earliest date from 1934, when he wrote for the cultural supplement to the newspaper *Crítica*, so they precede 1954, when he supposedly began to write them, by twenty years.

This agglomeration of "*retazos*" (fragments or remnants), once selected and ordered, becomes a book. The individual pieces in *The Maker* are not drafts but highly polished texts and certainly not fragments, but if these are the items selected, then there must be others that were found but rejected – their fate is unknown. "Ordered" implies a system or organization, that the fifty-four items (including the dedication to Leopoldo Lugones and the epilogue but excluding the elegiac note on John Kennedy arbitrarily added to later editions) that make up the collection are arranged in a certain way: the first twenty-three texts (again, including the dedication to Lugones) are prose, some autobiographical ("Dreamtigers" or "Delia Elena San

Marco") and some literary ("*Martín Fierro*" or "Parable of Cervantes and the *Quixote*"), while the next thirty are poems followed by the epilogue. Many of the poems ("Susana Soca," "In Memoriam A.R.," "Allusion to the Death of Colonel Francisco Borges (1835-74)," "The Borges,") are elegiac, like those in his first book *Fervor de Buenos Aires* (1921), while others are literary ("Ariosto and the Arabs," "Ars Poetica") or personal ("Rain," "Embarking on the Study of Anglo-Saxon Grammar"). Paradoxically, at the age of sixty, Borges becomes a revised version of the writer he was in 1921, but where that man alternated between essays and poetry this one writes vignettes and poems. The epilogue complicates this already complicated miscellany:

> God grant that the essential monotony of this miscellany (which time has compiled, not I, and into which have been bundled long-ago pieces that I've not had the courage to revise, for I wrote them out of a different concept of literature) be less obvious than the geographical and historical diversity of its subjects. Of all the books I have sent to press, none, I think, is as personal as this motley, disorganized anthology, precisely because it abounds in reflections and interpolations. Few things have happened to me, though many things I have read. Or rather, few things have happened to me more worthy of remembering than the philosophy of Schopenhauer or England's verbal music.
>
> A man sets out to draw the world. As the years go by, he peoples a space with images of provinces, kingdoms, mountains, bays, ships, islands, fishes, rooms, instruments, stars, horses, and individuals. A short time before he dies, he discovers that the patient labyrinth of lines traces the lineaments of his own face. (*CF* 327)

Borges deflects responsibility for finding and selecting the pieces he includes, denying that he would dare alter texts from the past because he wrote them having a different understanding of what literature was, although he did just that with any number of early poems and by simply consigning whole collections of essays to oblivion.

He again insists, without explaining what he means, on the personal nature of this collection, which he calls a "motley, disorganized anthology" or, in the original, "*colecticia y desordenada silva de varia lección*," which includes a reference to Pedro Mexía (1496–1552) and his 1543 *Silva de varia lección* (called the *Forest* by its Renaissance English translator), a Renaissance humanist's response to Aullus Gellius's *Attic Nights* or Macrobius's *Saturnalia*. The allusion to Pedro Mexía may be coincidental or it may be Borges's indirect way of alluding to his own wildly miscellaneous readings beginning in the 1920s. It also, in the style of "Kafka and his Precursors" (*SNF* 363–65), creates a pseudo-tradition of texts like *The Maker*, that is, a melange assembled using very personal criteria, books vaguely like this one but also very different.

The next sentences confirm Borges's idea that his reading experiences are much more significant than his life experiences, an echo of his delight at finding that Ben Jonson's literary testament was composed of quotations from the work of other authors rather than his own. In the last paragraph of the epilogue Borges makes clear that his "*biographia literaria*" would consist of things external to himself that he cherishes: a man tries to draw the world, and at the end of his life realizes his project is nothing more than a self-portrait: self and other fuse. Another version of this idea appears in the footnote appended to Borges's story "The Immortal," where the nominal editor of Cartaphilus's autobiography, that is, Borges, quotes Cartaphilus's statement that "*As the end approaches ... there are no longer any images from memory – there are only words*," to which the "editor" adds, "Words, words, words taken out of place and mutilated, words from other men – those were the alms left him by the hours and the centuries" (*CF* 195).

The epilogue and Borges's statement confirm the suspicion that all the texts assembled under the title of *The Maker* are ultimately autobiographical, that no matter what the putative subject may be in prose or poetry the text always reflects Borges. Ironically, exactly one year after publishing *The Maker*, his most "personal" book, Borges would publish the *Personal Anthology*, his own selection of his writings, a book unique among Borges's publications for having a cover composed entirely of a photograph of the author.

Borges's dedication of *The Maker* to Leopoldo Lugones continues a process Borges had begun with an article in the magazine *Sur* in 1938, when Lugones committed suicide. There, Borges sought to vindicate Lugones, to show him as the major influence on Borges's entire literary generation. That effort nullified the savage attacks Borges leveled against Lugones in *The Extent of My Hope* (1926), which the mature Borges must have recalled with chagrin. But at no time does Borges discuss Lugones's politics or his proto-fascistic militarism.

The dedication takes the form of a meeting between Borges and Lugones in the old National Library on Calle Rodríguez Peña. Borges enters Lugones's office, hands him *The Maker*, exchanges pleasantries with him, and then drifts into wishful thinking:

> Unless I am mistaken, you didn't dislike me, Lugones, and you'd have liked to like some work of mine. That never happened, but this time you turn the pages and read a line or two approvingly, perhaps because you've recognized your own voice in it, perhaps because the halting poetry itself is less important than the clean-limbed theory. (*CF* 291)

The phrase "you'd have liked to like some work of mine" (in the original, *"le hubiera gustado que le gustara algún trabajo mío"*) is grammatically and psychologically bizarre: the multiple subjunctives and repetitions are confusing, while imputing good will to Lugones is far-fetched. But to suggest that Lugones would have wanted to like something Borges had written transforms him into a metaphorical and insulted father the repentant son would like very much to placate. In the final paragraph, Borges reveals that we have been reading a dream:

> My vanity and my nostalgia have confected a scene that is impossible. Maybe so, I tell myself, but tomorrow I too will be dead and our times will run together and chronology will melt into an orb of symbols, and somehow it will be true to say that I have brought you this book and that you have accepted it. (*CF* 291)

The dedication is an apostrophe. Lugones is evoked, made present, and once more allowed to die ("and you, Lugones, killed yourself in early '38") only to be revived in the final sentence, where Borges postulates a time when he and Lugones will be thought contemporaries and where he really has given him a copy of *The Maker*. This idea, reminiscent of the one Borges uses to end his tale "The Theologians," says time erases differences.

But above and beyond the "vanity and nostalgia" Borges ascribes to himself, the dedication expresses the idea that all writers are one writer, that each adds a variation on eternal themes, that art transcends the historical and autobiographical context in which it was produced. This we see in Borges's first, dense paragraph, where he dreams himself walking through the library and catching a glimpse of the readers:

> rows of readers' momentary profiles in the light of the "scholarly lamps," as Miltonian displacement of adjectives would have it. I recall having recalled that trope here in the Library once before, and that other adjective of setting – the *Lunario*'s "arid camel," and then that hexameter from the *Aeneid* that employs, and surpasses, the same artifice: *Ibant obscuri sola sub nocte per umbras.* (*CF* 291)

Hypallage is a figure of speech which transposes the expected or natural relation between two elements, as in "scholarly lamps" or "arid camel" above.[4] And hypallage dominates the passage cited above (Borges in the original refers specifically to *"la hipálage de Milton,"* Milton's hypallage), but we must look beyond the rhetorical device and think about Milton, another blind poet, about Virgil's Aeneas about to descend into Hades where he will speak to his dead father, and about the relationship Borges imagines he has with Lugones. If *Paradise Lost* concerns the reconciliation of the Creator with His creature, if Virgil sends Aeneas to Hades in Book VI to reunite father and son, then this dedication has much more to do with Borges's acknowledgment of Lugones as a literary father than with his dexterity with hypallage. The father–son relationship permeates *The Maker*, beginning with the vignette that provides the book's title, and continuing into the poetry section with the sonnet "Rain," where Borges touchingly evokes his sorrow at losing his father.

In "The Maker," Borges, without mentioning his name, writes a succinct life of Homer, an echo of the "capsule biographies" he wrote during the years (1936–38) when he was in charge of the "foreign books and authors" page of the society magazine *El Hogar* (*The Home*). Borges defines the young Homer with a negation: "He had never lingered among the pleasures of memory" (*CF* 292). Homer, like the cat Dahlmann pets in "The South" or the Lombard warrior Droctulft in "Story of the Warrior and the Captive Maiden," lives in the present moment: "Keen, curious, inadvertent, with no law but satisfaction and immediate indifference, he had wandered the various world and on now this, now that seashore, he had gazed upon the cities of men and their palaces" (*CF* 292). The onset of blindness transforms him. He loses visual contact with the world, and "felt, inexplicably, the way one might feel upon recognizing a melody or a voice, that all this had happened to him before" (*CF* 292). Homer suddenly becomes two people: a blind warrior and someone who has already been that man, who is still that man, yet is another at the same time, as Borges says of himself in "Poem of the Gifts":

> Which of the two is setting down this poem –
> a single sightless self, a plural I? (*SP* 97)

Transformed, Homer is now able to descend into his memory, like Aeneas descending into Hades, and seek out specific experiences.

The first is his initiation into the life of violence. He remembers being insulted by another boy and turning to his father for advice. His father lets him speak "as though he weren't paying attention, or didn't understand," and then hands him a bronze dagger. His father cares nothing for the details of his son's humiliation; all he knows is that he must now give him the opportunity to be a man. He simply says: "*Let it be known that you are a man*," to which the narrator adds, "and there was a command in the voice" (*CF* 293). Homer heeds his father's admonition, but the Homer remembering the moment is not trying to re-create or re-live it but to capture the "precise flavor of that moment," its essence cleansed of autobiographical specificity, made abstract and applicable to a literary character.

Another memory, it too nocturnal and charged with "a foretaste of adventure," springs from the first. This one concerns sex, "a woman, the first woman the gods had given him" (*CF* 293). She waited for him, he says, "in the darkness of a subterranean crypt," that is in a hypogee, often used for burials in the ancient world, thus linking sex and death. He recalls having to seek her out "through galleries that were like labyrinths of stone and down slopes that descended into the darkness." Death and sex are inseparable for Homer, though memories of his inaugural experiences of both come to him "without bitterness, like some mere foreshadowing of the present" (*CF* 293). Again, the man who remembers is now two men, the one who had the experiences and the other, for whom all experience, all memory is an arch-ive for the creation of art. The final paragraph confirms this. Now blind, Homer can again look forward to love and risk, but as essential themes in the *Iliad* and the *Odyssey*, "that it was his fate to sing and to leave echoing in the cupped hands of human memory." Homer's good fortune, in Borges's version, is to have had experiences that he could turn into art, unlike Borges, as he says in the epilogue: "Few things have happened to me, though many things I have read" (*CF* 327). That is, Borges, like the inhabitants of Tlön, must make copies of copies rather than work directly from experience.

Borges's Homer is a warrior and only becomes a poet because he is simul-taneously cursed and blessed with blindness. Being cut off from experience makes him turn inward to his vast, unexplored library of memories, one of which is the first woman with whom he has sex. She could not be "the first woman the gods had given him" unless he had sex with her. A related text, "Borges and I," dramatizes what Homer experiences when, as he goes blind, he feels as if everything had happened before, that is, when he becomes a poet with a warrior's memory. "Borges and I" plays with the idea that the living Borges can comment on the author Borges as if he were someone else. There is irony in the relationship, but also symbiosis: "I live, I allow myself to live, so that Borges can spin out his literature, and that literature is my justification" (*CF* 324). The concept of justification through art reap-pears throughout Borges's writing (see, for example, his 1941 "A Fragment on Joyce," *SNF* 220–21), but it is the penultimate line of the vignette that contains the key to the whole: "So my life is a point-counterpoint, a kind of fugue, and a falling away – and everything winds up being lost to me, and everything falls into oblivion, or into the hands of the other man" (*CF* 324). A fugue is a composition of recurring themes, Borges's acknowledgment of his obsessive thematic repertoire, especially his focus on art as, simultan-eously, existential salvation and absorption by tradition or language – the "Borges" of the "Borges and I" dichotomy.

Two other vignettes from *The Maker* confirm this. First, "Parable of Cervantes and the *Quixote*," where Borges echoes his idea in the dedica-tion that time will confuse reality so that he will in fact hand Lugones *The*

Maker. Borges points out that Cervantes has Quixote go mad reading the marvels of chivalric literature and then seeking them out in the real world. Time, Borges says, erases the difference between the poetic reality of literature and the banality of reality, to the point that the dusty roads of La Mancha will be no less poetic than the adventures of Sinbad or Ariosto's magic universe.

"*Everything and Nothing*" is about Shakespeare's lack of identity, an idea Borges may have snatched from Hazlitt: "There was no one inside him; behind his face ... and his words ... there was no more than a slight chill, a dream someone had failed to dream" (*CF* 319). Borges's Shakespeare vainly seeks an identity in books and in sex (his relationship with Anne Hathaway). He only finds solace in London, where he becomes an actor who "plays at being another person, for an audience of people who play at taking him for that person." From lacking any identity he goes to having myriad. From acting he turns to writing, where he again creates identities not his own. Exhausted, he leaves London and assumes the role of a retired businessman. In death, he meets God and says, "I, who have been so many men in vain, wish to be *one*, to be myself" (*CF* 320), to which God responds "among the forms of my dream are you, who like me are many, yet no one." This is the writer's, that is, Borges's, destiny, as he presents it in "Borges and I."

While it is true that the Borges of 1957, the year he first published "Borges and I," was perforce an unhappy man – almost blind, bereft of love, under the thumb of his mother – that situation is not replicated in his text. "Borges and I" is playing with the opposition between the mortal man and the immortal but never-alive author, between living and writing. The final sentence, "I am not sure which of us it is that's writing this page," returns us to Homer, to the idea that the warrior of experience undergoes a metamorphosis through blindness and becomes the author.

In the vignette "Dreamtigers," Borges, like his Homer, describes himself remembering his childhood fascination with tigers: "In my childhood I was a fervent worshiper of the tiger" (*CF* 294). The tigers he saw in books and visited at the zoo become characters in his dreams. Like the magus in "The Circular Ruins," the dreaming Borges seeks to create a tiger ("*I am going to bring forth a tiger*"), but, absent divine aid, his attempts are as disappointing as those of the rabbi in the poem "The Golem," from his 1964 *The Self and the Other*. In the poem "The Other Tiger," Borges again describes himself thinking about a tiger. The library surrounding him disappears, and he sees the tiger prowling the jungle, but as afternoon advances he thinks:

> that the tiger I am calling up in my poem
> is a tiger made of symbols and of shadows,

> a set of literary images,
> scraps remembered from encyclopedias
> and not the deadly tiger. (*SP* 117)

Simply by conjuring up the word "tiger" he turns the image into a "*ficción del arte*," a fiction of art. What he now seeks is "a third tiger." This one will also be:

> a form in my dream like all the others,
> a system, an arrangement of human language,
> and not the flesh-and-bone tiger. (*SP* 119)

But this does not discourage Borges from searching for it:

> ... yet something
> drives me to this ancient, perverse adventure,
> foolish and vague, yet still I keep on looking
> throughout the evening for the other tiger,
> the other tiger, the one not in this poem. (*SP* 119)

It is the insufficiency of language, its inevitably metaphoric nature, that keeps him trying to replicate in life what his magus, aided by a god, does achieve, to bring something living into the world through words. He can neither succeed nor stop trying.

The existence of Borges the man is justified by the art of Borges the writer, but neither can be God. Unlike Mary Shelley's Frankenstein, who does bring the bits and pieces of bodies to life, Borges cannot create even a hideous, albeit living, monster. So he must be content to be an "*hacedor*," a maker, a poet, a being both proud of his work and distraught at its limitations.

NOTES

1 The prose section of *The Maker* is included in Viking Penguin's *Collected Fictions* (*CF*). A selection of the poetry appears in the *Selected Poems* (*SP*).
2 This statement is quoted in Alejandro Vaccaro's *Borges: vida y literatura*, Buenos Aires, Edhasa, 2006, 559 (my translation).
3 Edwin Williamson, *Borges: A Life*, New York, Viking, 2004, 324.
4 See Andrew Hurley, "What I Lost When I Translated Jorge Luis Borges," *Cadernos da Traduçao*, 4, 1999, 289–304. Hurley shows hypallage to be one of Borges's favorite rhetorical devices.

12

ARTURO ECHAVARRÍA

Brodie's Report

After *Fictions* and *The Aleph*, Borges did not publish another collection of stories until *Brodie's Report* (1970). In that interim, a few short fictions were included in *The Maker* (1960) and *In Praise of Darkness* (1969), but these resembled parables and prose poems rather than stories as such. It is not, then, until *Brodie's Report* that we once again find the master at work creating what we might truly call short stories. These in particular he calls "realistic" and "direct."

The book's initial reception was mixed, which is understandable if we consider that at first reading *Brodie's Report* lacks the verbal and thematic complexity we associate with the stories in *Fictions* and *The Aleph*. One might think that it was the turn toward "realism" that weakened Borges's narrative powers, but I believe the apparent "plainness" of these stories (for which Borges invoked as a model Kipling's *Plain Tales from the Hills*) is due rather to the author's tragic personal circumstances. During the early 1950s Borges had gone blind and had to turn to dictation. He "wrote" mainly poetry because it is possible to compose a poem within the realms of memory without recurring to the written page. Not so with the kind of prose one associates with his most famous stories, exacting and often oblique, but even in these circumstances *Brodie's Report* contains memorable stories and deserves to be read with the closest attention.

In the Foreword – which abounds in contradictions – Borges declares that the stories, save one, are "realistic," and as such contain an abundance of "circumstantial details" (*CF* 346). He then goes on to undermine the notion of "realism" by stating that it is a genre as convention-ridden as any other literary mode, including fantastic literature. But just the same, his appeal to "realism" should be given some consideration because a literary mode in some ways determines how a text is read, and therefore the way it signifies.

Translation by Andrew Hurley.

Taking into account the ambiguous light that Borges sheds on "realism," it might be useful to examine some of the stories to see if there are characteristics in the narrative discourse that go against the grain of traditional literary "realism."

One encounters time and again in these stories narrative techniques that undermine the notion of the text as a mere "mirror" of reality. The origins of several of the stories, for example, are made ambiguous and problematic, often relying on what the narrator heard from someone, who heard it from someone else, and so on. The verbal chain, plus the suspicion that some sources are unreliable, gives the impression that there are several versions of the story material. In one way or another, these circumstances can be found in "The Interloper," "Unworthy," "The Other Duel," "Juan Muraña," and "The Story from Rosendo Juárez." Often, too, the narrator confesses that he has retouched what he heard and thus "contaminated it with literature." As a result, as has been noted, the dichotomies history/fiction and truth/lie are introduced. Finally, Borges inserts into his Foreword the following sly tease: "Two of the stories – I will not say which ones – can be opened with the same fantastic key."

The circumstances discussed above undermine the notion of traditional realism vis-à-vis the "transparent" nature of the linguistic sign, whose relation to the social and economic world that surrounds it is grounded on that sign's nature as a mirror of "reality." Once this principle – the one-to-one relationship of word to "real world" – is called into question, the scaffolding that holds up the realistic story is dangerously weakened. In such a context, Balzac's proclamation, for example, that the story in *Père Goriot* "is not fictional ... All is true" becomes moot, and the novel's "realism" is indeed compromised.[1] A close reading of the stories in *Brodie's Report* reveals their complexity, and the notion of the "transparent sign," in most cases, becomes questionable. Notwithstanding the fact that these narratives allude to places, objects, and persons pertaining to referential "reality," they are not properly speaking "realistic," nor are they "direct." This, of course, does not mean that they do not comment on historical and social reality, as eighteenth-century satire (Voltaire and Swift, for example) attests.

Leaving aside the notion of "realism" *per se*, it might be useful to search for a different framework in which to insert these stories. In the Foreword, Borges says that the "curious reader will perceive certain secret affinities among the tales" (*CF* 346). The attentive reader will find that those affinities, which abound, go well beyond the mere variation of plots and manifest themselves by way of veiled allusions. The network of affinities, moreover, which often manifests itself figuratively or symbolically, imparts a sense of unity to the book as a whole. We might sum up the "rationale" for this internal network, and the principle that imparts cohesion to the whole, as follows: *Brodie's Report* presents a very harsh critique of the various hierarchies that make up Argentina. And, even though in some stories the negative comments are fairly evident, in many others the critique manifests itself indirectly. Of course, as is usual in Borges, there is no one way of reading his narratives. Stories as complex as "The Gospel According to Mark," "Guayaquil," and "The Interloper" can be read using differing symbolic keys. But I feel that there is solid textual support for the reading I am about to undertake. *Brodie's Report*, with only one story (the last) that does not relate directly to Argentina, can be understood as a whole, comprising a complex web of "secret affinities." For our purposes, I have grouped the stories to be discussed as follows: first "The Duel," "The Other Duel," "The Encounter," "The Story from Rosendo Juárez," and "Juan Muraña"; second, "The Interloper" and "The Gospel According to Mark"; third, "Guayaquil," "The Elderly Lady," and "Unworthy"; and finally, "Brodie's Report." Since limitations of space prevent me from analyzing all of them, I will only comment on those I feel to be representative of each group.

Most of the stories in *Brodie's Report* deal, directly or indirectly, with dueling, which is a recurrent theme in Borges's work. Sometimes the duel is presented directly: the encounter between knife-fighters, for example. Other times, it is presented figuratively, as in "Guayaquil" and, in a way, "The Interloper." "Unworthy" presents a moral, not physical, confrontation. The five stories that deal directly with dueling can be further subdivided. In two of them ("The Duel," "The Encounter"), the duel occurs between characters who belong to the upper class. Of the rest, two deal with gauchos or knife-fighters ("The Other Duel" and "Rosendo Juárez") while in the third, "Juan Muraña," the characters belong to a lower middle class whose past is related to the underworld of thugs and toughs.

"The Encounter," "The Other Duel," and "The Story from Rosendo Juárez"

"The Encounter" tells the story of an outing to a country estate. The young men in attendance belong to the upper-class "aristocracy." One, Uriarte, provokes another, Duncan, against whom he bears some vague ill will (an ill will, we find out, that is longstanding), to a game of poker. There is much drinking and an argument ensues: Uriarte challenges Duncan to a duel. Someone, perhaps maliciously, proclaims that there is a collection of knives in the house that once belonged to famous gauchos and knife-fighters. Uriarte and Duncan fight with two of these knives, which seem to have a life and will of their own. Uriarte kills Duncan and later repents.

"The Other Duel" is "the chronicle of a long-held hatred" of obscure origin between two gauchos, Cardoso and Silveira (*CF* 387). There are disputes over animals; later on, they play cards and the winner insults the other man. But the "duel" occurs only at the end. Although they don't quite understand why, they are drafted into an army during a civil war. Their side loses. The commander of the victorious forces orders the losers' throats slashed. But the officer had heard of the hatred between Cardoso and Silveira and so proposes a final "duel" between the two men – a duel that will be at the same time some sort of a spectacle for the rest. He orders them to run a race, once their throats have been slit, and see who gets to go farthest in those conditions. After running a few steps, blood gushing from their throat, they fall and Cardoso, extending his arms, "wins."

The two stories present two radically opposed social classes. The protagonists of "The Other Duel" are illiterate gauchos; those of "The Encounter" are "aristocrats" whose contact with the lower class seems merely sentimental and folkloric. But a single cultural pattern rules both classes and determines their behavior: the "cult of courage". The grudge between Silveira and Cardoso, like that between Uriarte and Duncan (and also between Clara and Marta in "The Duel"), is very loosely related, if at all, to specific circumstances. Its origin is hazy and "obscure." In both cases, a game of cards feeds the ill will ("The Other Duel") or brings it to the surface ("The Encounter"). In one, the game is a "native" one, *truco*; in the other, poker, imported. Unconsciously, it seems, they share a way of fighting: when the "aristocrats" fight they symbolically turn into gauchos: "As their forearms (with no ponchos wrapped around them for protection) blocked the thrusts ..." (*CF* 367). They employ knives which, as in the case of "Juan Muraña," seem to have a cultural personality of their own, and that autonomous personality appears to guide the weapons that bear the names of the knife-fighters who owned them. The fight between Uriarte and Duncan becomes literally phantasmagoric, the knives wielded by ghosts from an absurd and cruel past with the young men as their instruments. In "The Other Duel," things change a bit: the knives are wielded by intermediaries, the executioners.

Furthermore, the story which deals with gauchos ("The Other Duel") harbors an irony of significant proportions. It is an "aristocrat" belonging to the military class who organizes the cruel and barbaric "show." The young officer who invents the "prank" – a race between men whose throats have been slit – bears an Irish or English surname (Nolan) and his first name intensifies the irony: Juan Patricio (the latter name meaning both Patrick and "patrician" in Spanish). Given these facts, one wonders whether there really is a defining line in the dichotomy between "civilization" and "barbarism" that is a traditional feature of Argentine cultural discourse.[2] One might also ask, given the behavior of both the popular and the ruling classes, whether the redemption of such a society is possible.

"The Story from Rosendo Juárez" gives us a glimmer of hope. This tale refers back to a famous early story by Borges titled "Man on Pink Corner" (1935), which in turn points to an even earlier one, "Hombres pelearon" ("Men Fought," 1927). In "Man on Pink Corner," the young Rosendo had been depicted as a coward, but now the aging protagonist wants to tell "Borges," the narrator, what really happened that night. In "Man on Pink Corner" we are told that Rosendo refused to respond to an insult and walked away when his opponent, the Yardmaster, challenged him publicly to a knife fight. He was branded ever after as a coward. In "The Story ...," Rosendo relates that, prior to the encounter with the Yardmaster, two experiences had left a mark on him. One of them had to do with the advice he gave a friend not to seek the man he felt had affronted him. He didn't listen, there was a duel, and his friend was killed. Somehow, Rosendo felt guilty. A few days later, Rosendo, while watching a cockfight, thought: "What in the world's wrong with those animals ... that they tear each other to pieces this way, for no good reason?" (CF 362). Finally, on the fateful night he met the Yardmaster; he saw himself reflected in the drunken challenger and became ashamed of himself. That is why he turned and walked away. But this decision, which broke a dominant cultural pattern, ruined him forever. Rosendo, it is important to note, did not respond out of impulse, as so many other characters do – he thought through the situation; he proved capable of insight and reflection.[3]

The absence of thought or reflection, whether because one lacks the capacity or because of the pressures of dominant cultural patterns, is a recurrent motif in *Brodie's Report*. Some characters are incapable of analyzing circumstances, often culturally determined, that seem to make no sense. Other protagonists have difficulty formulating abstractions; that is, transforming experience from the concrete into a general or abstract pattern. Some simply cannot understand the symbolic nature of a verbal representation. The narrators of the stories often sum up these limitations with phrases such as "let's see if they understand," or "he seemed to understand nothing," or simply "they do not understand." The impossibility of "understanding" is another recurrent motif in *Brodie*.

"The Interloper" and "The Gospel According to Mark"

These two stories, though they appear to have little in common, present two similar situations that play an important role in their respective plots. The first has to do with the allusions to the European roots of the Nilsen family in

"The Interloper" and the Gutre family in "The Gospel" and the second refers to the cultural and intellectual limitations that are evident in both families.

"The Interloper" has been examined from different points of view: as an example of woman as sexual object; as an example of woman as an obstacle or mediator to possible homoerotic relations; as a portrayal of women's position in late nineteenth-century Argentine society and the hatred that position inspired; and in terms of the conflict between two ideologies, a conflict that arises when gauchos from the country move in to the outskirts of the city.[4] The story tells the tale of two brothers, descended from Irish or Danish forebears, who have become thoroughly "Argentinized" in the sense that they have absorbed the culture of the poor rural classes. They lead isolated lives and are very close to each other. One day the older brother, Cristián, brings home a woman, Juliana, as a sexual object. The younger brother, Eduardo, almost without realizing it, falls in love with her. A tacit rivalry ensues which is tempered somewhat when Cristián encourages Eduardo to share Juliana sexually with him. But soon the differences re-emerge, and so, to avoid further problems, they decide to sell Juliana to a whorehouse. But that solves nothing because both brothers continue to visit the woman. Cristián decides to bring her home; soon problems arise again. At last, Cristián decides to end the dissension between him and Eduardo once and for all by killing Juliana.

It should be stressed that the author presents Cristián and Eduardo Nilsen as examples of a "degraded" or "decayed" family, or race. Like the Gutre family in "The Gospel," the Nilsens are descended from Northern European emigrants. Aficionados of "saddles and short-bladed daggers" (*CF* 348), they live on the rural outskirts of the city, like so many other men, and their values seem no different from those of other knife-fighters and brawlers and cattle-drovers. Of the culture of their European forebears, nothing seems to be left save a Bible in which, as in the case of the Gutres, family birthdates, deaths, and marriages had once been written. In time, even that custom had been lost. The Nilsens' intellectual limitations and cultural indigence might relate to the fact, stressed by the narrator, that the Bible was "the only book they owned" (*CF* 348). The Nilsens seem to be illiterate, and the absence or scarcity of books is a significant and recurrent fact in many stories in *Brodie's Report*. Along with isolation, this absence seems to foster the harsh, brutal atmosphere in which the characters live. Noteworthy also is the Nilsens' inability to formulate verbally what they think and feel. The lack of verbal communication is, I think, one of the factors that contribute to the story's tragic conclusion.

"The Gospel According to Mark," with its evident religious overtones, has inspired varied interpretations. It has been analyzed in the light of the history of that particular Gospel, and in the context of other Borges stories that touch upon religious subjects. Another critic has discussed the role of metafiction and metaphysics, while Haberly inserts this story into the controversy over Borges the cosmopolitan writer versus Borges the writer of Argentine literature, and mentions a series of texts that I, too, see as important.[5]

In this story, a young medical student, Baltasar Espinosa, is invited by his cousin to spend the summer at his ranch. The cousin is then called back to the city and Espinosa is left in the company of three peons – two men and a woman – named Gutre. The Gutres' ancestral name was Guthrie, originally from Inverness. They had intermarried with Indians, and now culturally impoverished, no longer know how to read or write. A storm floods the ranch and strands the four characters in the main house. To entertain the Gutres, Espinosa decides to read to them sections of a novel and the Gospel According to St. Mark, "to see if they might understand a little of it" (*CF* 400). The Gutres, in their utter ignorance, begin to behold the student as an object of veneration. One day they ask Baltasar if the men who nailed Christ to the cross were also saved. Espinosa ("whose theology was a bit shaky") says yes, and he is later led by them to the shed at the back of the house where he sees the cross they have built. He is about to be crucified.

This story shares with the previous one the presentation of characters that are descended from Northern European stock now "degraded" in the Americas. If the Nilsens have fully assimilated the culture of the Argentine knife-fighters and in the process have lost all remnants of Danish or Irish culture, the case of the Gutres is even worse. They are illiterate and, like the Nilsens, they "rarely spoke" and therefore "conversation [with them] was not easy" (*CF* 398). They seem incapable of formulating daily occurrences in abstract patterns: "[The] Gutres, who knew so much about things in the country, did not know how to explain them" (*CF* 398). Their intellectual and cultural poverty is such that Espinosa doubts whether they are capable of understanding the Gospel he is about to read to them. But of their many limitations, the one that leads to tragic consequences is their inability to understand that what is written in a text is often figurative or symbolic. We see this twice: when Espinosa reads them a few chapters from the novel, *Don Segundo Sombra*, the Gutres take it literally, as though Ricardo Güiraldes's classic novel about the education of a young gaucho were a sort of manual for cattle-driving. And the result of the Gutres' *literal* interpretation of the Gospel that Espinosa reads to them is the crucifixion of Espinosa himself, perhaps ironically abetted by the "dim current of the Calvinist's fanaticism" that still ran in their blood alongside "the superstitions of the pampas [Indians]" (*CF* 400).

One of the most notable differences between "The Interloper" and "The Gospel According to Mark" is the presence of the *criollo* "aristocracy" in the latter. The narrator implicitly subdivides this class into ranch-owners and educated professionals. It is obvious that Baltasar, a university student, a thoughtful and avid reader, belongs to the latter category. The landowning class, on the other hand, is not so culturally well-endowed. The owners of the ranch possess very few books. Espinosa's cousin is a frivolous young man with an "indefatigable interest in the vagaries of men's tailoring" (*CF* 398). Similarly in "The Encounter," the upper-class young men gathered at the country house talked mainly about "racehorses, tailoring, automobiles, [and] notoriously expensive women" (*CF* 365). In contrast, Baltasar Espinosa, the studious reader who reflects upon and defends "debatable ... opinions," as did his namesake the philosopher Baruch Spinoza, is subjected to martyrdom.

In addition to the metaphysical and religious dimensions present in the story, there is the subject of "civilization and barbarism" seen from the viewpoint of what some interpret as the cultural "degradation" of the European race in the New World. Haberly brings out the significance of the few books mentioned in the story – *The History of the Shorthorn in Argentina*, for example, is about the importing of "English shorthorn bulls" to produce a superior breed of cattle, but also recalls the repeated attempts by the Argentine ruling class to "improve the race" by encouraging the immigration of Europeans. There are, in addition, two subtexts that are not directly mentioned: one, by José María Ramos Mejía, and the other, by Esteban Echeverría. The protagonist Espinosa attended an English school in a city near Buenos Aires named Ramos Mejía. Among the various Ramos Mejía, a well-known family, José María (1842–1914) was a psychologist and reformer, and the author of *Las multitudes argentinas* (*The Argentine Masses*, 1899), in which he declared that "Argentine history and culture was a case-book study in abnormal psychopathology."[6] He believed that the gauchos and their leaders were "degenerate and inferior," and that mixing with other "inferior" races, such as Negroes and Indians, was the cause of the race's "degeneracy."

The other subtext is the story "El matadero" ("The Slaughterhouse," 1838), by Esteban Echeverría, in which a young liberal student is ridiculed, tortured, and, once tied to a table as if to a cross, finally dies, victimized by a small mob of thugs and illiterates. In this context, I do not believe that "The Gospel" constitutes a discourse of redemption. Despite the rather docile, even cowering behavior of the Gutres (they seem to harbor no evil), it is their failure to "understand" Baltasar Espinosa in his own terms, and the strangeness that his intellectual and imaginative powers generates in their presence, that leads to the tragic ending.

"Guayaquil"

"Guayaquil" shares certain characteristics with "The Elderly Lady." In both there are protagonists descended from heroes and statesmen of the Wars of Independence; both deal with a historical past; and in both, that "aristocracy" is now bankrupt. Here I will discuss "Guayaquil" and only mention "The Elderly Lady" and also "Unworthy" when relevant.

"Guayaquil" has attracted critical attention because, among other reasons, it depicts the presence of a new class in Argentine society, the immigrant Central European Jews, and the challenge their presence represented to the *criollo* "aristocracy." There is, of course, some relationship with another story, "Unworthy," which narrates the struggle for integration in Argentine society of a descendant of immigrant Jews, the will to be "a good Argentine" – a goal that is not altogether understood (again the notion of mis-"understanding") by the authorities who represent the abstraction that is the nation-state. But in the case of "Guayaquil," it is the immigrant who manages to conquer the descendant of those "fathers of the nation"; it is the newcomer who wins the "duel" of wills between the "aristocrat" and the Jewish immigrant. They both aspire to be appointed Argentina's official representative on a historic mission abroad. The object of the mission is to rescue a letter written by Simón Bolívar discovered in a Latin American "republic" in the Caribbean. In that letter, the Venezuelan "Liberator of the Americas" supposedly reveals what happened in a secret meeting in Guayaquil between him and San Martín, the Argentine national hero. What motivated San Martín in that meeting to transfer his troops to the command of Bolívar is still a mystery. As a result, Bolívar became the commander-in-chief of the continent's armies and the hero of its wars of liberation.

The story is quite complex and has been assessed by, among others, Balderston, Fernando Iturburu, and Martín Kohan. For Balderston it constitutes a paradigmatic example of the ways fiction and history may intertwine and "contaminate" one another to produce a text of indeterminate genre, rich in possible meanings. Iturburu argues that the story is about the destruction of both the *criollo* ideology/society and its hegemonic discourse and, at the same time, undermines the nationalist epic, while for Martín Kohan it portrays the triumph of immigrants over the *criollo* patricians who "did not know how to link their *I* (*yo*) to the destiny or the will of the nation."[7]

Borges assumes a very critical stance vis-à-vis the *criollo* "aristocracy" descended from the founding fathers of the country, one of whose representatives is Sra. de Jáuregui in "The Elderly Lady," and the class to which Borges's own family belonged.[8] The unnamed first-person narrator of "Guayaquil" is also depicted in very caustic terms. He is shown to be conceited and frivolous. Vain and prejudiced, he portrays himself, perhaps unknowingly, in a negative light. He admires his own prose as "at once melancholy and pompous"; he lives, "as most people know," on Calle Chile; he opens the door to the Jewish immigrant himself, with "republican simplicity"; and he frequently contradicts himself. But of his negative qualities, the most serious are xenophobia and anti-Semitism.

The narrator claims for himself the right to act as the nation's historian not because he holds university degrees and even less because he has studied books and documents (as Zimmermann has), but rather because he carries Argentine history "in [his] blood." That irrational "privilege" is a warrant of his authority as a specialist. Looking at the web of interrelations between the stories, we see that the issue of "blood" appears also in "The Gospel." There the context is tragic: when Espinosa reads the Gospel to the Gutres "to see if they understand," he seems surprised that they listen attentively, and he thinks, in allusion to their Scottish Calvinist background, that "it is in their blood." We already know what the "understanding" in the Gutres' blood leads to.

Expressions of anti-Semitism abound. The narrator of "Guayaquil" seems to approve Heidegger's denunciation of Zimmermann as "of Hebrew, not to say Jewish, descent." Zimmermann's wanderings in exile (his "exodus and subsequent nomadism") are referred to as "*actividades* trashumantes": the adjective *trashumante* is generally used in Spanish to denote the transfer of *cattle* from one pasturage to another. Although Zimmermann is a naturalized citizen of Argentina, he is constantly referred to as a foreigner – "our guest" – and one of his gestures is described as "Oriental." Finally, in a fit of xenophobia and anti-Semitism, not even the Germans are spared: "The servility of the Jew and the servility of the German were in his voice" (*CF* 396). In a story about historians, one wonders how reliable any "history" written by such a person could be.

Finally, one factor that further complicates the story is the allusions to Joseph Conrad. Critics have noted his presence, and Balderston in particular has commented on some aspects and characters of *Nostromo* (1904) which postulate the history–fiction duality in "Guayaquil." I believe one can go a bit farther – *all* historiographical accuracy in the story is called into question. The first paragraph written by the *criollo* "historian" is a description of a landscape and a geography that are totally imaginary – the region called "the Western State" is an invention of Conrad's, who, under his Polish name, is even called "its ... most famous historiographer" (*CF* 390). Bolívar's letter, as Balderston has noted, is to be found in the collection of documents owned by a character in *Nostromo*, "Dr. [José] Avellanos," who lives, as noted by the narrator of "Guayaquil," in Sulaco, the capital of that imaginary republic. All of this is disturbing, but what is indeed confusing is that both "historians," the narrator and Zimmermann, seem to *believe* in the objective existence of an invented place and invented characters. At the end, the mystery deepens when the narrator sees the itinerary on Zimmermann's airline ticket, which reads "Ezeiza (Buenos Aires)-Sulaco." It is as though the existence of another of Bolívar's letters were discovered in one of the libraries of Tlön. Borges seems to have endowed "Guayaquil" with this fantastic geography and "list of characters" in order to further undermine the story's historicity. I tend to think that a reading of "Guayaquil" in the light of Conrad's *Nostromo* might prove to be very productive.

"Brodie's Report"

The manuscript that constitutes "Brodie's Report" was found in a copy of *The Thousand and One Nights*, a detail that underscores its fantastical nature, and aspects of the plot are linked to Gulliver's last voyage in Swift's *Gulliver's Travels*. The Borges–Swift relationship has been discussed by several critics, but there is still room for more research.[9] Swift's work, as we know, is an acerbic satire aimed at the political and social situation of the England of his time. In that sense, the title story accords with the Swiftian tradition. It can be read as a transposition, into a grotesque and much bitterer context, of many of the critical observations, direct and indirect, that have been pointed out in this volume's "realistic" stories.

David Brodie is a Scottish missionary whose work takes him to Africa and Brazil. During his travels he comes across a barbarous people called, like those of Swift, Yahoos. They "walk about naked." Their language has no vowels. Only a few of them have names, and their notion of personal identity is linked to mud ("to call one another, they fling mud at each other"). Their political system is founded on mutilation and cruelty: when they identify the new king, "he is gelded, blinded with a fiery stick, and his hands and feet are cut off, so that the world will not distract him from wisdom" (*CF* 404).

Brodie alludes repeatedly to an almost complete lack of imagination in the Yahoos. They cannot imagine much beyond visual impressions. Their numerical system responds to the fingers of their hand: "They count on their fingers thus: *one, two, three, four, many*; infinity begins at the thumb." They cannot relate events to one another; they lack any notion of cause and effect. Their lack of imagination, of course, has serious consequences. In our daily world our imagination creates, on the basis of a series of successive and diverse perceptions, a unified and coherent world that allows us to relate one thing to another and thus allows us to reason, and to act. This concept is not far from some of the ideas expounded by the (also) Scottish philosopher Hume. Without imagination, then, one can neither think nor orient oneself: "A house of several rooms would be for [the Yahoos] a labyrinth" (*CF* 404). Brodie summarizes: "Their lack of imagination makes them cruel." Finally, they lack any notion of history, conceived as a time continuum, because, except for the "witch doctors" who can remember what happened a few hours ago, they have no memory (like, at the end, the widow Jáuregui in "The Elderly Lady," whose memory, now replaced by a gaping void, is ironically declared an "eloquent archive" of Argentine history). They have difficulty formulating abstractions, and those provided to them by their language, which contradictorily are many, are so chaotic that they are actually useless. Finally, the Yahoos both venerate and mistreat their poets, especially if they manage to "surprise or astound" their listeners. In that case, even the poets' mothers will not speak to or look at them, and "anyone may kill" them.

There is no space here to list in detail the relations between the attributes of the Yahoos and the circumstances narrated in the earlier stories in the volume, but though there are not exact equivalences, there are clear similarities. The treatment allotted to the poets by the Yahoos is not that different from the "treatment" given Baltasar Espinosa. We should recall, besides, that the Gutres, for example, are descended from Scotsmen from Inverness; we know that Brodie is the name of a castle located just kilometers from Inverness. Borges being Borges, might this not be an indication that Brodie and the Gutres are related by "Calvinist fanaticism," which would make the minister's chronicle ambiguous and biased, at the very least? In his conclusion, the missionary declares that the Yahoos are not a primitive people, but rather a "degenerate" one, just as the Nilsens and Gutres are "degraded." Finally, in an appeal that is not lacking all compassion, Brodie states that despite all he has described, the Yahoos have a culture and should be saved.

In summary, in *Brodie's Report* a series of internal relationships give significance not just to the individual stories but to the volume as a whole. Using narrative devices and a language that do not easily accommodate to the notion of traditional "realism," the "report," which, figuratively, constitutes almost the entire book, presents a very critical picture of Argentine society. It reminds us of an essay that Borges published in *Sur* in 1931 – "Our Inabilities" – in which the critique is equally severe and in which the author, pained because he is conscious that he is one of them, imputes to his compatriots exactly the tendency to rancor, grudge-holding, intolerance, and lack of imagination that we find in the stories collected in *Brodie's Report*.[10] These stories examine with equal harshness the upper classes, the working class, and the gauchos and cattle-drovers. The author sometimes seems to go harder on the privileged class than on the less privileged, yet never falls into pamphleteering or moralizing except when he opts for the satiric mode. There are several stories of high literary quality that link this volume with his earlier work. And last, beyond satire, beyond irony, beyond the bitter tone that sometimes emerges, there are traces of melancholy and tenderness that allow us to glimpse the Borges who repeatedly celebrated Buenos Aires with deep fervor (read: love). It is the same Borges who in the 1931 essay concluded: "I have been an Argentine for many generations and express these complaints with no joy."

NOTES

1 Honoré de Balzac, *Père Goriot*, New York, W. W. Norton, 1994, 6.
2 On "civilization" and "barbarism" in Borges, see Rafael Olea Franco, "El íntimo cuchillo en la garganta: ¿civilización o barbarie?" in *Los dones literarios de Borges*, Frankfurt Madrid, Vervuert; Iberoamericana, 2006, 37–66.
3 Helene Weldt, "Borges: diálogo entre tres textos, 'Hombres pelearon,' 'Hombres de la esquina rosada' e 'Historia de Rosendo Juárez'," *Texto Crítico*, 8 (1983), 214–27, underscores the impulsiveness of knife-fighters' behavior, and contrasts the narrators of the two stories in this respect.
4 See, respectively, Jesús Freire Álvarez, "Mujer objeto," *Baquiana: Revista Literaria*, 6 (2005), 133–38; Herbert J. Brant, "The Queer Use of Communal Women in Borges' 'El Muerto' and 'La Intrusa'," *Hispanófila*, 125 (1999), 37–50; Perla Sassón-Henry, "North Meets South: Jorge Luis Borges' 'La intrusa' and Natalie Bookchin's Media Experiment *The Intruder*," *MACLAS: Latin American Essays*, 19 (2009), 159–69; Guillermo Tedio, "'La intrusa' o las herejías del suburbio," *Espéculo: Revista de Estudios Literarios*, 15 (2000), www.ucm.es/info/especulo/numero15/intrusa.html.
5 See, respectively, Nora de Marval-McNair, "'El Evangelio según Marcos' según Borges," *Círculo: Revista de Cultura*, 24 (1995), 63–73; Rodolfo A. Borello, "El Evangelio según Borges," *Revista Iberoamericana*, 43 (1977), 503–16; Silvia Schönhals, "Metaficción y metafísica en 'El Evangelio según Marcos'," *Alba de América: Revista Literaria*, 20 (2001), 291–98; David T. Haberly, "The Argentine Gospels of Borges," *Bulletin of Hispanic Studies*, 66 (1989), 47–54.
6 Haberly, "The Argentine Gospels of Borges," 52.
7 See, respectively, Daniel Balderston, "Behind Closed Doors: The Guayaquil Meeting and the Silences of History," in *Out of Context: Historical Reference and the Representation of Reality in Borges*, Durham, NC, Duke University Press, 1993, 115–31; Fernando Iturburu, "'Guayaquil': judíos, argentinos y el fin del nacionalismo criollo," in Gregory J. Racz (ed.), *Jorge Luis Borges (1899–1986) as Writer and Social Critic*, New York, Edwin Mellen Press, 2003, 115–29; Martín Kohan, "El enigma de Guayaquil: el secreto de la Argentina," *Variaciones Borges*, 16 (2003), 35–44 (43).
8 Edwin Williamson identifies Borges's maternal grandmother, Leonor Suárez, as the model for Sra. de Jáuregui. See *Borges: A Life*, New York, Viking, 2004, 362.

9 See Luis Martínez de Mingo, "El decálogo ciego y los Yahoos," *Cuaderno de Investigación Filológica*, 11.1–2 (1985), 59–69; Viviana Plotnik, "Colonialismo y aculturación en 'El informe de Brodie' de Jorge Luis Borges y *El entenado* de Juan José Saer," *Monographic Review/Revista Monográfica*, 12 (1996), 345–54; José A. Rivas, "El último viaje de Alvar Núnez Cabeza de Vaca," *Salina: Revista de Letras*, 9 (1995), 111–15.

10 "Our Inabilities" (*SNF* 56–58). Originally published as "Nuestras imposibilidades," in *Sur* 4, 1931, and later reprinted in *Borges en Sur, 1931–1980*, Buenos Aires, Emecé, 1999, 117–20.

13

EFRAÍN KRISTAL

The Book of Sand and *Shakespeare's Memory*

Jorge Luis Borges would often say that he preferred *The Book of Sand* (1975) over his other books, perhaps as a rejoinder to critics who dismissed the thirteen stories of the collection as exercises that pale in comparison to his signature tales of the 1940s. Borges insisted on the opposite view: "It would be better to forget all the other ones I wrote, because they are nothing more than drafts of this one."[1] Borges had a consistent sense of his attainments and limitations, and neither corresponded to the critical assessment of his later work as evidence of his literary decline. He identified flaws in a number of the tales that made him famous, and thought he had addressed some of those blemishes in his later fictions. In public, Borges embraced his fame as a pleasant surprise, and was both amused and disappointed by the response to his work. His expressions of amusement vanished in one of his last short stories, in which a character named Jorge Luis Borges offers an observation about the book he considered his finest: "I was taken for a clumsy imitator of Borges" (CF 492).

The Book of Sand, Borges's most carefully crafted compilation, explores new ground and revisits older conceits in ways that shed retrospective light on his more celebrated tales. He attains greater heights in *Shakespeare's Memory*, a collection of four stories composed in the twilight of his life, when his health was beginning to falter.[2] Borges worked on these stories with the same care with which he composed and polished poems in his mind, after losing his sight and with the help of María Kodama, who transcribed the advanced versions. It took Borges two years to complete the story that gave the title to *Shakespeare's Memory* after the ominous line, "I will sell you the memory of Shakespeare," came to him in a dream.[3] Borges's final four stories surpass the pathos and emotional intensity of any of his previous tales. The posthumous collection has received less critical attention than *The Book of Sand*, but it is a high point of his literary career.

The last two collections have more in common with each other than with *Fictions* and *The Aleph*, rightly admired for their dazzling complexities, philosophical aura, and the sense that fictional worlds with impossible objects, characters with preternatural attributes, and outlandish circumstances, can feel urgent and compelling; or with his intermittent attempts to practice realistic narrative modes in some tales such as "Man on Pink Corner" or *Brodie's Report*. In the last two collections Borges returns to the fantastic genre, disarmingly.

Many readers of Borges's signature tales were likely to accept his most preposterous narrative twists and turns because they were outmaneuvered by a writer with many tricks up his sleeve, including the false start and the use of unreliable narrators with a limited, perverse, or distorted understanding of unaccountable situations. Borges was also masterful in his ability to endow absurd objects with plausibility by presenting them in stories with an array of erudite and apocryphal sources, or in elaborate and intriguing plots in which matters of life and death endow his impossibilities with an air of necessity. In stories like "The Garden of Forking Paths" and "Tlön, Uqbar, Orbis Tertius," studied ambiguities, lacunae, and contradictions abound; for that reason they have lent themselves to a myriad of engaging but incompatible philosophical projections which tend to reveal more about a critic's theoretical commitments than about the stories themselves. The last stories do not allow for projections of this kind with the same ease. In them, the reader is presented with Borges's impossibilities without subterfuges, and is invited to consider the consequences of situations that could only take place in fictional realms. In "A Weary Man's Utopia," for example, time travel happens without explanation so that the reader can consider an encounter between a man of the past and a man of the future.

The later stories have other novelties: they directly allude to Borges's personal life. In some, he transforms prejudices and speculations about his political convictions or his purported sexual inadequacies into ironic self-parody. The last collections are also keenly informed by Borges's preoccupation with dreams. It is instructive that the book he published after *The Book of Sand* was his *Book of Dreams*, an edited collection in which he is interested in exploring "the influence of dreams in literature,"[4] and that Borges included "Ulrikke" from *The Book of Sand* in the edited volume.

After writing *The Book of Sand* Borges readily pointed out deficiencies in some of his previous short stories; and these observations offer insights into his mindset when composing the later tales. He indicated, for example, that "The Immortal" was overwritten: it can become lost on the reader that the story is not about a Roman who meets Homer after drinking from the waters of immortality, but about Homer who forgets he composed the *Iliad* and the *Odyssey*, and confuses his life with that of an uncultured Roman soldier. Borges also felt that "Death and the Compass" could be edited to underscore that it rehearses the suicide of a detective who expects that the endpoint of his investigation will be his death. In his self-critique Borges would say that in the 1940s he wanted to be brilliant, but in the later stages of his life he preferred to be intelligible, and to experiment with impossibilities worthy of a fictional world: "If the imagination accepts something, it does not make a difference what mere logic might say."[5] In the later stories, Borges remains a master of the fantastic genre, but his erudition and philosophical concerns are not intended as concealments. As he put it more modestly: "In these exercises of a blind man I wanted to remain faithful to the example of [H. G.] Wells, and bring together a style without glare, at times as if it were spoken, and an impossible plot."[6]

The Book of Sand

Each of the stories in *The Book of Sand* is self-contained, but they are also deliberately interconnected. Some are variations on a theme: "The Mirror and the Mask," "Undr," and "The Book of Sand," for example, explore Borges's speculation that a book, a sentence, or even a single word can evoke a universe. The neologism "undr," for example, can be read as a contraction of two words, the Sumerian "ur" (origin) and the Germanic "und" (and), which suggests a beginning and something else, in other words, the structure of any possible story.

Other stories of the collection share similar narrative tropes. "The Other" and "Ulrikke," for example, explore the momentary union and separation of two unlikely characters in a dream. Several of the stories offer insights and passing comments that shed light on other stories of the collection. Together, the stories exemplify a literary vision informed by his lifelong adherence to the literature, history, and popular culture of the River Plate region; his interest in philosophy, religion, and mythology; and his fascination with dreams. He also creates new metaphysical parables inspired by one of his most enduring literary influences, Wilkie Collins's *The Moonstone* (1868), in which the possession of an object with an exotic provenance and supernatural powers becomes a curse. Collins transformed the Midas myth into a contemporary fable, and Robert Louis Stevenson refined the conceit in his short story "The Bottle Imp." The nightmarish conception of a magical object as a bane rather than a boon emerges in numerous Borgesian stories premised on a certain kind of wishful thinking intrigued by the possession of magical objects or impossible attributes such as immortality, a perfect memory, the imposition of our will on nature, the ability to control the passing of time or to undo what has been done, and the like.

"The Book of Sand" is an apt title for a story about an impossible object which brings initial joy but subsequent horror to its owner. Borges's "book of sand" has an infinite number of thin pages, but lacks a first or a last page. The book's pagination is random, but once a reader turns a page, she will never be able to find it again. The narrator of the story, an Argentine rare book collector, purchases the book from a Scotsman who had acquired it from an illiterate man in India. The original owner makes a connection between the book of sand and the metaphor in its name, "because neither sand nor this book has a beginning or an end" (*CF* 481). The narrator comes to feel that the infinite book without a beginning or an end, without closure or continuity, is monstrous, a nightmarish obscene object which corrupts reality.[7] He considers destroying the book by fire, but is afraid the combustion of its infinite pages might engulf the world in smoke. He decides to leave the book on a shelf in the Argentine National Library, thinking that his act is analogous to hiding a needle in a haystack.

The story recalls Borges's speculations on the frustrating disproportion between what a reader could read, and what she is actually able to read. According to Peter Sloterdijk, Borges's "book of sand" is a searching philosophical image, which suggests that "to begin and to begin from the beginning are two very different things."[8] For Sloterdijk, our entry into any narrative of our own life is as belated as our entry into Borges's book of sand because the most acute memory cannot account for its own beginnings. Sloterdijk's observations resonate with the conversation, in a popular coffee-house in Buenos Aires, about beginnings, in the opening of "The Night of the Gifts." A participant in the discussion argues that "nobody remembers the first time they saw yellow or black, or the first time they tasted some fruit – most likely because they were little and had no way of knowing they were at the beginning of a long, long series" (*CF* 446).

"The Night of the Gifts" is also an exploration of beginnings through the prism of degraded motifs taken from the literature and popular culture of Argentina. Like the protagonist of Ricardo Güiraldes's gaucho novel, *Don Segundo Sombra*, the protagonist of Borges's tale is an adolescent initiated into male adulthood by an older man from the pampas. Borges transforms Güiraldes's wise gaucho into an unwholesome farmhand who takes the boy to a brothel accustomed to violent brawls. In the brothel the boy encounters characters who happen to be archetypes of Argentine lore, including a woman who has returned to "civilization" after escaping from a period of captivity in an indigenous tribe (a foundational motif in Argentine literature in Esteban Echeverría's poem "La cautiva" [The Captive], and in José Hernández's *Martín Fierro*); and Juan Moreira, the legendary Argentine outlaw. On the same night the boy remembers his sexual initiation by the captive, and witnessing the death of Juan Moreira at the hands of a corrupt policeman. As an adult, however, he cannot tell for certain if his first encounters with sex and death at the brothel were experienced or imagined, which turns the story of an individual whose experiences are archetypal into a vexed dream-like recreation of Argentine national beginnings.

"Avelino Arredondo" is inspired by the assassination of the Uruguayan president Juan Idiarte Borda, on August 25, 1897, by a member of his own political party. The narrator warns that the story is not so much about the events as they happened, but as he can "dream" them.[9] The story of a terrorist act performed by an isolated individual is an illuminating rewriting of "Emma Zunz" in a political key. Like Emma, Arredondo is determined to kill a powerful man he thinks has committed grave injustices; he keeps his private plan a secret until he executes it, and his motivations will never be understood by himself or by those who remember the deed. Arredondo is plagued with contradictions: he is aloof but longs for human company, his eyes are both sleepy and energetic, he is a superstitious "freethinker." He is one of the last descendants of an erstwhile powerful oligarchical family who moves to Montevideo from a rural province to execute his project. He frequents a café for decent poor men, and falls in love with a young woman of a lower class. He decides to isolate himself to protect his girlfriend and other acquaintances from guilt by association. Arredondo assassinates the president and subsequently makes a statement to justify his self-appointed role as arbiter of justice. Borges undermines his character's self-righteousness, suggesting that beneath Arredondo's moralism lies the humiliation of a fallen oligarchy, and the secret source of his insanity. Borges's protagonist, who longs for love but does not know how to love, who longs for friendship but does not know how to be a friend, is a pathetic figure. He is also Borges's most poignant image of the political fanatic.

The pathos of "The Other" depends on the fictional premise that it is not a fiction but an autobiographical confession. The narrator, named Jorge Luis Borges, recalls an experience in 1969 during a visit to Cambridge, Massachusetts, when he encountered his double: his own self, as a nineteen-year-old high-school student in Geneva. The narrator claims that he had wanted to forget the event to keep his sanity, but since he could not forget it, he hopes that his confession might become a fiction for others, and perhaps for himself as well. The narrator is under no illusion that the experience, terrifying for himself, will move his readers, who will probably dismiss it as just another one of Borges's fantastic tales. In fact, it is a version of a fantastic tale by Giovanni Papini, "Due immagini in una vasca" ("Two Reflections in a Pond"), in which, inexplicably, a man meets his own self as he was seven years earlier, and finds himself insufferable.[10] Borges improves on Papini's fantastic tale by oscillating between an autobiographical and an oneiric register: his version of an encounter with his younger double can be read as a haunting dream the narrator has confused with his awakenings. Immediately before the encounter, the narrator remembers the "gray" waters of the rivers dragging blocks of ice. Gray, in Borges's short stories, is often the color of those characters who are the product of the dreams of others, as in "The Circular Ruins," and, more generally, it suggests impersonality, anonymity, and even non-existence. The young man acknowledges that the face of the older man resembles his own, but is puzzled by the older man's "gray" head. To prove to the younger Borges that he is not lying, the older Borges mentions things that only the younger Borges could have known, including embarrassing secrets such as the hiding place of a book of Balkan sexual practices he kept hidden on a bookshelf behind his copies of the *Arabian Nights*, *Don Quixote*, and Carlyle's *Sartor Resartor*.[11] The older Borges does not hide a staunch anti-Communism, or a flippant attitude toward the indigenous peoples of Latin America. These views are at the antipodes of the young Borges who had Bolshevik sympathies and the conviction that poets cannot turn their back on history. The older Borges notices that the young man is holding a novel by Dostoyevsky, and after alluding to *The Double*, an obvious antecedent to the situation they are experiencing, he disparages the young man's interest in novels.

As poets, their concerns could not be further apart: the young man is seeking to discover unprecedented explosive metaphors, whereas the older Borges aims to identify satisfying metaphors that the imagination has already accepted. They both love Walt Whitman for incompatible reasons. They have some common ground in their appreciation of a poetic line by Victor Hugo, in their scruples, and in their inability to deceive each other. The narrator arrives at the conclusion that the meeting was real, but that his younger self spoke to him from a dream, which he had long forgotten. The blind narrator's realization is belied by the precision of his visual memories, and other contradictions.

"Ulrikke," like "The Other," is the story of a fraught encounter. Here Borges explores feelings of love, and the fear of expressing them, in the guise of a dream in which a sexual encounter is a subterfuge for the protagonist's emotional inadequacies. In the story, set in Yorkshire, a reserved and celibate Colombian professor (who specializes in Nordic mythology) is smitten with a Norwegian woman who takes an interest in him. The professor, and first-person narrator of the tale, promises to be as faithful as he can to the reality he experienced, but dilutes the promise by pointing out that being faithful to reality and being faithful to one's personal memory of reality amount to the same thing; and by acknowledging the inevitable literary propensity to embellish. The professor's concern with the accuracy of his account is humorously belied by the fantastic setting informed by his wishful thinking, and by his knowledge of old Icelandic lore. The couple takes a walk in a place called "Thorgate," alluding to the pagan thunder god, and the professor is certain he has heard the far away howling of a wolf whose presence heralds the Nordic twilight of the gods. Ulrikke lets the shy man know she is available to him, and reveals that she will be dying soon. His callous indifference to her revelation underscores his narcissism. Before they make love, the couple playfully call each other Sigurd and Brynhild (the lovers of the *Song of the Nibelung*). Since the professor lacks the courage to declare his love, or to ask about her feelings, their sexual encounter suggests an emotional failure. The Old Norse epigraph to the story ("He took Gram, his sword, and placed its naked blade between the two of them") referring to the sword that separates chaste lovers, is famously inscribed on Borges's own tombstone. An illuminating commentary to the pathos of "Ulrikke" is found in "The Other," in which a character insists that lovemaking by the sea in a section of *Leaves of Grass* in which Whitman's poetic voice claims to have felt a sense of fulfillment, is an imaginary compensation for a hidden failure: "The poem gains if we sense that it is the expression of a desire, a longing, rather than the narration of an event" (*CF* 416).

In the afterword to *The Book of Sand* Borges calls "A Weary Man's Utopia" the most honest and melancholy story of the collection, but its tone is of understated, sardonic humor. The story is a poignant variation on the Borgesian theme of a willful suicide or of relief in impending death, of the kind that the Minotaur feels in "The House of Asterion" when Theseus puts an end to his misery. Here, a man from the present meets a man in the future in a world that has eradicated decease, difference, and diversity. The man of the future can hardly be a sympathetic character for Borges: in the four hundred years of his life, he has not read more than six books; and the future he inhabits cannot be agreeable to Borges, as there are no libraries. The man lives in a drab home he built himself, identical to any other. Nothing surprises him, not even the apparition of another man from the past. Nothing interests him or sustains him, and nothing gives him pleasure, not even his artistic endeavors. He is a painter who has experimented with many styles. This vision of the future lacks many aspects of the contemporary world that Borges found disagreeable (advertising, politicians, and the profit motive), but it is also a world in which love and friendship are perceived to be weaknesses. Its inhabitants, who could live indefinitely, agree that there is no point in perpetuating the human race, and that it is worth considering gradual or collective suicide for every human being on the planet. If Borges considers this tale to be his most honest and melancholy, it is perhaps because it captures a gloomy mood that evokes the pessimism of his admired Schopenhauer. The man from the future offers his visitor a strange painting that appears to disturb him, before taking his other works of art to the crematorium where he has elected to destroy his possessions and end his life. In this unsavory world, Adolf Hitler is remembered as the philanthropist who invented the death chamber. Borges's story is an unwholesome utopia, which generates longing for the imperfections of our imperfect world.

In "A Weary Man's Utopia," a character speaks of St. Thomas Aquinas's *Summa Theologica* as a work of fantastic literature. This observation would be apt for the engineer in "There Are More Things," who is interested in the literary possibilities of Philosophy and Theology. The engineer sold his home to Max Preetorius, a mysterious man who closes up the house to the outside world after hiring architects to redesign it before he abandons Buenos Aires. Preetorious is a reincarnation of an evil character conceived by Borges for a detective story he never wrote with Bioy Casares.[12] The architects consider him to be insane. The narrator enters the house and realizes from the shapes of the furnishings that it has been appointed for a monster he encounters at the close of the story. The narrator does not need to describe the monster for the reader to feel its terrifying presence: a German shepherd is found decapitated and mutilated near the house, and the narrator associates the word "amphisbaena" (the two-headed monster born of Medusa's blood) to the monster. The most intriguing mystery of the story – an homage to H. P. Lovecraft's fantastic tales of horror – is not the nature of the monster, but the relationship between the monster and Max Preetorious, the sinister man who prepared the abode for the creature in the first place.

In "The Congress," a group of unpleasant characters who meet in a coffee shop in Buenos Aires before the outbreak of the First World War conspire to impose a utopia on the world, and they come to the realization that their scheme was successful beyond their expectations, but that the consequences of their conception were not necessarily what they had hoped for or antici-pated. The story is both incredible and impossible, because the scheme will retroactively inform the universe from the beginning of time. The themes of "The Congress" had informed many of Borges's signature tales, like "Tlön, Uqbar, Orbis Tertius," in which a group of conspirators conceive of an alternative world which they impose on our own; "The Garden of Forking Paths," where a Chinese ruler renounces his worldly power to draft a book that would anticipate the experiences of this world and all other possible worlds; "The Lottery in Babylon," where complex adjustments to a lottery transform the institution into one that controls all aspects of society; or "*Deutsches Requiem*," where an unrepentant Nazi meditates on the success of National Socialism even though Germany lost the Second World War. In

"The Congress," Borges is not interested, as he was in some of the previous stories, in making his readers believe in the plausibility of his impossible tale, but in the feeling that a plan of this kind could have an impact: "What matters is having felt that that institution of ours, which more than once we had made jests about, truly and secretly existed, and that it was the universe and ourselves" (*CF* 435–6). The narrator is the only surviving conspirator, and thus the only man aware that his benign universe is the product of a conspiracy, which had intended to cause evil.

Shakespeare's Memory

The stories in *Shakespeare's Memory* lack the self-deprecating touches of *The Book of Sand*, and gain from a greater directness, as in "August 25, 1983," Borges's most intense exploration of the double. The story is set on the day after Borges's birthday, when the narrator, a sixty-one-year-old Borges, meets his own self when he is eighty-four years old. The encounter takes place in a dream. The younger Borges goes to a hotel room in Adrogué which he had frequented in his youth, but which no longer exists, and in that hotel room he meets his older self. The eighty-four-year-old Borges has just taken a lethal dosage of pills. The two men meet in the same place, but the eighty-four-year-old Borges is in his Buenos Aires apartment. He finds it amusing that even though he is about to die, he keeps dreaming of the double. The younger Borges is not altogether surprised that this could happen in a dream because he had written a story anticipating a suicide of this kind. The older Borges lets the younger one know that he is still to write his best poem, and that he will realize "that your supposed career has been nothing but a series of drafts, miscellaneous drafts, and you will give in to the vain and superstitious temptation to write your great book" (*CF* 491). The younger Borges assumes that this quest will be a failure, but the older Borges says that something more disappointing would take place: he would write his masterpiece, publish it under a pseudonym in the hope of attaining invisible glory, but his reviewers would consider its author to be "a clumsy imitator of Borges" (*CF* 492). The younger Borges is brutally honest when he says: "I loathe your face, which is a caricature of mine, I loathe your voice, which is a mockery of mine, I loathe your pathetic syntax, which is my own" (*CF* 492). The older Borges shares the feelings, which is why he has decided to kill himself. In a striking statement that underscores the multiple infinite regresses of this story, the older, lovelorn Borges says to the younger one, concerned about his literary fate, that one day he will write the story, the story we are now reading, but that he will think it is a fantastic tale.

"Blue Tigers" offers a sobering twist on Borges's previous explorations of nightmarish objects as subterfuges for experiences that might be all too real. In the story, a Scottish professor of Western and non-Western logic, obsessed with tigers since he was a child (as Borges was), hears of a mysterious blue tiger in a town far away from the Ganges river.[13] He dreams of the blue tiger, and when he arrives in the town in India the inhabitants deceive him, pretending that there are blue tigers in their midst. In his search for the animals, the professor comes across some rocks, which, inexplicably, are of the blue color of his dreams. Unaccountably, the stones increase and decrease in number. In his attempts to figure out the logic of the rocks he is able to determine one pattern that satisfies his logical mind: he finds that an isolated stone cannot multiply or disappear. He prays to God to relieve him of the burden of the impossible objects that defy his understanding. A beggar appears, asks for all the stones, and the man, with some hesitation, relinquishes every single one. The beggar leaves as in a dream, and the Scottish logician gains intimations that the nightmare of the blue stones may be over, but that it was a subterfuge to the true nightmare of his life.

"The Rose of Paracelsus" is a poignant parable about Borges's self-perception as a misunderstood fabulist whose reputation has obfuscated the nature of his craft. Borges summarized one of his most enduring views about literature when commenting: "Reality is unreachable by art, even though art can create other realities."[14] In the story, reality is reached by art but only as a fictional conceit. Borges's Paracelsus, a magician, meets a doubting Thomas in the guise of Johannes Grisebach, a potential disciple. The master tries to convey to the young man that in his search for wisdom the process ought to matter more than the results, but the young man is not willing to engage in the search until he has tangible evidence of the master's prowess, in particular his reputed ability to be able to resurrect a burnt rose from the fire. The insolent young man throws a rose into a fireplace, and his feelings of impatience turn to pity and embarrassment when he feels he has humiliated a pitiful charlatan. He feigns respect and departs. In his absence, the master utters a magic word, and the rose resurges from its ashes. The miracle of the story can only take place in a work of fiction, but the impossible event is a touching image by Borges of the attainments and the limitations of fiction as a compensation for the burdens of life.

"Shakespeare's Memory" is a meditation on the limited role that memory, understanding, or the will might play in the creative process. In the tale, Hermann Sörgel, a pedantic Shakespearean scholar, is offered the bard's memory. Before the impossible occurrence, the man had written erudite trivialities about Shakespeare. When he acquires Shakespeare's memory his critical understanding of the works remains conventional, but he gains unexpected insights that are initially exhilarating, and ultimately terrifying, as with most other impossible gifts in Borges's fictional world. Sörgel realizes that the memory he has inherited includes shadowy areas of matters that Shakespeare must have wanted to forget. Shakespeare's *œuvre* was renewed for the specialist, not because he gains special insights about the writer's creative process, but because he comes to terms with the pitfalls of his once prickly approach to erudition. Sörgel realizes, for example, that cases of apparent carelessness in Shakespeare were deliberate gestures to give his characters' lines more spontaneity. He begins to realize that Shakespeare had access to the very same things that are available to anyone else, but "it was his gift to be able to transmute them into fables, into characters that were much more alive than the gray man who dreamed them" (*CF* 514). In an observation that rivals Proust's notion of involuntary memory, Borges's narrator says: "A man's memory is not a summation; it is a chaos of vague possibilities" (*CF* 513). What lies beyond the once pedantic literary scholar is the ability to transform the disorder of indefinite possibilities into a persuasive realization, or even the ability to understand how Shakespeare transformed those possibilities into his own work. The original joy of Sörgel turns into a feeling of oppression and fear that he might lose his sanity as his own memory becomes confused with the memory of another. Sörgel's personal appreciation of Shakespeare's works does not diminish after he inherits the bard's memory, but he prefers the burdens of his own memory to wrestling with the burdens of both his own and that of another; so he relinquishes the impossible gift. Borges's last four stories are arguably the most compelling he ever wrote. They are certainly his most mature statement on both the compensations and the subterfuges of the literary imagination.

NOTES

1 *El otro Borges. Entrevistas (1960–1986)*, Fernando Mateo (ed.), Buenos Aires, Equis Ediciones, 1997, 188. Unless otherwise indicated, all translations into English are mine.
2 It was edited posthumously in 1989 by María Kodama, and includes three stories published in journals before 1983; the title story was published for the first time in the *Obras completas* (1989).
3 *Borges el memorioso. Conversaciones de Jorge Luis Borges con Antonio Carrizo*, Mexico, Fondo de Cultura Económica, 1982, 58. In the final version of the story, he modified the thought from "selling" to "offering" the impossible gift of Shakespeare's memory.
4 *Libro de sueños*, Buenos Aires, Torres Agüero, 1976, 7.
5 *Borges el memorioso*, 45.
6 In J. L. Borges, *Œuvres complètes*, vol. II, ed. Jean Pierre Bernès, Paris, Gallimard, 1999, 1326.

7 For a brilliant analysis, see Mercedes Blanco's "Nouer une corde de sable: À propos de la nouvelle 'El libro de arena'," *Variaciones Borges*, 10 (2000), 97–118. Whereas the books in "The Library of Babel" have the benefit of continuity, the "book of sand" eliminates continuity, making it impossible for a reader to ascertain any meaning to the work. Blanco's essay is also an instructive meditation on Borges's impossible objects.

8 Peter Sloterdijk, *Zur Welt kommen. Zur Sprache kommen. Frankfurter Vorlesungen*, Frankfurt, Suhrkamp, 1988, 38.

9 For the historical sources, and other references to Arredondo in Borges, see Pablo Rocca, "Uno o dos destinos sudamericanos. Ficción y realidad y 'Avelino Arredondo'," *Revista Iberoamericana*, 67, 194–95 (2001), 161–72. Rocca shows that Clementina (a former slave of the family who continues to serve Arredondo and who finds it unbecoming that he should undertake any manual labor) is an invention which helps to underscore the significance of Arredondo's status as a member of a fallen oligarchy. The lawyer who defended the historical Avelino Arredondo was an older relative of Borges.

10 The attitude of the older Borges to his younger self echoes the sentiment expressed by Papini's protagonist: "questo giovine ridicolo e ignorante, è stato, in altri tempi, me stesso" ("This ridiculous and ignorant young man was once my own self"), in "Due immagini in una vasca," *Il pilota cieco*, Naples, Ricciardi, 1907, 7. Borges pays tribute to Papini's story as the antecedent to "The Other" in his *Biblioteca personal*, OC IV 473.

11 The narrator of "The Book of Sand" also hid the book in a bookshelf, behind a copy of the *Arabian Nights*.

12 This earlier Dr. Preetorius killed and tortured children. See Adolfo Bioy Casares, *Borges*, Buenos Aires, Ediciones Destino, 2006, 28.

13 This is Borges's last story about a tiger; his first was written when he was twelve years old. See a facsimile in Waldemar Verdugo-Fuentes's *En voz de Borges*, Mexico City, Editorial Offset, 1986, xi.

14 *Borges el memorioso*, 280.

14

RAFAEL OLEA FRANCO

The early poetry (1923–1929)

Borges published his first three books of poetry in the 1920s, but his output would decrease markedly by the end of this period. *Fervor de Buenos Aires* (1923) consists of forty-nine poems; *Moon Across the Way* (*Luna de enfrente*, 1925), twenty-seven; and *San Martín Copybook* (*Cuaderno San Martín*, 1929), only twelve. Given the variety and abundance of these poems, it will only be possible to discuss the three collections in general terms. Furthermore, I shall be referring to and citing from the original first editions of all three books, now out of print.[1]

Of the seven years the Borges family lived in Europe (1914–21), the last two were spent in Spain, where the young Borges joined an avant-garde group of poets who called themselves "*ultraístas*."[2] On his return to Argentina, he championed *ultraísmo*, defining it in opposition to two other trends: the *sencillismo* ("plain poetry") of the Argentine Baldomero Fernández Moreno, who aimed to poeticize everyday reality using plain language, and the *modernismo* founded by the great Nicaraguan poet Rubén Darío, whose reputation dated from the last years of the nineteenth century. While *sencillismo* had not caught on outside Argentina, *modernismo* had spread throughout the Spanish-speaking world and had produced several poets as renowned as Darío himself, including the Argentine Leopoldo Lugones.

Modernismo, however, came under fire from a younger generation for the affectation of its language, its taste for the ornamental and the exotic, and its references to the Hellenic world, all of which supposedly distanced the poet from "social reality." Borges condemned the outworn rhetoric of *modernismo*, claiming it was no longer capable of surprising the reader. Instead, he advocated *ultraísmo*, summing up its principles as follows: primacy of metaphor, synthesis of various images into a single image, elimination of syntactical connections, and abolition of what he termed "confessionalism" and "circumstantiation" (*circunstanciación*).[3] Nevertheless, by the time

Translated by E.W.

172

he published his first book in 1923, he was no longer using metaphor as the main technical resource of his poems, and the latter, moreover, were grounded in a very specific location – the city of Buenos Aires, for which the poet confessed great "fervor."

Borges himself explained his move away from *ultraísmo* thus:

> Were the poems in *Fervor de Buenos Aires* ultraist poetry? When I came back from Europe in 1921, I came bearing the banners of ultraism. I am still known to literary historians as "the father of Argentine ultraism." When I talked things over at the time with fellow-poets … we came to the conclusion that Spanish ultraism was overburdened – after the manner of futurism – with modernity and gadgets. We were unimpressed by railway trains, by propellers, by airplanes, and by electric fans. While in our manifestos we still upheld the primacy of the metaphor and the elimination of transitions and decorative adjectives, what we wanted to write was essential poetry – poems beyond the here and now, free of local color and contemporary circumstances.[4]

Fervor de Buenos Aires is not without local color, but it does lack the usual trappings of avant-garde poetics. In the original prologue to the first edition of the book,[5] the author explains: "Rather than the decoratively visual and polished poetry bequeathed to us by Luis de Góngora, through his 'executor' Rubén [Darío], I wanted to produce another kind of poetry, a more meditative lyric, based on adventures of the spirit" ("A quien leyere," *FBA*).[6] Although there is no space to go into the matter at length, this "meditative lyric" gives rise to a number of reflective poems of a philosophical or metaphysical nature, rooted in the idealism of Berkeley, as when in "Truco" (*SP* 13), he resorts to the popular Argentine card-game of the title in order to demolish the concept of time.

Borges now adopts a more direct language, far removed from the *modernista* style, but different too from the everyday idiom of the *sencillistas*. He also rejects rhyme and meter, as well as discarding regular classical forms. His alternative technique is free verse, which leads him to experiment with excessively long lines that tend to lack a sense of rhythm. And while his declared model is Heine, who composed without regular rhyme or meter, he regrets not having quite succeeded in his experiments: "The unequivocal precision of Spanish pronunciation, together with its abundance of vowels, does not tolerate the making of totally free verse, and demands rather the use of assonance" ("A quien leyere," *FBA*). In other words, he regarded assonance and a degree of metric regularity as intrinsic qualities of the Spanish language, irrespective of the stylistic intentions of the individual poet.

As Guillermo de Torre noted:

> Rather than persisting with a particular poetic "manner" [i.e. *ultraísmo*], Borges favoured the discovery of a "tone." He replaced a Whitmanian enthusiasm for the plurality of the universe with a "fervour" for the circumscribed

space of a city, more specifically, for a few neighbourhoods and for a certain period in the past. He returned to his childhood, as well as to the early days of his country's independent history, idealizing them both with fond nostalgia.[7]

The desire to poeticize the city is confirmed in an essay from the same period in which he asserts: "Nothing has happened yet in Buenos Aires, whose grandeur has not been validated by a symbol, a surprising fable, or even an individual destiny comparable to Martín Fierro's" (*SNF* 11).[8] While the rural world of the gaucho and the pampas has been represented fully in literature, the city lacks "poeticization": "The city is in me, like a poem / which I have not yet managed to capture in words."[9] The fundamental aim of his early poetry – particularly in *Fervor* – is, therefore, the creation of "symbols" and "fables" commensurate with the "grandeur" of Buenos Aires.

There is a clear nationalist motivation here, but of the many visible aspects of a cosmopolitan city, Borges picks out the following:

> My *patria* – Buenos Aires – is not the extensive geographical myth that these two words suggest; it's my home, the friendly neighbourhoods, together with the streets and gardens to which I lovingly devote my time, and in which I have known love, pain and doubt. ("A quien leyere," *FBA*)

His writing, then, offers a very personal appreciation of the homeland, restricted not just to the nation's capital city but to a few of its neighborhoods. Furthermore, his concept of the city includes a familial, domestic dimension. A number of his poems are not urban as such but are consonant with his purpose of investing the city with personal significance: these texts, for example, sing the praises of the heroic exploits of his ancestors such as his great-grandfather, Colonel Isidoro Suárez, or Colonel Francisco Borges, his grandfather, both of whom achieved distinction in the patriotic wars of the nineteenth century.

A topic of this period is the expression of his dismay at not being able to realize a heroic destiny worthy of the feats of his forebears. Nevertheless, he justifies his vocation as a poet – he will save his ancestors from oblivion by extolling their exploits in his verse. For instance, in the closing lines of a poem dedicated to his grandfather, he declares: "I pray destiny / will bestow all good fortune on you, / and that immortality will be your just reward."[10]

Fervor de Buenos Aires, then, restricts its vision to a few aspects of the city, as indicated in the first poem of the collection:

> The streets of Buenos Aires
> Are already at the core of my soul.
> Not the energetic streets,
> troubled by hustle and bustle,
> but the gentle neighborhood street
> softened by trees and sunsets.[11]

This is an urban geography in which the center of the city (its streets "troubled by hustle and bustle") is replaced by "the gentle neighborhood street." In the prologue of *Fervor* he rejects the motley reality of Argentina in the 1920s, marked as it was by a diversity of cultural and linguistic registers:

> I have purposely rejected the vehement claims of those in Buenos Aires who have regard only for what is foreign: the rowdy energy of some downtown streets and the pitiful multinational rabble of the ports, both developments which, with unwonted disquiet, have put paid to the indolence of the *criollo* population.[12]

Borges here adopts the dichotomy between the *criollo* or "true Argentine" on the one hand, and the upstart immigrant or *extranjero* on the other, an opposition which underpinned and purported to legitimize the nationalist discourse of the period.

Whenever elements of modernity appear, they violently disrupt the young Borges's quiet, spiritual identification with the city of his birth:

> Bright advertisements tug at one's weariness
> Vulgar celebrations
> storm into the quiet of the soul
> Impulsive colours
> Scale the astonished façades
>
> .   .   .   .   .
>
> I walk the streets disheartened
> By the insolence of false lights.[13]

To escape this unpleasant prospect, the poetic "I" retreats to the neighborhood, choosing, moreover, the most propitious time to wander there. Evening is the favored hour, for at sunset he can find the perfect moment to savor the peace he so desires, thanks to the absence of "annoying" crowds.

> In search of the evening
> I roamed the streets in vain
>
> .   .   .   .   .
>
> The whole evening had settled in the square,
> serene and seasoned,
> beneficent and subtle as a lamp.[14]

The poetic "I" defines his *patria* through a particular set of desires. He yearns to create the sense of a "homeland" by poeticizing a city of empty squares, low houses, patios, balustrades, and porches. On the temporal plane, he longs to recover the tranquil flow of time past, and deplores the accelerated tempo measured by modern clocks. In short, he wants to recreate that *criollo* world of nineteenth-century Buenos Aires, which moves at a slow patriarchal pace, where the rush of modernity has yet to be felt, and buildings have not yet shot up to transform the old town into a vertical metropolis.

This idyllic and mythical image of Buenos Aires is elaborated by a *flâneur*, wandering the city streets on his own, a theme which is also found in *Moon Across the Way*, although one can observe a number of changes in this second collection. In the prologue, the author notes: "The city in *Fervor de Buenos Aires* is never other than intimate, but there is something ostentatious and public about it in this volume."[15] *Moon Across the Way* is less intimate in tone than *Fervor* but the phrase "ostentatious and public" refers also to a certain spatial displacement. In effect, if the errant "I" of the first book constructs his image of the city by withdrawing from the center and the port, and finding shelter in the "modest" and "gentle neighborhood streets," this process of withdrawal is accentuated in the second book, and even takes the poet to the edge of the open spaces of the pampas:

> I have been walking the whole night long
> And its restlessness has left me
> In this street which is like any other.
> Here once more the spectacle of the pampas on some horizon
> And the vacant lot that frays into weeds and wire fencing
> And the tavern bright as last evening's new moon.[16]

In *Moon Across the Way*, then, Borges begins to exalt the countryside, just as he had earlier done with the neighborhood streets. Here, too, the presence of the immigrants causes him to lament a lost world, and he nostalgically contrasts the neighborhood as it now is, with the way it was in the past, when the influence of the immigrants was not yet perceptible:

> Calle Serrano
> No longer are you as you were at the Centennial:
> Then you were more sky and now you are just façades.
>
> .   .   .   .   .   .
>
> Now you are honored by the warm hubbub of a coffee-house
> With its signboard, red as an insult.
> On the swaying backs of your little Italian girls
> There is not a single braid with which to strangle one's tenderness.[17]

The growth of the city, alluded to by the loss of the "sky," is represented by the appearance of the modern coffee-house, a sign of immigrant influence, and by the Italian girls who lack the *criollo* braids cherished by the poet. The kind of establishment Borges tends to favor is the "*almacén*" or "*pulpería*," a traditional *criollo* tavern-cum-general store. In the poem "Street with a rose-colored *almacén*" ("Calle con almacén rosao"), the gentle adjective "rose-colored" ["*rosao*"] contrasts with the aggressive "red as an insult" ["*punzó como una injuria*"] of the coffee-house's signboard in the previous poem.

176

I will now examine the most obvious difference between *Fervor* and *Moon Across the Way*: the use of language. When he returned to the city of his birth Borges did not immediately resort to Argentine idioms in his poetry; although *Fervor* demonstrates a distinct inclination for local themes, its language is not much different from that used by the author in his early European poems. In fact, the Argentine flourishes of the first book are few, and mostly confined to the use of diminutives ("austeras cas*itas*," "past*ito* precario," "manoj*ito* de patio"), some *criollo* noun or adjective ("*gauchaje*," "*chacotera*," "*barullero*"), and the odd image which is given a certain local color (e.g. the night is "fragrant as a *mate* tea" ["*olorosa como un mate curado*"]). Furthermore, these words retain the standard Spanish spelling; the "Argentine" character of the language is limited to the lexical level as there are no phonetic variants peculiar to the Spanish of Buenos Aires.

By contrast, the language of *Moon Across the Way* provides evidence of the intensification of Borges's *criollo* nationalism toward the middle of the 1920s. The use of self-consciously *criollo* words illustrates Borges's innovative and experimental kind of writing, which was integral to his project to establish a new *criollo* aesthetic. The poems exhibit linguistic traits that are meant to represent Argentine pronunciation, such as "ros*ao*," "eventualid*á*," "intensid*á*." There are plenty of expressions designed to give the poems a *criollo* flavor (impossible to convey in English): "*pampa sufrida y macha*," "*manso como un yuyal*," "*barrio guarango, corazonero*," "*tristona gustación*," "*almacén malevo*." Some of this is overdone, and may be attributed to the use of *criollo* dictionaries that provided the author with words which were not typical of his own speech, as he was to acknowledge in the prologue he appended to the edition of *Moon Across the Way* in the *Obras completas* (OC I 55).

Borges, moreover, employed a new stylistic device: he tried to represent through spelling certain phonetic traits of Buenos Aires Spanish. This technique had been much used in the reproduction of dialogue by "gauchesque" writers of the nineteenth century in order to emulate the speech of the Argentine cowboys, but to use it in lyric poetry was a risky innovation. Thus, in this second collection, the significant increase in Borges's use of idioms and other *criollo* features was also an attempt to establish a new literary language. First, at a basic level, the final "*d*" is elided in words with stressed endings, especially those ending in "*-dad*": "oscurid*á*," "crueld*á*," "eventualid*á*"; and in some past participles ending in -*ado*: "nombr*ao*," "ros*ao*," "solt*ao*." Secondly, he begins to use "*vos*" in his poems, the non-standard second person singular vocative pronoun which in Argentina replaces the standard "*tú*." The first poem in the collection employs this "*voseo*."[18] Lastly, he distorts the standard spelling of some words so as to reflect demotic pronunciation, such as writing *güellas* for *huellas* ("traces"), or in order to render colloquial speech, such as *"menudiaron"* instead of *"menudearon"* ("they were plentiful").

Even so, there are vacillations and inconsistencies. For example, even though the elision of a final *"d"* is common in Argentine speech, it is not a constant feature of Borges's poems. Similarly, the standard *"tú"* forms and the *criollo "vos"* at times appear side by side, even though incompatible in everyday speech.[19] Such inconsistencies were criticized by his contemporaries for evincing a lack of regular principles, and although Borges acknowledged this, he asserted that in general he was only following actual Argentine usage, which itself was inconsistent.[20] This shows that Borges's project did not entail a comprehensive effort to "Argentinize" the language in defiance of the precepts of the Royal Spanish Academy. All the same, he reaffirms his desire to raise the oral Spanish of Buenos Aires, with its inherent inconsistencies, to the status of serious literary writing. These creative innovations led Erwin Rubens, co-editor of *Megáfono*, the literary review which in 1933 featured the first survey of critical opinion on Borges's work, to praise the oral quality of his writing and his desire to give literary status to the conversational style of Buenos Aires.[21]

Already in the prologue to *Moon Across the Way*, one finds Borges writing in this Argentine vernacular style as he describes his personal engagement with the city:

> Let every versifier extol the things that best agree with his "I," for poetry is nothing more or less. I have celebrated those that suit me, those that bring out the most intense feelings. The sky-blue walls of the suburbs and the little squares opening like fountains to the heavens above. Here you have my modest fortune, for that is what I offer you in this book. (*Luna de enfrente* [*LE*], 7)[22]

And as regards the verse forms he employs, he tells the reader:

> Today I don't want to talk to you about technique. The truth is I'm not interested in the auditory qualities of verse and I like all stanza forms so long as the rhymes are not strident. Many of the poems in this book are spoken in *criollo*; not in *gauchesco* or *arrabalero*, but in the heterogeneous vernacular language of Buenos Aires-style conversation. Others employ that timeless, eternal Spanish (neither from Castile nor the River Plate) that is registered in the dictionaries. (*LE* 7)[23]

Moon Across the Way does indeed contain compositions in classic meters. For example, the oddly titled poem "Versos de catorce" ("Verses of Fourteen" [i.e. syllables]) indicates its use of alexandrines. This proclivity for composing verse in traditional meters became accentuated in later years owing to his blindness: "One salient consequence of my blindness was my gradual abandonment of free verse in favor of classical metrics ... It is obviously easier to remember verse than prose, and to remember regular verse forms rather than free ones. Regular verse is, so to speak, portable."[24]

In rejecting "strident" rhymes ("*barulleras*"), he was probably thinking of the *modernista*, Leopoldo Lugones, who had indulged in far-fetched rhymes, such as *ampo–crisolampo, apio–Esculapio, garbo–ruibarbo, insufla-pantufla*, in his celebrated book, *Lunario sentimental* [1909]. In contrast, Borges defines his own poetic language in two distinct yet complementary ways. He differentiates it from the pseudo-demotic style of the traditional "gauchesque" genre, as well as from the plebeian *arrabalero* (derived from the slang of the Buenos Aires underworld known as *lunfardo*). Secondly, he draws attention to the intrinsic qualities of his own language, such as its orality (he refers to "spoken" poems) and its specific character ("*charla porteña*" or Buenos Aires-style conversation), although he does acknowledge that some of his poems employ a neutral, standard Spanish ("neither from Castile nor the River Plate").

A wide range of linguistic registers can generally be found in any society, but this phenomenon was even greater in the Buenos Aires of the 1920s, a city formed through migratory fluxes, above all of Spanish and Italian peasants, who immigrated in the last third of the nineteenth century. As indicated earlier, Borges had distanced himself from the city center in the prologue to *Fervor de Buenos Aires*, reacting against its perceived "foreignness" and the rowdy energy of some of the downtown streets. His reaction also entailed a rejection of the dynamic *porteño* language that was actually spoken in Buenos Aires at the time, marked as it was by inflections from the enormous immigrant population, whose particular dialect of Spanish may have been different (in the case of Spaniards from the Peninsula), or whose mother tongue was not Spanish (which applied mostly to the Italians), not to mention the fact that the immigrants played little part in Argentine literary culture.

In this respect, Borges implicitly shared the prejudices of the elite "Florida" group of writers attached to the avant-garde magazine *Martín Fierro* (1924–27), who boasted: "All of us are effortlessly Argentine because we don't have to disguise any kind of exotic *pronunzia* [sic]."[25] This contemptuous dismissal was directed against members of the so-called "Boedo" group, named after a working-class district of the city, and comprising writers from proletarian or immigrant backgrounds (hence their alleged need to hide their foreign accents). For members of the "Florida" group, writing in the Buenos Aires "vernacular" Spanish of the *criollos* was "authentically Argentine," and thus became a manifestation of a linguistic nationalism which the young Borges supported up to a point.

Still, from an aesthetic perspective, Borges's experiments with this "vernacular" *criollo* Spanish produced some notable literary successes, such as the title of the poem "El general Quiroga va en coche *al muere*" ("General Quiroga Rides to His Death in a Carriage"), where the vernacular "… *al muere*" replaces the standard "… *a la muerte*" (*SP* 41). Also, in the same poem, we have an effective neologism: "Y la luna *atorrando* por el frío del alba" (literally: "And the moon *lazing* along the cold of the dawn"), where the gerund *atorrando* is derived from the adjective "*atorrante*," Buenos Aires slang for "lazy" or "shiftless."

Borges's third collection, *San Martín Copybook* (*Cuaderno San Martín*, a school exercise-book of the period named after the Liberator, General San Martín), contains very few poems, although it includes some now famous texts, such as "The Mythical Founding of Buenos Aires" (*SP* 53–55), which is written in lofty assonanced alexandrines. It opens with a question: "And was it along this torpid muddy river / that the prows came to found my native city?" (*patria* in the original), suggesting that the true object of the foundation of Buenos Aires by the conquistadors was to create a *patria* expressly for this particular poet.[26] Borges thereby relates his own "myth" of Buenos Aires to the city's origins, which the poet relocates to Palermo, the neighborhood in which he was raised, and, more precisely, to the city block bounded by the four streets named below:

> On the coast they put up a few ramshackle huts
> and slept uneasily. This, they claim, in the Riachuelo,
> but that is a story dreamed up in the Boca.
> It was really a city block in my district – Palermo.
>
> A whole square block, but set down in open country,
> attended by dawns and rains and hard southeasters,
> identical to that block which still stands in my neighborhood:
> Guatemala–Serrano–Paraguay–Gurruchaga.[27]

The original center of Buenos Aires has shifted to Palermo, with the Calle Serrano, where stood his childhood home, as one of its privileged borders. By claiming his own neighborhood as the true origin of the city and the *patria* (Argentina), Borges invests his creative will with a legitimacy that is absolute and timeless. Thus, the last lines reaffirm a vision of an eternal Buenos Aires: "Hard to believe Buenos Aires had any beginning. / I feel it to be eternal as air and water."[28] The creation of the myth is complete: the poet recalls the geographical origins of his native city and attaches himself to these origins in order, finally, to elevate that space onto a timeless plane: poet, city, and *patria* are conjoined in an absolute, symbolic unity which is proof against contingency. In short, one might say that "Borges invents a city that is made to measure, a Buenos Aires which he founds as myth."[29]

Borges's third collection all but abandons the project of reproducing phonetically the *criollo* "vernacular" of Buenos Aires, which was such a marked feature of *Moon Across the Way*. Standard Spanish is the norm in *San Martín Copybook*. Even a text with a theme as Argentine as "The Mythological Foundation of Buenos Aires" (written in 1926) employs few regionalisms, other than the occasional diminutive ("barqu*itos*," "estrel-l*ita*," "noche*cita*") and the odd spelling imitating colloquial phonetics (e.g. "*mitá*" [from *mitad*]).

To sum up, contrary to his avant-garde contemporaries, Borges adopts a nostalgic and old-fashioned tone to create poems that refer to the Buenos Aires of the last third of the nineteenth century, when the effects of modernity and the influence of the immigrant population were not yet much in evidence. His poetry exhibits two impulses in creative tension with each other: a strong *criollismo* and an incipient vanguardism; in other words, tradition and renovation. On the one hand, his perceptions and memories align him with the past, with a bygone Buenos Aires which he wants to turn into myth; on the other, his project also inclines partially toward "the new," toward the creation of what the manifestos of the ephemeral avant-garde magazines of the period repeatedly called a "new aesthetic." It is fair to say that Borges in this period wrote "under the impact of the movement of aesthetic renovation and of the modernization of the city: he produced a mythology with pre-modern elements but employing the aesthetic devices and theoretical ideas of the avant garde."[30]

By way of a provisional conclusion, I will cite the view of the Chilean writer Enrique Lihn, since it is a prime example of a certain trend in the critical reception of Borges, the poet. According to Lihn, the founders of modern Spanish American poetry are the Chileans Pablo Neruda and Vicente Huidobro, the Peruvian César Vallejo, and the Argentine Oliverio Girondo. As for Borges, Lihn delivered this scathing judgment:

> His conservatism in poetry amounts to a "revival," to the parading of outworn literary materials without revitalizing them by changing their function … His rhyming is uncommonly poor, a mere coincidence of identical sounds as opposed to proper semantic rhyme … Nor does Borges display much sense of polyvalent meaning: his writing is literal, grammatically correct and regular. And frankly, even if it doesn't tell stories, Borges's poetry often recycles the narrative and intellectual subject matter of his fiction and essays, but to less felicitous effect than in those two genres. In short, he strikes me as an antiquated poet who lacks the qualities that are essential to *the kind of poetry one would call modern*. (My emphasis)[31]

Certainly, Borges did not write the kind of poetry that Lihn would have accepted as "modern." But I would say that one must take literary history into account when evaluating a writer's work, and this requires that one consider the circumstances in which that work was produced. The bias evident in Lihn's assessment puts one in mind of Walt Whitman's famous reproach that Edgar Allan Poe had never written about American democracy, which was a subject, as Borges himself observed, that Poe had never set out to write about in the first place. The fact is that Borges's blurring of genres, which Lihn criticizes, is a distinctive trait of what critics have called "postmodernism," itself a modern kind of writing. And while it is true that Borges's rhyming (when it occurs) is generally monotonous, this is not due to a lack of creativity but to a conscious authorial decision, in line with the contemporary movement generally known as "colloquial poetry." In this respect, it is likely that these early poems of Borges would have been taken as a model by more than one budding poet of the period.

In conclusion, Borges wanted to create a distinctive and innovative style of poetry, in relation both to the contemporary writing of the 1920s and to that of an earlier generation, as is always the case in art. One must identify and understand the characteristics of a poet's style in order to form an appropriate evaluation of his artistic achievements. In the case of Borges's early poetry, his themes (particularly his perennial love of Buenos Aires) and his verbal innovations (from free verse to phonetic spelling) produced a fruitful new aesthetic. However, the multiple revisions of these early poems undertaken by Borges himself from the 1940s onward served to erase some of their original features.[32] In general, these changes were intended to suppress certain themes or formal traits which the author had come to repudiate in later life.

The most obvious example of this process was the "cleaning up" of his first three books of poetry, from which he removed avant-garde techniques and *criollo* elements (linguistic as well as thematic), including his efforts to render Buenos Aires speech in poetic form. Love also disappeared, since various texts not only expressed amorous feelings but were even dedicated in some cases to named women, notably Concepción Guerrero, who was his girlfriend for most of the period in which he wrote *Fervor de Buenos Aires*. Borges's revisions were not motivated solely by aesthetic considerations; the changes he introduced were designed to conceal the fact that these poems had been composed at a specific juncture in Argentine literature and culture, and their effect was to disguise the ideological and literary meaning of his early writing.

In the 1920s, the young Borges was in quest of a style, in both his poetry and his essays. His style of writing was apt to change from one book to the next, and sometimes even within the same book (for example, free verse could coexist with regular metrical forms and assonance). All in all, these "successive ruptures" contributed to the making of an exceptionally rich body of work for a writer who was still at the beginning of his literary career.[33]

NOTES

1   Given Borges's revisions of the original poems in later years, the three "books" of early poetry currently in print fail to convey the idiosyncratic character of the texts Borges actually wrote in the 1920s. Since the English translations in Penguin's *Selected Poems* are taken from these later revised versions, quotations in the main text have been translated into English by E.W., and the original Spanish texts given in the endnotes.

2   See Edwin Williamson, *Borges: A Life*, New York, Viking, 2004, chapter 5, 68–89.

3   J. L. Borges, "Ultraísmo," *Nosotros*, 151 (1921), 466–71.

4   "An Autobiographical Essay," in *The Aleph and Other Stories (1933–1969)*, London, Jonathan Cape, 1971, 225–26.

5   "A quien leyere" ("To Whomever May Read This") was the title of the original prologue to the first edition of *Fervor de Buenos Aires*, Buenos Aires, Imprenta Serantes, 1923, (FBA), which was published by Borges at his own expense. There was no pagination in this first edition.

6   Luis de Góngora was one of the great poets of the Spanish Baroque, famous for his Latinate syntax, and complex, sensuous imagery.

7   Guillermo de Torre, "Para la prehistoria ultraísta de Borges," in *Al pie de las letras*, Buenos Aires, Losada, 1967, 173.

8   See, "Después de las imágenes," *Inquisiciones*, [1925], Buenos Aires, Espasa Calpe/Seix Barral, 1993, 31.

9   "La ciudad está en mí como un poema que aún no he logrado detener en palabras" ("Vanilocuencia," *FBA*).

10   "Ruego al justo destino / aliste para ti toda la dicha / y que toda la inmortalidad sea contigo" ("Inscripción sepulcral," *FBA*).

11   Las calles de Buenos Aires
        ya son la entraña de mi alma.
        No las calles enérgicas
        molestadas de prisas y ajetreos,
        sino la dulce calle de arrabal
        enternecida de árboles y ocasos.
                    ("Las calles," *FBA*).

12   De propósito pues, he rechazado los vehementes reclamos de quienes en Buenos Aires no advierten sino lo extranjerizo: la vocinglera energía de algunas calles centrales y la universal chusma dolorosa que hay en los puertos, acontecimientos ambos que rubrican con inquietud inusitada la dejadez de una población criolla ("A quien leyere," *FBA*).

13   Anuncios luminosos tironeando el cansancio
        charras algarabías

entran a saco en la quietud del alma.
Colores impetuosos
escalan las atónitas fachadas

. . . . .

Yo atravieso las calles desalmado
por la insolencia de las luces falsas
("Ciudad," *FBA*)

14 En busca de la tarde
fui apurando en vano las calles

. . . . .

la tarde toda se había remansado en la plaza serena y sazonada

bienhechora y sutil como una lámpara.
("La plaza San Martín," *FBA*)

15 "La ciudad de *Fervor de Buenos Aires* no deja nunca de ser íntima; la de este volumen tiene algo de ostentoso y de público" (OC I 55).

16 Toda la santa noche he caminado
I su inquietud me deja
En esta calle que es cualquiera.
Aquí otra vez la eventualidá de la pampa en algún horizonte
I el terreno baldío que se deshace en yuyos y alambres
I el almacén tan claro como la luna nueva de ayer tarde.
("Calle con almacén rosao," *Luna de enfrente* [*LE*] 9).

17 Calle Serrano.
Vos ya no sos la misma de cuando el Centenario:
Antes eras más cielo y hoy sos puras fachadas.

. . . . . .

Ahora te prestigian
El barullo caliente de una confitería
I un aviso punzó como una injuria.
En la espalda movida de tus italianitas
No hay ni una trenza donde ahorcar la ternura
("A la calle Serrano," *LE* 27)

18 "I sólo a *vos* el corazón te ha sentido, calle dura y rosada" ("Calle con almacén rosao," *LE* 9–10). "And only you, tough, rose-colored street, have touched my heart."

19 "Acaso todos me dejaron para que *te* quisiese sólo a *vos*." ("La vuelta a Buenos Aires," *LE* 54). "Maybe they all left me so that I should love only you."

20 J. L. Borges, "Sobre pronunciación argentina," *Nosotros*, 227 (1928), 152.

21 Quoted in María Luisa Bastos, *Borges ante la crítica argentina, 1923–1960*, Buenos Aires, Hispamérica, 1974, 87.

22 "Ensalce todo verseador los aspectos que se avengan bien con su yo, que no otra cosa es la poesía. Yo he celebrado los que conmigo se avienen, los que en mí son intensidá. Son las tapias celestes del suburbio y las plazitas [*sic*] con su fuentada de cielo. Es mi enterizo caudal pobre: aquí te lo doy," (*LE* 7).

23 "Hoy no quisiera conversarte de técnica. La verdá es que no me interesa lo auditivo del verso y que me agradan todas las formas estróficas, siempre que no sean barulleras las rimas. Muchas composiciones de este libro hay habladas en criollo, no en gauchesco ni en arrabalero, sino en la heterogénea lengua vernácula de la charla porteña. Otras asumen ese intemporal, eterno español (ni de Castilla ni del Plata) que los diccionarios registran" (*LE* 7).

24 "An Autobiographical Essay," 250.

25 "Todos somos argentinos sin esfuerzo, porque no tenemos que disimular ninguna *pronunzia* exótica," in "Suplemento explicativo de nuestro «Manifiesto»," Revista *Martín Fierro*, 8–9 (1924), 2.

26 "¿Y fue por este río de sueñera y de barro / Que las proas vinieron a fundarme la patria?" (*Cuaderno San Martín* [*CSM*], 9).

27   Prendieron unos ranchos trémulos en la costa,
        Durmieron extrañados. Dicen que en el Riachuelo
        Pero son embelecos fraguados en la Boca.
        Fue una manzana entera y en mi barrio: en Palermo.
        Una manzana entera pero en mitá del campo
        Presenciada de auroras y lluvias y suestadas.
        La manzana pareja que persiste en mi barrio:
        Guatemala, Serrano, Paraguay, Gurruchaga (*CSM* 10).

28 "A mí se me hace cuento que empezó Buenos Aires: / La juzgo tan eterna como el agua y el aire," (*CSM* 11).

29 Jean Andreu, "Borges, escritor comprometido," *Texto Crítico*, 13 (1979), 59.

30 Beatriz Sarlo, *Una modernidad periférica: Buenos Aires, 1920 y 1930*, Buenos Aires, Nueva Visión, 1988, 103.

31 Pedro Lastra, *Conversaciones con Enrique Lihn*, Xalapa, Universidad Veracruzana, 1980, 88.

32 See Rafael Olea Franco, *El otro Borges, el primer Borges*, Mexico, El Colegio de México-Fondo de Cultura Argentina, 1993, and Antonio Cajero, *Estudio y edición crítica de "Fervor de Buenos Aires,"* Doctoral thesis, El Colegio de México, 2006.

33 Daniel Balderston, "Borges, las sucesivas rupturas," in *"In memoriam" Jorge Luis Borges*, ed. Rafael Olea Franco, Mexico, El Colegio de México, 2008, 19–36.

In memoriam Joan Marik.

15

JASON WILSON

The late poetry (1960–1985)

As a poet, Borges existed "in a kind of splendid isolation" after the 1950s.[1] His poetry was not at the forefront of taste or innovation. Few younger poets read him as an act of discovery or to commune with a master: Roberto Juarroz said that one could learn nothing from Borges; Guillermo Sucre deemed him marginal.[2] However, after reading *The Unending Rose*, his contemporary Pablo Neruda thought that he should be rescued as a poet.[3] Developing these insights, I argue that Borges's late poetry is read because it is by Borges and often self-referentially about Borges, thus seducing readers into searching for clues to the man. He projects such a complex literary persona in his devious fictions of the 1940s that his later poems, often grafted on a notion of sincerity, allow a critical reader immediate understanding. At the same time, Borges reread his favourite poets – often English, Anglo-Saxon, or Norse – and cared little for contemporary writing: "I'm a nineteenth-century writer … I don't think of myself as a contemporary of surrealism."[4]

After going blind, Borges conjured the words in his mind before dictating them aloud, much as blind John Milton did when he composed. He defined the poem as involuntary. The lines created in his head, and then recited, obeyed his craft and metrics, ensuring their survival in this elaboration imposed on him by blindness. A consequence of letting a poem "happen" is that the late collections collect whatever he dictated, without an underlying order. When he reached a certain number, he had them published. Formally, little changes from *The Maker* (1960), *The Self and the Other* (1964), *In Praise of Darkness* (1969), *The Gold of the Tigers* (1972), *The Unending Rose* (1975), through *The Iron Coin* (1976) to *The History of the Night* (1977), *The Limit* (1981), *Atlas* (1984), and *Los Conjurados* (*The Confederates*, 1985). In these ten books we have a homogeneous series of poems or musical variations composed by a poet when he was over sixty years old. He called *The Maker* a "miscellany" (*SP* 142); *The Self and the Other*, a "compilation" (*SP* 147). He even carried over poems from one collection to another to fill out the book, aware that the poems were circumstantial, sometimes monotonous, and repetitious. The last twenty-six years were prolific in comparison to the years between 1930 and 1958 when he penned only twenty-one new poems.

However, as Borges often asserted, a poem belongs equally to a reader. In a lecture on "Blindness," he noted that when we read a good poem we think that we too could have written it (*OC* III 281), an insight about reading intrinsic to the Borgesian revolution which postulated that the reader creates the text as much as the author. Yet contrary to such a subjective reading, he resonates in his readers not only because he is Borges, but because he writes in a lyrical way, in his own voice. In his later thinking about poetry he suspected that intonation and the poet's voice were essential, and not metaphors.[5] He long opposed Baroque attitudes, which put formal structures that generated surprise above expressing feeling. His voice speaks quietly and quirkily to us: Jaime Alazraki evoked a "music unheard before: an austere, poised, dignified, and quiet music."[6] A source of voice is Montaigne, chosen in a poem "To France" as one of his masters (*OC* III 194). Montaigne is explicit that "I desire therein to be delineated in mine own, genuine, simple and ordinary fashion, without contention, art or study; for it is myself I portray."[7] Montaigne shuns words and artifice: it is the subject that matters, not the words that evoke it; his style "is a natural, simple, and unaffected speech … so written as it is spoken." Close to Borges, he picks out valor, "not pedantical, nor friar-like, nor lawyer-like, but rather downright, soldier-like."[8] Here then, in Montaigne, Borges finds manly, soldier-like values and defines for himself an old man's poetics. A constant device in Borges's late poetry is the dramatic monologue where, following Browning, he impersonates another's voice in the poem.[9] Behind all his later verse, as Alazraki has shown, is a will to be intimate that undermines his more "impersonal" earlier poems; he avoids facile confession, Romantic intimacy, and existential egocentrism.[10]

In his late books Borges continues exploring the paradox of time, but less analytically, more with what I call the emotion of time. Most critics agree that Borges's obsessive allusions to Heraclitus's aphorism – "One cannot pass twice through the same river" – best capture this inexorable rushing of time. Old age forced a new emotion on to this awareness that nothing can stop time's flow. It is almost as if Borges had invented Heraclitus's succinct epigram, so well does it convey a lifetime of pondering the mystery and anguish of time. The oddest Heraclitean allusion – in which Borges typically hides behind an apocryphal Latin writer called Gaspar Camerarius – is titled in French "*Le regret d'Héraclite*." It reworks the sexual envy of his narrator "Borges," in his fiction "The Aleph," for Beatriz Viterbo. It reads: "I who have been so many men, have never been the One in whose embrace

Matilde Urbach swooned" (*SP* 141).[11] Here the poet mocks his own belief in the ability of the river of time to abolish his pain, his sense of betrayal, for some memories do not vanish, hence the "regret" of the title.

Yet, contrary to this sense of relentless time, the poem itself, echoing a vast poetic tradition (Homer, Dante, Quevedo, Milton, Browning, Verlaine, Lugones, Yeats, Frost, etc.), seems to halt time's torrent. At the least, this truce between the ephemeral now and time rushing past happens during the act of reading. So, fugitive time, the act of reading, a living tradition of poems, the poem itself, and art in general, become pressing topics that spread beyond a restricted literary life. Another cluster of topics, reminiscent of Wordsworth's "growth of a poet's mind" (the subtitle to his *Prelude*), emanates from blindness and aging, as both curse and blessing, and involves life and solitude, and also the reader. A third cluster of themes is the emotional resonances of place, valour, and *patria*. I will glance at a constant in all his work – the journey toward identity, and indirectly at the fame he attained from 1961 onward. Finally, surprisingly, late love lyrics emerge in *The History of the Night*.

But we begin with diction and voice. Juan José Saer broke down the famous Borgesian style into five elements: a colloquial tone, fixed lexical components, abrupt contrasts, his use of adjectives, and "incorrigible enumerative tendencies" (derived from Whitman, as Alazraki showed).[12] Saer's features do not separate prose from poetry. In fact, countless poets have been indebted to the prose. The Argentine poet Alberto Girri was struck by Borges's epigrammatic concision and strict syntax: "Borges's prose was absolutely decisive for me."[13] Girri does not mention the debt to English syntax, but in the epilogue to *The Maker* Borges notoriously confessed that nothing much had happened in his life except reading Schopenhauer and "the verbal music of England" (*SP* 143). Years later, talking about Shakespeare, he said that "the English language was then a secret miracle."[14] So essential is this English music that a perceptive critic observed that his "tone is English," and suggested that Thomas Gray's "Elegy Written in a Country Churchyard" shares an equivalent tone.[15] In the prologue to *The Unending Rose*, Borges claimed that compositionally he could not predict if a poem or a story would emerge after fixing the opening and closing lines (*SP* 343). Indeed, in the wake of *The Maker*, prose and poems are intermingled in all the late collections, so Saer's stylistic categories apply equally to poems.

Blindness and aging

In his "A Prayer for Old Age," W. B. Yeats saw decrepitude as wisdom and youth as passion and ignorance, and in "An Acre of Grass," he sought "an old man's frenzy," echoing Timon, Lear, and Blake with his "old man's eagle mind."[16] We look toward the old as fountains of insight. Images of bearded Merlins, gurus, biblical prophets, "elders," and old wise men (a Jungian archetype) haunt our culture. There is a peculiar freedom in old age. In the magnificent poem "In Praise of Darkness," Borges defines it as a kind of "bliss" ("dicha"), for "the animal has died or almost died" (*SP* 299). The poet can now face death beyond sexuality, fashion, and ambition.

How Borges's old man's poetry copes with this pressure to be "wise" and "free" will now be outlined. But as well as old age, we must add the theme of blindness as both a biographical and literary experience. Borges tended to appeal especially to Milton in his poems, and he turned to Milton because of the way the English poet had dealt with finding himself totally blind. Although there is much in Milton which is alien to Borges (he does not explore Milton's Latinate syntax or epic intentions, although the use of "blank verse" finds resonance), the main affinity was blindness. For Milton, blindness was not a sin or a calamity, but rather the chance to pierce "things merely of their colour and surface"; blindness forced both Milton and Borges to look inside, to contemplate what is real and permanent. Physical weakness led to moral strength, a Christian reversal evident in Borges too. Indeed, Milton thanked God for granting him an "inward and far surpassing light": he can "see and tell / of things invisible to mortal sight." Such is the calm acceptance of the "inward happiness" of blindness, but, as in Borges, there are shadow sides, especially in his last sonnet of 1658, about his second wife's death. Milton "saw" her in a dream: "But o as to embrace me she inclined / I waked, she fled, and day brought back my night." Not seeing his beloved because she was dead and he was blind, led to his cry of loss.[17] Borges's sonnet "A Rose and Milton," one of his own favorites, rescues Milton's unseen rose from oblivion and begs that it magically abandon its past in his lines. Both blind poets share this mental rose (*SP* 199).

"The Maker" (in the collection of that name), is a literary parable about the first poet, blind Homer. As he slowly lost the world of appearances on becoming blind, he shouted in despair at being forced to live on in his memories. But blindness had given him a future as a poet: "it was his fate to sing" (*CF* 293). Another crucial poem is "Poem of the Gifts," equating blindness with a gift. In 1955, as he was becoming blind, Borges was appointed Director of the National Library, a "splendid irony," for he can no longer see books but only dream them in "senseless paragraphs"; walls of books offer him hopelessness; he experiences a "vague and holy dread" as he feels the presence of a previous Director of the National Library, Paul Groussac, who was also blind. Which of the two is writing the poem? he asks, as he did in the prose piece "Borges and I." It does not matter, for the world is now "a pale uncertain ashy-gray / that feels like sleep, or else oblivion" (*SP* 97). The tone is not desperate, but accepting. In "Ronda" (*The Limit*), he evokes blindness as a "delicate penumbra" and acknowledges the blind man's enhanced senses of smell and hearing: "leisure of jasmine / and a gentle murmur of water that conjured up / memories of deserts" (OC III 291).

The poet offers wisdom from the tower of age and blindness. Nearly every poem concludes with some perception about place or identity or art. "The Unending Rose" plays on the possibility of imminent death through the surrogate figure of blind Attar, the Persian poet, contemplating a rose – "Which the Lord will finally show to my dead eyes" (*SP* 367). "Proteus" ends with "you, who are one and many men" (OC III 96), which encapsulates Borges's unique version of identity. Quite a few poems end with the word "nothing" ("nada"), with its suggestion of a Buddhist-like extinction of personality, and a vanishing of the self into literature, as in the poem "I Am": "I am echo, emptiness, nothing" (*SP* 357). Borges was preparing his death. "The Dream" ends with the poet "resigned and smiling" (*SP* 349), that smile of compassion for us reading mortals. In this he is akin to Milton, whose Samson moans, "O loss of sight, of thee I most complain! / Blind among enemies, O worse than chains, / Dungeon, or beggery, or decrepit age!"; but Milton's *Samson Agonistes* concludes with a coming-to-terms with destiny: "And calm of mind all passion spent."[18] In his essay on "Blindness," Borges sees a parallel with Milton, "who pulled through blindness and carried out his work," dictating "to casual people" (*Siete noches*, OC III 283). Here we have the privilege granted Borges of being "aged" and "blind," once freed from the body's animal passions.

At the same time, aging increased the poet's sense of wonder and his refusal to pretend or boast. In the prologue to *The Limit*, he reveals his self-awareness as a poet whose work lacks magical cadences, curious metaphors, long poems, and which fits in a tradition of "intellectual" poets headed by Emerson. This modesty is convincing for there is modesty in the choice of words themselves. Even the devices are limited to obvious meters (especially the hendecasyllable and the alexandrine), to the "protean" sonnet, to end rhymes, to enumeration (Borges loves lists), and overused anaphora. Such a verbal and rhythmical modesty lifts these poems out of fashion and history, and plunges them and us, the readers, into the "now" of reading outside time. In "Ars poetica," he declares that poetry is "immortal and poor" (*SP* 137).

But blindness also helps us respect the poet's suffering; blindness is a key, a freedom, a cry of self-pity. "La rosa profunda", which is the Spanish title of "The Unending Rose", suggests the peeling away of the appearances that sight establishes, and a return to the archetypal and universal that lies underneath: the Dantean *rosa mistica*; and the poet is aware of these strata of experience: "O endless rose, intimate, without limit" (*SP* 367).[19] There are countless references to blindness and patchy memory – everything fades, even books are shams of memory. Condensation and ellipsis are crucial devices – Borges shrinks writers to generic names like "the Greek," "the Persian," "the Saxon," and often impersonates Virgil, Shakespeare, Judas, or Browning, for in writing and reading there is no individuality, just tradition and associations. A reader can also expect Borges to continue to probe key themes: the tensions between the pen and the sword, the nature of dreams, nostalgic notions of *patria*, mirrors, tigers, elusive identity, labyrinths, love for books and reading, and, always, irreversible time.

Time

Nothing stops us dying. Dreaming, reading, creating art, idealist philosophy are but consolations for insatiable time. The poem "You Are Not the Others" ends with this reiteration: "Your matter is time, its unchecked and unreckoned / Passing. You are each solitary second" (*SP* 385). In "Adam Is Your Ashes" the poet yearns to be Heraclitean water, but a long solitary day leaves him "irrevocable and alone" (*SP* 411). Thus, there lies a paradox behind life and art. The epitome of poetic beauty, the rose, can also be a nightmare, an obscenity. In "The Panther" (*OC* III 84) the imprisoned animal can never grasp his reality, just as the poet himself can grasp nothing with thought and language. The panther is unaware of the varied world outside his cage; he is "blind," like Borges, and all is in vain. In *"The Thing I Am,"* Borges is just the shadow projected by his ancestors, a "prisoner in a house / full of books which have no letters" (*OC* III 196), to echo the panther self-image. No wonder Borges often appeals to "nothing," "never," oblivion, and nobody. "The Suicide," a grim poem mitigated only by its alliterative music, ends with what I call wisdom: "I bequeath nothingness to no one" (*SP* 353). Borges's poems deal with a Janus-like reality. Old age in these poems is partially a confession of defeat: "The Limit" ("La cifra") ends: "Take a good look [at the moon]. It could be the last" (*SP* 453). Nevertheless, a sense of impending death also brings an awareness that things must start again. As Borges declared in "Happiness," "Everything happens for the first time, but in a way that is eternal" (*SP* 435). This constant rediscovery of life by each person centers on love: "To live without love I think is impossible, happily impossible for each one of us" (*OC* III 284).

Wisdom, serenity, despair, and fear underpin Borges's late poems. "The Iron Coin" invokes the spinning of a coin, "a magic mirror," and reveals that its "reverse / Is no one, nothing, shadow, blindness. You are that" (*SP* 387). The topic of the double-sided coin is constantly reworked. In the bipartite "Poem," the "Obverse" section ends with the line: "The taste of grapes and honey," which clashes with the last line of the "Reverse" section: "It is to desecrate the waters of Lethe," and thus hints at the unavoidable reality of paradox (*SP* 443).

Borges's most notorious poem of the 1970s is the moving sonnet "Remorse," first published in the newspaper *La Nación*, soon after his mother's death. It deals personally with failure, art, guilt, and aging. The poet states bluntly, "I have not been / Happy" (*SP* 381). His parents gifted him birth and valor, but he let them down. He repeats the line about not attaining happiness, which he calls a "sin." Part of the cause of this failure has been his dedication to "the symmetrical challenges / Of art, which inter-weaves nothings" (my translation of "*entreteje naderías*"). He echoes this in "Baltasar Gracián," a poem on the Spanish Baroque writer: "A cold and overintricate nothingness – / that, for this Jesuit, was poetry" (*SP* 185). His "sin" was also cowardice, another insistent Borgesian theme: "They willed me bravery. I wasn't brave." The closing couplet recalls the Spanish title of Gérard de Nerval's famous poem, "*El Desdichado*": "It doesn't abandon me. Always at my side / the shadow of having been a wretched man" ("*No me abandona. Siempre está a mi lado / la sombra de haber sido un desdichado*"). Any reader of poetry will catch the allusion to the love-less archetype of Nerval's "*desdichado*," lamenting the cruel loss of a lover. Borges has evoked Nerval as a confession of an identical fate, but in the last line he stresses the word "always," setting this loss into a temporal frame which suggests a continuous mental torment. The poem appears so direct and free of cultural allusions that critical commentary does little to increase its emotional honesty.

The irruption of direct personal phrases characterizes the best of his late poems. In "Descartes," for example, we suddenly hear the old poet's aware-ness of death: "I feel a little cold, a little fear" (*OC* III 293); fear of dying is tackled by his valor – his last battle will be with death. As Paul Cheselka has observed, Borges began to write self-revealing, confessional poems that "expose raw feelings" in 1934, with two prose poems written in English but left unpublished until 1964, when they appeared under the titles "*Two English Poems*" in *The Self and the Other*.[20] The second poem ends thus: "I can give you my loneliness, my darkness, the hunger of my heart; I am trying to bribe you with uncertainty, with danger, with defeat" (*OC* II 239–40).

That same year he published another brace of poems under the title "1964," both of them sonnets, the second of which opens with the line "I will not be happy now. It may not matter," and which suggests the strange thrill of unhappiness: "All that remains is the pleasure of being sad" (*OC* II 298). The sonnet form itself asserts a long self-conscious tradition. Borges reread Shakespeare's sonnets continually, and these sonnets, he said, were intricate and obscure precisely because they were intimate; they were "confidential remarks that we will never end deciphering, but that we feel are immediate, necessary."[21] This definition is the key to the Borgesian sonnet, as epitomized in "Remorse."

Valor and *patria*

A theme that shines through the late work is the stress on valor and cowardice. The nostalgic elegies to his ancestors' bravery, his admiration for the thugs of Buenos Aires, and his constant shrinking of all these moments of bravery into the word "sword" are well known to critics and readers, and are repeated in the late poetry. In "To Johannes Brahms," he confesses: "I am a coward. I am a sad man" (*SP* 378).

The dialectic between the pen and the sword is linked to time passing and nostalgia for a vanished *patria*. In "Conjectural Poem" (1943), he assumes the voice of his heroic ancestor Francisco Laprida, finding his "destiny as a South American" through his murder by gauchos (*SP* 159). Another ancestor, Francisco Borges, also dies in battle "hardly touched by verse," as if action is purity and integrity and writing is failure and cowardice ("Allusion to the Death of Colonel Francisco Borges (1833–1874)," *OC* II 206). Borges's studying of Anglo-Saxon, Icelandic, and Norse texts is grounded on notions of bravery. The slipping of exotic male names into poems in Spanish invokes his admiration for primitive virility. The poem "Einar Tambarskelver" refers to a moment in Icelandic history, with the poet confessing: "I now translate it [the story] / so far from those seas and that spirit" (*OC* III 146). Temporal distance and an alien mindset leave the modern poet as a copier, a transcriber. "Elegy to the *Patria*" associates the past with valor: "Always bravery and always victory," while the present time is nothing but ashes and vestiges of "that ancient flame" (*OC* III 129). Borges has arrived too late to share this history: the *patria* is locked in the past. In the sonnet "Manuel Mujica Lainez," he reminds his friend: "We once had / A *patria* – do you remember? – and we lost it" (my translation, but see also *SP* 375). The sonnet "Hilario Ascasubi" locates happiness in the past, together with love and war and singing with gauchos. Ascasubi knew "the joy of a sword, " but the poet concludes: "Today we are night and nothing" (*OC* III 130). The poem "Buenos Aires, 1899," his birth year, alludes to his mythical city of cisterns, turtles, patios, swords, hallways, and vines, and culminates in "oblivion" and "elegy" (*OC* III 186). *Patria* has become a very private, local space.

Another of Borges's best-known poems reflects his thinking on the Malvinas/Falklands War of 1982. "Juan López and John Ward" is a prose poem which confronts both sides of Borges's identity as a patriot: the *criollo* and the Englishman, two sides of his literary persona meshing Buenos Aires and London, *Don Quixote* and Father Brown, Conrad and the Calle Viamonte. López and Ward could have been friends yet each embodied both Cain and Abel. Both died in this duel over land, buried under snow and corruption. This political poem, based on archetypes of conflict, ends with irony: "The deed I refer to happened in a time that we cannot understand" (*OC* III 496). That Borges adopted this view, contrary to countless patriots on both sides during the Falklands/Malvinas war, is another sign of his valor. The poem first appeared in the newspaper *Clarín* on August 26, 1982, and it was copied, photocopied, pasted on walls, and commented on all over the world.

Identity

The journey to the self is a great Borgesian pattern epitomized in the epilogue to *The Maker*, where Borges imagines a man spending his life drawing the world – with its bays, mountains, islands, fish – only to discover that he has drawn his own face (*SP* 143). "Borges and I," the last of the prose texts in *The Maker*, is grounded in a divided self – one is Borges the private man who meanders the streets of Buenos Aires, loves biographical dictionaries, Stevenson, and the taste of coffee; the other is the famous, public man, the vain actor. Their relationship is not hostile: one just lives, the other writes. But the real author of all literature is language itself or tradition. The private Borges does not recognize himself in the other's books. The short piece ends confusing the two Borgeses with the oblivion of passing time: "Thus my life is flight and I lose everything and everything belongs to oblivion or to the other one. I don't know which of the two writes this page" (my translation, but see *CF* 324). In 1978 Borges added a gloss to these two warring Borgeses: "It would be awful to think that I would go on being Borges. I am fed up with myself, my name, my fame and want to free myself of all this."[22] In the sonnet "On Waking" ("El despertar," *OC* II 272), he begs that death leave him without memory "of my name and all that I have been! / Ah, if on that morning there could be oblivion!"

Much of Borges's thinking in these poems hinges on the notion of an archetype, a deep sense of repeating a pattern or a gesture. The "ego" is illusory, and it screens the archetype where the "ego" is both the "other" and everybody, an insight that Borges based partially on the experience of reading and on the nature of language, which empties us of particularities. It is stating the obvious to tie Borges's notion of archetype to C. G. Jung's. For both, archetypes are emotional images that bond humans to basic, recurring experiences such as birth, death, love, the moon, the rose. Archetypes, for Jung, are buried in our brain, while for Borges they are literary and linguistic (a word is an archetype). He cites the concept in poems as an unarguable fact of experience. He would agree with Jung that "not even our thought can clearly grasp them [archetypes], for it never invented them."[23]

The crucial point is that archetypes undermine linear time. The poem "Sleep" (*OC* III 81) portrays the self as Proteus, as nobody, as past selves: repeats this formulated phrase: "I shall be all or nobody. I shall be that other / I am without knowing it." In "All Our Yesterdays" the poet mutates from a Genevan ["*ginebrino*"], to a "child" ["*niño*"], to a man who kissed a dead face: "I am those who are no longer. Uselessly / in the evening I am those forgotten people" (*OC* III 106). The present self is inevitably shallow, and aging adds to this loss. In "The Exile" ("El desterrado," *OC* III 107), the poet, through identificatory reading, becomes Ulysses, who explores Hell, sees Tiresias, and today, always impoverished, walks the streets of Buenos Aires, and could be happy, or not. It ends in a melancholic subjunctive mood: "What would I not give to be him." Age has separated the future from his multiple pasts. He is a nobody, unable to wield a sword. The poem "That Man" (*SP* 425) rehearses Borgesian identity: he is a "minor poet" who struggles to forget "personal history," a childless, sightless man.

Insomnia, another biographic constant in his work, reveals the horror of being. In "Two Forms of Insomnia," the poet is condemned to his body, to "a voice I detest," to "being and continuing to be" (*SP* 427). Borges wrote in "Dreams" (*OC* III 428) that he always dreamt of Buenos Aires; he dreamt of a narrow street in Palermo or in the Southside, and despite being blind (evoked as "a vague luminous mist") he saw, without surprise, the National Library on Calle México and knew that he was a *porteño*, a native of the city. The last poem of *Los Conjurados*, which lends its title to the collection, praises the Swiss Confederation, with its diverse languages, its claim to rationality, and names eminent Swiss like Amiel, Jung, and Paul Klee. As death approaches, Borges insists, perhaps without the emotion of his earlier patriotic poems, that "Geneva, the latest canton, is one of my *patrias*" (*OC* III 497). And indeed, he was buried there the following year, 1986.

In the poem "Fame," the aging poet lists what we as readers now know about Borges. The list is generated from the opening line by the verb "to have" ("*haber*") – "To have seen Buenos Aires grow, grow and decline" (*SP* 447) – and we revisit a patio, a vine, a hallway, a cistern, his knowledge of English, of Anglo-Saxon, German, and Latin; his chatting with "an old murderer," the pleasure of reading Macedonio Fernández "in his remembered voice," his not having left his library, his not daring to have been Don Quixote, his being a devotee of Conrad, and being an Argentine. We reach the last defining category: "To be blind." Then, we get the twist – all these features in the list are not random and have given the poet "a fame I have yet to understand" (*SP* 447). Ending on that unknowingness is more than ironic self-deprecation because it touches that deeper paradox of life which reason and language cannot explain but which feelings can – when a life shrinks to words it belongs to everybody. In the poem "Andrés Armoa," the poet describes a gaucho telling his tale of the long march from Junín to San Carlos, and shows how language splits – in a Borgesian way – from the facts of experience: "Maybe he tells it with the same words, because he knows it by heart and has forgotten the facts" (*OC* III 313). The wonderful opening poem of *Los Conjurados*, "Christ on the Cross," links the poet's experience of time and identity to Christ's, who could be anyone and who never saw what happened after his death. It closes: "Of what use is it to me that this man has suffered, / if I am suffering now?"(*SP* 465).

Old man's love

Just a glance at Borges's dedications and titles in the later poems – Susana Soca, Elvira de Alvear, Silvina Bullrich, Susana Bombal, and especially María Kodama – reveals his amorous endgames, tactfully narrated by Edwin Williamson.[24] In *The History of the Night*, a little love poem titled "Gunnar Thorgilsson (1816–1879)," with six general lines about the past, full of swords, empires, and Shakespeare, ends emphatically: "I want to recall that kiss, the kiss / You bestowed on me in Iceland" (*SP* 403). The word "that" stresses kissing and the thrill of Icelandic associations. Nought is worth remembering in history but *that* kiss. The poem is similar to Yeats's late poem "Politics," where *that* girl standing there mocks Roman, Russian, and Spanish politics, wars and alarms, and leads the poet to exclaim: "But O that I were young again / And held her in my arms!"[25]

Yeats's wish differs from Borges's old man's kiss. The poem "Hymn" ("Himno") includes a long list of historical events but ends denying the importance of history – just "because a woman has kissed you" (*OC* III 305). The love song, "A Man in Love" ("El enamorado"), establishes an anaphora of "I must pretend" (*"debo fingir"*) with mental illusions about the world, and closes with: "Only you are. You, my misfortune / and my fortune, inexhaustible and pure" (*OC* III 190).[26] The muse, beyond the senses and sex tortures, excites the poet, like any doubting lover. Age has not dimmed this uncertainty. How odd that Borges should echo the Spanish Romantic poet

Gustavo Adolfo Bécquer in his famous invocation to his muse: "Poetry …
is you!" ("*Poesía … ¡eres tú!*" *Rimas* XXI). In "Causes", Borges recites a
long list of events, objects, sensations, images, and legends, that ends with
the destiny of lovers: "All those things were required / So our hands could
meet" (*OC* III 199, but see also *SP* 409). "Waiting" ("La espera") describes
a lover's waiting for his beloved in tremulous anticipation – "In my chest,
the clock of blood measures / the fearful time of waiting" (*OC* III 192). And
Borges elaborates a conceit about what must happen in the universe before
the arrival of the woman he loves – a monk will dream of an anchor, a tiger
will die in Sumatra, and nine men will die in Borneo.

These adolescent-like experiences of love are mediated by the reality of
old age. In "The Mirror", the poet sees his soul "wounded by shadows
and by guilt" (*OC* III 193). "*Things That Might Have Been*" enumerates the things that he has lacked in his life, including "the son I never
had" (*OC* III 189). In "I Am Not Even Dust," a dramatic monologue voi-
cing Cervantes's old hidalgo of La Mancha, who wants to become Don
Quixote, he repeats "I do not want to be who I am" – an old man "in my
celibate, sad flesh" (*SP* 397). And in "G. A. Bürger," an old man evokes
once more the Heraclitean river of time: "He knew that the present is
nothing but / a fugitive particle of the past / and that we are made of
oblivion" (*OC* III 191). In a lecture on blindness, Borges cites lines from
Spain's "greatest" poet, Luis de León, in which old age is seen as living
alone, "free of love, of envy, / of hate, of hope, of suspicion," a view which
he qualifies by adding the already cited comment that to live without love
is "happily impossible" (*OC* III 284).

Borges had always been attracted by the possibility of happiness but had
been thwarted by life until old age (see his poem "Happiness," *SP* 435). In
1970, he wrote that "I no longer regard happiness as unattainable; once, long
ago, I did."[27] His late love poems reveal fragments of this love of a woman
as personal experiences, but without any confessional details. The "kissing"
removes it from Platonic or purely mental love, but it lacks the sensuality
of Rubén Darío's "ardent red kiss" ("*rojo beso ardiente*").[28] According to
Borges, Emily Dickinson's uniquely passionate and solitary life, where she
preferred to "dream love and maybe imagine it," offers a literary key to
grasp these late love poems.[29]

Conclusion

The old poet's poems are his own. There is no old poet's poetics, for each poet
is old in unique ways. Borges is not like the passionate elder W. B. Yeats, nor
like the aged Robert Graves; his old man's verse is classical, and his techniques

and metrics obvious and repetitive. There is nevertheless a delicacy and sincerity that invoke the themes he had already pondered in his complex fictions from the 1940s, but the later verse is linked to hearing, smell, and taste as compensations for becoming, like Milton's Samson, "eyeless in Gaza." Hearing is linked to the subtle music of his colloquial but not slangy diction; the smell, to the roses and jasmines that abound in his poems; and taste, to several references to drinking water. His "Poem of the Fourth Element" calls on water to "Remember Borges, your friend, who swam in you," and closes: "Be present to my lips in my last moment" (*SP* 165). This element – water – passing through one's throat hints at the omnipresent Heraclitean river that summarizes Borges's experience of time and refreshes the poet's voice, like a fountain, a source. In the poem "Someone" he listed the "modest alms" of everyday life, one being "the taste of water" (*SP* 225). This sensation of watery freshness is momentary, for it ends – like time and life.

We approach here the archetype of the old man, imparting wisdom about sensation and fugitive time. In "Góngora" (*OC* III 488), the Spanish seventeenth-century Baroque poet admits to being over-reliant on mythologies, on Virgil, on Latin, in poems that are arduous labyrinths, with metaphors replacing the world (pearls instead of tears). Góngora's self-criticism ends at the point Borges has reached in his last book: "I want to return to common things: / water, bread, a jug, some roses," a list of archetypal associations. The form this elementary poetics takes is found in the way the poems end: always with a summary, an intuition, an assertion. Like fables, these are close to becoming didactic, but are experiential and hard-won. They teach readers approaching the endgame of old age about the function of poetry. From that combination of blindness and longevity, Borges found consolation in Milton, a poetic rather than a philosophical consolation.

NOTES

1 Donald L. Shaw, *Spanish American Poetry after 1950: Beyond the Vanguard*, London and Rochester, NY, Tamesis, 2008, 44.
2 See Jorge Fondebrider, "El Borges poeta y los poetas," in "Borges 1899–1986. Veinte años después," *Ñ, Revista de Cultura, Clarín*, 141, 10 de junio 2006, 12–14, and Guillermo Sucre, *La máscara, la transparencia*, Caracas, Monte Avila Editores, 1975, 161.
3 Roberto Alifano, "Neruda y Borges. Una breve y secreta relación literaria," *Proa*, junio 1999, 25.
4 Willis Barnstone, *Borges at Eighty: Conversations*, Bloomington, Indiana University Press, 1982, 35.
5 J. L. Borges, *El círculo secreto. Prólogos y notas*. Edición al cuidado de Sara Luisa del Carril y Mercedes Rubio de Zocchi, Buenos Aires, Emecé, 2003, 236.

6   Jaime Alazraki, "Language as a musical organism: Borges' later poetry," in *Borges and the Kabbalah and other Essays on his Fiction and Poetry*, Cambridge University Press, 1988, 135.

7   *Essays of Montaigne*, selected and edited, with a Prefatory Note, by Percival Chubb, in John Florio's translation, London, Walter Scott, no date, xv. In 1957 Borges praised Montaigne as the progenitor of literature itself in "Montaigne, Walt Whitman," *Textos recobrados, 1956–1986*, Buenos Aires, Emecé, 2003, 37–40.

8   Montaigne, *Essays*, 65–68.

9   See Julie Jones, 'Borges and Browning: a Dramatic Monologue,' in Carlos Cortínez (ed.), *Borges the Poet*, Fayetteville, The University of Arkansas Press, 1986, 207–18.

10 Jaime Alazraki, "El difícil oficio de la intimidad," in Angel Flores (ed.), *Expliquémonos a Borges como poeta*, México, Siglo Veintiuno Editores, 1984, 145–48.

11 Juan Bonilla discovered that Borges had lifted the name of this woman from a novel by William Joyce Cowen which he had reviewed for *El Hogar* in 1938 (see *Textos cautivos*, OC IV, 392), but without citing her name. See http://es.oocities. com/juanbonillaweb/matilde.htm.

12 In *La Nación*, 11 de junio, 2006, 2. Jaime Alazraki placed Borgesian enumeration and Whitman in clear perspective in his "Enumerations as Evocations: On the Use of a Device in Borges' Latest Poetry," in Cortínez, *Borges the Poet*, 149–57.

13 Alberto Girri in *Plural*, 58 (July 1976), 51. Borges on Girri's complex poems, in *Textos recobrados, 1956–1986*, 353.

14 Borges, *El círculo secreto*, 168.

15 Howard Young, "Blindman with the Gift of Vision," *The Times Higher Education*, July 2, 1999, 24.

16 W. B. Yeats, *Collected Poems*, London, Macmillan, 1961, 326, 301, and 346–47.

17 John S. Diekhoff, *Milton on Himself*, New York, Oxford University Press, 1939, 101, 105 and 106.

18 John Milton, *Samson Agonistes*, in W. H. Auden and Norman Holmes Pearson (eds.), *Restoration and Augustan Poets*, Harmondsworth, Penguin, 1978, 85 and 134.

19 See Humberto Núñez-Faraco on the rose in *Borges and Dante. Echoes of a Literary Friendship*, Bern, Peter Lang, 2006, 166 ff.

20 Paul Cheselka, *The Poetry and Poems of Jorge Luis Borges*, Bern, Peter Lang, 1987, 126.

21 Borges, *El círculo secreto*, 186–87, my translation.

22 *Borges oral* (1979), OC IV, 175.

23 Frieda Fordham, *An Introduction to Jung's Psychology*, London, Penguin Books, 1953, 28.

24 See Edwin Williamson, *Borges: A Life*, New York, Viking, 2004, 416–92.

25 Yeats, *Collected Poems*, 392.

26 Williamson, *Borges: A Life*, 424, relates this poem to Borges's secretive love for María Kodama.

27 "An Autobiographical Essay," in *The Aleph and Other Stories 1933–1969*, ed. and trans. Norman Thomas di Giovanni in collaboration with the author, New York, E. P. Dutton, 1970, 260.

28 Rubén Darío, "*Ite Missa Est*," in *Antología poética*, Madrid, EDAF, 1979, 57.

29 Borges, *El círculo secreto*, 264.

16

EDWIN WILLIAMSON

Borges in context
The autobiographical dimension

Borges's work poses the challenge of exploring the complex relations between text and context. He is widely perceived to be a somewhat frigid writer concerned exclusively with things of the mind, but this does not accord with his own view. In the 1960s he observed: "There is emotion in my stories. It isn't possible to write without emotion."[1] And even after he became world famous, he would point out:

> I have felt my stories so deeply that I have told them, well, using strange symbols so that people might not find out that they were all more or less autobiographical. The stories were about myself, my personal experiences.[2]

This explanation was rooted in an abiding conception of the nature and purpose of writing. In "A Profession of Literary Faith" (1926), he had written that "all literature, in the end, is autobiographical"; the autobiographical substance might at times be rendered invisible by the "accidents" that embodied it, but it subsisted all the same "like a heart beating in the depth" (my translation, but see also *SNF* 23, 25).

How, then, does one reconcile the Borges who is acclaimed for his cerebral fictions with the "autobiographical" author who wrote with "emotion" about his personal experiences? It hardly needs pointing out that the myriad inventions and subtleties of a literary text cannot simply be reduced to context, nor should one diminish the intrinsic importance of philosophical ideas for Borges. Nevertheless, context is also important in as much as it can reveal new dimensions of the work and enrich our understanding of the writer's values and concerns. Too little attention has been given to the evolution of Borges's writing; there are continuities certainly, but also crucial differences between his youth and his middle or late years: the Borges of 1926, for instance, was radically different from the Borges of 1946 or 1976. By contextualizing the work in chronological perspective we may discern the contours of experience that stimulated and gave shape to his ideas and practice.

Jorge Luis Borges was born in Buenos Aires in 1899 into a middle-class family. His mother was of *criollo* stock – native-born Argentines of Spanish descent – and her family enjoyed a certain patrician status thanks to their ancestor Colonel Isidoro Suárez, who had been praised by Simón Bolívar for turning the tide of battle at Junín, the second-last engagement in the Wars of Independence against Spain. On his father's side, too, there had been warriors: the paternal grandfather, Colonel Francisco Borges, had distinguished himself in frontier wars against the Indians of the pampas, but this side of the family was more modest: Borges's grandmother was an English immigrant who would bring up her two infant sons in straitened circumstances after her husband's early death in battle. Young "Georgie" was raised in Palermo, a working-class barrio bordering the pampas, once notorious for its knife-fighters but then becoming gentrified. He was tutored at home by his English grandmother and an English governess until he was about eleven, so he grew up speaking and reading English as well as Spanish, his mother tongue.

His parents were poles apart in character and values. Leonor Acevedo, a strict Catholic, was an intelligent, domineering woman, who instilled in her children a fierce pride in their lineage of heroic warriors and nation-builders. She was to live with Borges, almost without interruption, until her death at the age of ninety-nine. In contrast, his father, Dr. Jorge Guillermo Borges, was a reluctant lawyer by profession, a free-thinking anarchist, and a compulsive philanderer, who tried and failed repeatedly to become a writer. "Georgie" became an omnivorous reader in his father's library of mostly English books, where he would spend hours devouring tales of adventure and intrigue. The enchantment of poetry was revealed to him while listening to Dr. Borges and his friends reciting at the family house. He was especially taken with the "cult of courage" celebrated by the anarchist poet Evaristo Carriego in poems extolling the bravery of gaucho outlaws and the knife-fighters (*cuchilleros*) of Palermo.

The contrary influences of his parents were to provide Borges with a store of material for his writing. From his mother's obsession with her ancestors he developed his fascination with the epic figure of the warrior. Carriego's "cult of courage" gave him a repertoire of gauchos, *cuchilleros*, duels, and daggers. This produced a notable opposition in his work between, as it were, the sword of honor, deriving from his mother's imposing rectitude, and the illicit dagger, associated with his bohemian and womanizing father. Even so, there was a hidden connection between sword and dagger, and it lay in the matter of destiny, for the man of action, the hero, whether illustrious soldier or lowly bandit, is capable of clinching in combat a defining moment of true being. Thus, in "A Page to Commemorate Colonel Suárez, Victor at Junín," he wrote: "What do they matter now … / the pointless days … / when he had at least his burning hour on horseback / on the plateau of Junín …? / What is time's monotony to him, who knew / that fulfilment, that ecstasy, that afternoon?" (*SP* 169). This idea is more fully articulated in "A Biography of Tadeo Isidoro Cruz (1829–1874)," a story about a renegade gaucho, which has for an epigraph a quotation from W. B. Yeats's "The Winding Stair": "I am looking for the face I had / Before the world was made," lines that are glossed in the story thus:

> (In the future, secretly awaiting him, was one lucid, fundamental night – the night when he was finally to see his own face, the night when he was finally to hear his own name. Once fully understood, that night encompasses his entire story – or rather one incident, one action on that night does, for actions are the symbol of our selves.) Any life however long and complicated it may be, actually consists of *a single moment* – the moment when a man knows forever more who he is. (*CF* 213)

If the figure of the hero was so compelling it was because it seemed to provide the key to self-fulfillment – the revelation of who you really were. The opposite of the hero was the coward, the nonentity, drifting on a treacherous sea of solipsism, of "unreality," plagued by doubts and ambivalence. Hence Borges's horror of repetition – of mirrors, doubles, fakes, and copies. This opposition between hero and coward brings us to Borges's fundamen- tal preoccupation – the debate between self and non-self. His father played a crucial role in creating this dialectic: "From the time I was a boy, it was tacitly understood that I had to fulfil the literary destiny that circumstances had denied my father. This was something that was taken for granted … I was expected to be a writer."[3]

The quest to discover a "literary destiny" provides the thread that runs through Borges's writing and gives it an underlying unity and coherence. It also led to a particular conception of the ultimate purpose of writing. Borges knew he was no hero, "As most of my people had been soldiers … and I knew I would never be, I felt ashamed, quite early, to be a bookish kind of person and not a man of action."[4] For all the thrills of reading, books afforded a second-hand picture of the world, a kind of "unreality." In fact, the library is often a negative trope for Borges, a dystopian symbol of solipsism: the whole point was to get out of the library and plunge into a direct, authentic experience of the world. And so, if he was to discover a literary destiny, writing would have to become a form of action, the pen must become a surrogate for the sword or the dagger: like the hero, the writer must engage with the Real in order to capture something essential and vital in his work.

Borges's career may be divided into three broad phases: the period of his youth, when he pursued an ideal of the author as hero; the middle years, which correspond to a notion of the author as reader; and the late period, when he gradually came to conceive of the author as a "weaver of dreams."

The young Borges (1914–1930): the author as hero

In 1914 Borges's father took the family to Europe, where they were surprised by the outbreak of the First World War and took refuge in neutral Geneva for the duration. It was in Geneva that Borges had his beginnings as a writer. He came across the German expressionist poets, and through them, Walt Whitman, whom he idolized because he felt his writing was so expansive and alive. He also discovered love. Shy though he was, he managed to get himself a sweetheart. An early prose poem tries to emulate Whitman's impassioned tone in a fantasy about making love to his girlfriend:

> Oh Beloved, our kisses will light up the Night! (Oh Adamic phallus!). Throw open the Windows, for I want to invite the Universe to my Nuptials: I want the Air and the Sea and the Waters and the Trees, to enjoy your astral flesh, to partake of the febrile, brief feast of your beauty and my strength.[5]

Here we encounter two abiding themes: first, the romantic aspiration to experience the Real or the Absolute, an essential union of self and world in a rapturous whole, and secondly, the lover as the muse who will inspire him to "create life" through his writing:

> Kiss me. Kiss me. All my doubts have already been extinguished. Already my woes have died, and with you by my side I feel strong as a God. I am a God. I can create life.

Love, then, is the key to original creation, for it empowers the artist to become a creator-god. However, not long after falling in love, young Georgie was to have his first actual experience of sex, when it occurred to his father to have him initiated by a prostitute, a traumatic experience that caused a nervous breakdown and contributed to lifelong difficulties with women.

When the war was over, the family went to Spain, where Borges joined a group of young avant-garde poets known as "the Ultra," and wrote some of their manifestos. Originality was the overriding aim: each poet must strive to be different from all the others. He believed a poem should not be a "passive mirror" of reality, it must refract experience through the "active prism" of feeling and imagination in order to rise above contingent circumstances and "convey naked emotion."[6] On his return to Buenos Aires in 1921, he formed a group of *ultraístas* and led a rebellion against the conservative literary establishment. However, the assertive individualism of his *ultraísta* poetics was gradually undermined by his sense of alienation from his native city after his long absence in Europe, and this alienation began to sow doubts about selfhood. He began to doubt the existence of an objective reality, and in "The Nothingness of Personality," he repeated the phrase "The self does not exist" and observed:

> The thought came over me that never would *one full and absolute moment,* containing all the others, justify my life, that all of my instants would be provisional phases ... and that outside of the episodic, the present, the circumstantial, we were nobody. (*SNF* 6, my italics)

Nevertheless, this radical skepticism would itself be called into question after he fell in love with Concepción Guerrero. Love acted as an antidote to solipsism. In "Year's End," for instance, as 1922 turned into 1923, he marveled at "the miracle / that, though the chances are infinite, / allows something in us to endure / never moving" (*SP* 19). Many poems of his first book, *Fervor de Buenos Aires,* show how Concepción enabled him to recover a sense of belonging in his native city. Love, then, has a distinct philosophical value for Borges: it gives definition to the self by connecting it to another, and through the lover, to an external, objective reality.

In 1923, he accompanied his family on a year-long visit to Europe, which rather strained his relations with Concepción. He continued to see her for several months after his return but he was becoming fascinated by a girl called Norah Lange, who was Argentine-born of Norwegian descent. She was also a budding poet, tall, fair-skinned, and slim – and widely admired for her striking mane of red hair. Borges adopted her as his protégée and would see her first book into print, heaping praise on her in the prologue – she was "'illustrious for the double brilliance of her hair and her haughty youth," she was "light and haughty and passionate like a banner unfolding in the breeze."[7]

While in Europe, he had conceived of a new project, having become jaded with *ultraísmo,* which he thought was too obsessed with metaphor. He now urged the young poets of Argentina to write poems that had "the flavour of the *patria,*" and in 1925 announced plans to write a "history in verse of Argentina."[8] However, he made little headway due to his difficulties with Concepción, which produced troubled poems that were collected in *Moon Across the Way* (1925). It was after he finally broke up with Concepción that he returned to this project, but thanks to his growing emotional involvement with Norah Lange, his creative aspirations became correspondingly ambitious – he now resolved to fashion a poetic myth for Buenos Aires. But first he needed a unifying principle, of the kind which in the new mathematics, he wrote, was represented by the sign of the "Alef" [*sic*], "the infinite number which encompasses the others."[9]

His new muse would inspire him to find the "Alef" he needed for the new project of mythologizing Buenos Aires. Norah Lange's house on the Calle

Tronador was in the barrio of Villa Urquiza in the far north-west of the city, and these outlying suburbs were known as the *orillas* or "shores" of Buenos Aires, because they bordered the open plains or pampas. The *orillas* provided the unifying idea Borges needed because, unlike the cosmopolitan streets of the city center, they were permeated still by the influence of the pampas and therefore represented a continuity between the rural past of the *criollos* and the present-day realities of the city, with its indiscriminate melting-pot of *criollos* and immigrants. The *cuchillero* of the *orillas* was a kind of urban gaucho, and so the heir to the knife-fighting tradition of the pampas, while the blend of foreign and native musical traditions had already produced the primitive tango. The *orillas* thus mediated the traditional and the modern, the native and the foreign, and in this mediation Borges saw the possibility of creating a new Argentine identity, centered on Buenos Aires. With this aim in mind, he conceived the idea of an "epic" – a "novel" in either prose or verse – which would provide a new "mythological foundation" of Buenos Aires; it would draw on the popular culture of the great metropolis – the legends, anecdotes, songs, and sayings of the common people – and sum up in a symbolic way the essential character of the great city.[10]

Why an epic? Borges was opposing conservative nationalists who feared that mass immigration would swamp the culture of the native-born Argentines. The leading poet Leopoldo Lugones had argued that the celebrated verse-narrative, *The Gaucho Martín Fierro* (1872, 1879) by José Hernández should be regarded as the national epic because it expressed the essential spirit and character of the *criollos*. However, this insistence on the cultural supremacy of the *criollos* – with the gaucho and the pampas as the true symbols of Argentine identity – was nostalgic and inherently reactionary. The fact was that millions of immigrants had settled in the country, and Buenos Aires, not the pampas, had become the dynamic center of Argentine life. Borges wanted to create a new epic which would make Buenos Aires the symbolic locus of Argentina, just as the *Martín Fierro* had made the pampas the representative landscape of the nation when it was predominantly rural. This was a new kind of cultural nationalism, a forward-looking urban *criollismo*. Borges urged the *criollos* to forget their pride in their honorable lineage and become "confederates" (*conjurados*) with the immigrants in order to create what he termed a "new man," a new kind of Argentine, in a tolerant, hospitable country where people "from various nations of the world" might find a home.[11]

Borges had now found himself a role as a nation-builder: his forebears may have helped to build the *patria* as soldiers and politicians, but he would become a comparable hero with his pen. So grand was his ambition that he aspired to be, not simply an author-hero, but a kind of author-god, capable of bringing a whole cultural world into existence. In "The Extent of My Hope" ("El tamaño de mi esperanza," 1926), he issued a rallying call to young writers and artists, inviting them to become creator-gods and "incarnate" a new culture, no less:

> More than a city, Buenos Aires is a country, and we must find for it the poetry, the music, the painting, the religion, and the metaphysics appropriate to its grandeur. This is the full extent of my hope, which invites all of us to be gods and to work toward its incarnation.[12]

By the middle of 1926, Borges's *criollismo* was fully formed – it was an ambitious, comprehensive vision of the poet's role in shaping a new identity and culture for his people.

The year 1926 was indeed an *annus mirabilis*. Norah Lange had joined his group of *ultraístas*, and the Lange family villa on Calle Tronador became the inner sanctum of Borges's circle. Every Saturday they would meet there to discuss and recite their work, and then they danced to tangos played on the piano. Being in love with Norah confirmed his sense of self once more. When we are happy, he argued in "Writing Happiness," we cannot imagine "the negation of all consciousness, of all sensation, of all differentiation in time or space," since happiness entails "the satisfaction of the will, not its loss."[13]

His feelings for Norah, his fellow-poet, impelled him to elaborate an extreme confessional poetics. In "A Profession of Literary Faith" (1926), he likened the transaction between an author and a reader to "a confidence," based on "the trust of the listener and the veracity of the speaker" (my translation). "Everything is poetic that confesses, that gives us a glimpse of a destiny" (*SNF* 23); and so, "all poetry is the confession of an I, a personality, a human adventure" (*SNF* 26) and, correspondingly, readers had "a craving for souls, destinies, idiosyncrasies," and if fictional lives did not suffice, they would lovingly probe the life of the author (*SNF* 24).

Nevertheless, he recognized an intrinsic problem in this romantic-expressionist poetics: "How can we interject into the heart of others our humiliating truth?" (*SNF* 26). The difficulty lay in the fact that the poet's very medium was an obstacle to sincerity – verse, rhyme, metaphor, language itself, tended to obscure rather than lay bare genuine feeling. His solution was that "words must be conquered, lived" (*SNF* 26): language, though generic and impersonal, must be imbued with the writer's experience of the world so that the work should bear the stamp of its maker's personality. This distinctive configuration of meaning would rescue the author from the "nothingness of personality," for it amounted to the shaping of a unique personal destiny:

> I have now conquered my poverty, recognizing among thousands the nine or ten words that get along with my soul; I have already written more than one

book in order to write, perhaps, one page. The page that justifies me, that *sum-marizes my destiny*, the one that perhaps only the attendant angels will hear when Judgement Day arrives. (*SNF* 27, my italics)

This hope of justification, of salvation by writing, would remain with him to the end, for just as the hero might discover who he really was in a supreme moment of destiny, so too might an author "summarize" his destiny in a self-defining work that would rescue him from the void of the non-self. He now invoked the "Aleph" once more, but in a more exalted vein than before. The Aleph, he wrote in "A History of Angels" (1926), was the Hebrew letter used by the Kabbalists to denote the chief of the ten emanations of God: it was "the brain, the First Commandment, the sky of fire, the divine name 'I Am Who Am'" (*SNF* 17–18). The Aleph would come to symbolize a sense of the Absolute, in which the individual self could perceive its true place within the total reality of God's universe.

But then, suddenly, in November 1926, Norah Lange fell head over heels in love with another man – the poet Oliverio Girondo, Borges's most hated rival in the Buenos Aires avant-garde. For over two years Norah would oscillate between the two rivals, creating a love-triangle which brought great anguish to all three.[14] Borges was devastated by the desertion of his muse, and his idea of the author-hero (let alone the author-god) began to disintegrate. He questioned the belief that poetry entailed a full confession of the self based on the trust of the listener and the veracity of the speaker. Already in "A Profession of Literary Faith," he had realized that language itself could be a barrier to direct communication with the reader, but he had asserted that intensity of feeling and experience would enable the poet to "conquer" the impersonality of language and make words his own. That optimism evaporated now. In an essay titled "An Investigation of the Word" (1927), he observed that language possessed a "hemisphere of lies and shadows" which betrayed one's expressive intent; linguistic meaning was "fickle and contingent," so that the sense of a sentence could differ according to the reader; and yet, there was no choice but to submit "to syntax, to its treacherous concatenation, to imprecision, to the maybes, to the excessive emphases, to the buts"; this inherent opacity of language he called "the general tragedy of all writing" (*SNF* 39, but my translation here).

As he waited for Norah to choose between him and Oliverio Girondo, his future as a writer hung in the balance. He wrote that "For love unsatisfied the world is a mystery, a mystery that satisfied love appears to understand."[15] Love, indeed, held the key to his literary destiny, for if language itself prevented the poet from communicating his feelings to the reader, if he could not "conquer" words in order to mesh them with his heart, what would be the point of writing? He railed against the infidelity of words: it

Devil

was the Devil – "that mocking serpent, that inventor of equivocation and adventure, that core of the fruits of chance, that eclipse of an angel" – who had baptized the things of this world (my translation).[16]

When Norah Lange finally rejected him around February 1929, he abandoned forever the project of writing an epic of Buenos Aires. His poetic output had declined markedly anyway – there were forty-six poems in *Fervor de Buenos Aires* but only twelve in his third collection, *San Martín Copybook* (1929), of which six were concerned with death. In June, in a postscript to "The Duration of Hell" (1929), he wrote of a dream in which he found himself in a strange room: "I thought fearfully, 'Where am I?' and I realized I didn't know. I thought, 'Who am I?' and I couldn't recognize myself … Then I really woke up, trembling" (*SNF* 51). Gone were the ties that bound him to a familiar world, gone the dream of the realized self; the promise of the Aleph had vanished, and Hell was a room in the middle of nowhere in which you had lost all sense of who you were.

The middle years (1930–1964): the author as reader

The 1930s were a bleak period for Borges. He was racked by insomnia, nightmares, depression, and even thoughts of suicide. Over the next two decades, he would scarcely write any poetry at all. Instead, he turned to fiction in order to find a way of coming to terms with the "general tragedy of all writing" – how to write from within the prison-house of language but without draining writing of purpose altogether.

In 1932 he published two essays which are key to understanding the evolution of his literary ideas. In "Narrative Art and Magic" he questioned the premises of the psychological novel, which "attempts to frame an intricate chain of motives similar to those of real life" (*SNF* 80). Fiction did not depend on the illusion of reality, but was an "autonomous sphere" ("*un orbe autónomo*") fashioned by the author from the "overwhelming disorder of the real world" (*SNF* 81). The way narrative worked was akin to sympathetic magic, where, for example, sticking pins in a wax effigy was believed to harm an enemy. Any narrative – including film – was based on a comparable "teleology": its causality functioned as "a rigorous scheme of attentions, echoes, and affinities." What mattered ultimately was an author's success in generating "poetic faith" in the reader.

In "The Postulation of Reality" he restated his belief that all art is essentially expressive. Nevertheless, he distinguished between the "romantic" writer, who "wishes incessantly to express himself," and the "classical" writer, who "is not really expressive: he does no more than record a reality, he does not represent one." The facts we are given in a "classical" story may

1932

well be laden with the author's experiences, but these can only be inferred from the story and are not contained within it: "The author presents us with a play of symbols, no doubt rigorously organized, but whose eventual animation is up to us" (*SNF* 60).

As in his earlier *ultraísta* theory of the poem as an "active prism," fiction creates an "autonomous sphere" in which experience is refracted through the feeling and imagination of the author. In other words, fiction retains an expressive function as far as the author is concerned. What Borges discarded was the idea of communication with the reader. In 1926 he had described writing as a "confidence" based on the trust of the listener and the veracity of the speaker, but now he was proposing an aesthetics of radical mistrust, in which the author disguises the primary experience and disappears behind the text, leaving the reader to create meaning for himself. The text thus becomes a screen between author and reader. Writing is still a crystallization of the author's response to the world, and thus potentially a form of self-realization, while the reader, for his part, can relish the pleasure of the ambiguous, polysemic, and "un-authoritative" text.

Borges had effectively formulated the ideas that would underpin his *ficciones*, but it would take him another seven years to realize them in practice. Between 1932 and 1939 he embarked on a number of experiments, of which the main extant examples are those collected in *A Universal History of Iniquity* (1935) – fictionalized biographical sketches of notorious rogues, plus a few pseudo-Oriental tales. It was a complex personal crisis that finally spurred him to make the breakthrough that resulted in "Pierre Menard, Author of the *Quixote*," the fiction that inaugurated the second phase in his development.

In 1938, after his father had become terminally ill, Borges got his first full-time job as an assistant in a municipal library, earning a pittance. He felt an acute sense of humiliation and failure, made even worse by a curious request from his dying father. Dr. Borges had managed to publish a few poems and only one novel, *The Caudillo* (1921), but he could not resign himself to literary failure: he asked his son to rewrite *The Caudillo* "in a straightforward way, with all the fine writing and purple patches left out," and the two of them would discuss ways of improving the work.[17] Father's request brought the question of "literary destiny" to a head, for how could the son save his father from failure when he had himself been mired in failure for the past ten years? In any case, rewriting his father's novel would nullify the creative personality of each writer and would effectively destroy the idea of original authorship.

Dr. Borges died in February 1938, and in the following months, his son would work up an idea for a story about the implications of rewriting somebody else's work. "Pierre Menard, Author of the *Quixote*" is a review of the works of the eponymous French writer whose most ambitious project was the rewriting of Cervantes's great novel. It was not a question of copying the work but of "repeating" it – making it coincide word for word and line by line with the Spaniard's text. However, it turns out that when Menard recreates from scratch the words of *Don Quixote* in the twentieth century (he only managed two short passages), they take on a very different meaning from Cervantes's. The result of Menard's enterprise, then, is to dissolve the concept of the author as the sole origin of meaning and, furthermore, to suggest that it is the reader who effectively invents the meaning of a text as he reads. Menard's rewriting of the *Quixote* is an attempt to subvert the status of Cervantes as the unique, original author of the great classic, by confusing the two roles, turning the author into a reader and the reader into a kind of author.

In "Pierre Menard," Borges presents a conception of writing which is radically new, indeed revolutionary, and which seems to anticipate by some twenty years certain ideas developed by French theorists. Like Michel Foucault, Menard questions the existence of an objective historical reality and suggests that the reader constructs the so-called truths of history; like Julia Kristeva, Menard wants to show that a text is not an original piece of writing but a web of "intertextual" relations; and like Jacques Derrida, Menard denies the possibility of discovering the "presence" of an author in a literary text. Above all, the story heralds what Roland Barthes would famously call the "Death of the Author" – Menard's project undermines the idea that a text communicates a message from what Barthes called the "Author-God."[18] Barthes replaced the author by an impersonal agent – language or writing – which, he argued, destroys authorial voice, origin, and personality. Every reader, therefore, is a kind of Pierre Menard who repeats the words of the text as he reads and changes their meaning as he adjusts them to his own subjectivity.

Roland Barthes may have celebrated the liberation of the reader from the tyranny of the Author-God, but in Borges's case, the "death of the author" was certainly no cause for joy, for in "Pierre Menard, Author of the *Quixote*" he had willfully destroyed the most cherished ideal of his youth – salvation by writing. A bitter, self-mocking irony pervades his story, for if Menard's rewriting of Cervantes's work had succeeded, if time changed the meaning of words, then it would be impossible for an author to capture his unique destiny with his pen: a literary text would have no particular connection with the author's experience or emotion, and would indeed be no more original than the work of a scribe "repeating" a pre-existing text.

Still, with "Pierre Menard" Borges had found a way of relating "the general tragedy of all writing" to anxieties about selfhood and destiny, and from this he would generate his great themes – solipsism, the limitations of language and rationality, the elusiveness of the Real, the evanescence of the self, the mystery of time, the horror of infinity, and the yearning for a moment that would raise one beyond time's relentless flow. "Pierre Menard" was followed by fables reminiscent of Kafka, such as "The Library of Babel," "The Lottery in Babylon," or "The Circular Ruins," but he would strike out on his own, experimenting with a range of formats in order to deploy philosophical ideas in narrative, and often blurring the boundaries between different genres. Thus, "Tlön, Uqbar, Orbis Tertius" is a blend of mystery story and science fiction in which a group of conspirators invent a planet whose inhabitants have no sense of objective reality. "The Garden of Forking Paths" negates the purposive thrust of a thriller by ramifying time into an infinite labyrinth in which roles become interchangeable and all the characters might end up as one and the same.

Nowhere is the "general tragedy of all writing" – the disconnection of the author from his reader – more strikingly realized than in "Death and the Compass," which brings together fantasy, pseudo-theology, and metaphysics within the framework of a detective story. The murder of a Jewish scholar of the Kabbalah is being investigated by Erik Lönnrot, whose hubris impels him to seek the killer by a process of pure reason. In fact, he is being manipulated by a Jewish criminal called Scharlach, who encourages Lönnrot (implicitly a Christian) to elaborate a hypothesis based on Kabbalistic ideas regarding the secret "name" of God. The plot turns on a treacherous dialectic between the numbers 3 and 4, associated respectively with the Trinity (the Christian "name" for God) and the Tetragrammaton (the Jewish alternative). Moreover, there are allusions to pogroms, and indeed the action itself mimics a pogrom as the Christian detective hunts down the Jewish criminal. However, when Lönnrot arrives at the precise spot where he calculates the fourth murder will take place, he finds himself in a villa called Triste-le-Roy, where he is shot dead by Scharlach.

Among other things, this multilayered fantasy allegorizes Borges's new-found aesthetics of mistrust, as expounded in "The Postulation of Reality." Lönnrot (the reader) is tempted to find meaning (i.e. the solution to the mystery) by interpreting clues laid by Scharlach (the hidden author), but when he expects to get at the truth he discovers that he is to become the fourth victim of Scharlach, the author of the other crimes. And yet, there are clues which suggest that when the criminal shoots the detective, he is killing a mirror image of himself. The "tragedy of all writing" is enacted here – the prison-house of language may prevent the author from communicating with his reader, but this, in turn, deprives the reader of interpretative certainty, so meaning becomes treacherous and unreachable. Author and reader are thus divided by – yet also mirrored in – their respective solipsism, and the only place they can meet is in the negative utopia of Triste-le-Roy, where they finally cancel each other out. Thus the story may be read as an allegory of the "death of the author," but it also entails the death of the reader, for in the end it makes no difference who actually kills whom.

Curiously, Borges was to hint at an autobiographical subtext even in this outlandish fantasy: the story, he said, was about "a man committing suicide."[19] After all, Triste-le-Roy, where detective and criminal, author and reader, discover they are reflections of each other, may be taken as a figure of that "sad king," the solipsistic subject, sovereign in himself, yet unable to engage with anything other than himself. No wonder, then, that "pointless symmetries and obsessive repetitions" abound in the villa. The exception, however, is a "single flower" in a bedroom, but this figure of love, this promise of human connection, has withered – at the first touch, "the ancient petals crumbled away" (CF 154).

Despite the mutual "death" of both author and reader, Borges's desire for salvation by writing subsisted all the same. It is made explicit in "The Secret Miracle," where the Jewish writer Hladík is about to be shot by a Nazi firing squad and prays to God to spare him for long enough to finish *The Enemies*, a play he believed capable of "rescuing (albeit symbolically) that which was fundamental to his life" (CF 160). Hladík is on the point of being executed, so for whom is he writing? For no one but himself – and for God. He prays to the Almighty:

> If I do somehow exist, if I am not one of Thy repetitions or errata, then I exist as the author of *The Enemies*. In order to complete that play, which can justify me and justify Thee as well, I need one more year. (CF 161)

This is salvation by writing in its purest form – writing as a means of giving the author's life a purpose, and thereby saving the universe also from absurdity. Yet without a woman's love, such a saving work was impossible. Indeed, this is precisely the subject of Hladík's play: *The Enemies* concerns the rivalry between a nobleman and a writer for the love of a woman, but the audience later discovers that the jilted writer has gone mad, and the entire action of the play is but a "circular delirium" which he "endlessly experiences and re-experiences" (CF 160).[20]

After 1941, fantasy largely gave way to stories focusing on the figure of the hero, for with the "death" of the author-hero (or author-god), Borges would call into question the destiny of the hero. Thus, in "The Theme of the Traitor and the Hero," an Irish historian discovers that his own grandfather, a leader of the separatist cause, had secretly betrayed his comrades. "The Shape of the Sword" is the confession of an Irishman who has been impersonating the hero whom he has himself betrayed to the British. "Three Versions of Judas" portrays the great traitor as the true redeemer because his betrayal of Jesus made possible the salvation of mankind. All three stories enmesh the hero in violent paradoxes involving honor, shame, betrayal, and salvation, so that his true destiny proves as maddeningly fugitive or deceptive as Borges's own.

Borges had come to terms with the "general tragedy of all writing" by converting philosophical ideas into figurative vehicles for his own desolation and angst. After *Fictions* was published in December 1944, he spoke of the stories having been "nourished on dangerous poisons" – "darkness, bitterness, frustration, interminable useless evenings, and neglect."[21] At about this time too, he embarked on a new story about the saving role he had once accorded love in his conception of writing. "The Aleph" describes the extreme amorous obsession of a character called "Borges" for Beatriz Viterbo – even after she dies, he still visits her house on her birthday every year, bringing a gift. The name "Beatriz" is an allusion to the Beatrice of the *Divine Comedy*, and Borges took from Dante the theme that the poet's love of a woman may lead to a vision of universal wholeness and inspire the writing of an autobiographical masterpiece describing the author's salvation. But this great Dantean theme is parodied in the figure of a leaden versifier, Carlos Argentino Daneri, a cousin and sometime lover of Beatriz Viterbo, who is trying to describe the entire world in a laughably inept poem. In this respect, Daneri could be seen as a self-mocking *alter ego* of Borges himself, for he claims to draw inspiration from a magic orb set in the wall of a cellar in Beatriz's house, which he calls an "Aleph," a "place where … all places of the world, seen from every angle, coexist" (*CF* 281). One day, Daneri calls "Borges" to say that Beatriz's house is due to be demolished, and then shows him the Aleph, through which "Borges" gazes upon "the inconceivable universe." He tries to convey this vision to the reader as best he can, even while realizing that it is impossible to capture in language (another manifestation of "the general tragedy of all writing"). The experience leaves him with "a sense of infinite veneration, infinite pity" (*CF* 285). "Borges" then spitefully advises Daneri to consent to the demolition of the house, even though it may allude "infinitely to Beatriz."

Borges had first used the term "Aleph" at the height of his infatuation with Norah Lange, and there are aspects of the story which recall this muse of his youth. He had lost Norah forever in 1929, the year of Beatriz Viterbo's death, and the Lange villa on Calle Tronador, where he had once been so happy with Norah, had been put up for sale when he started to write this story in late 1944. However, he had not yet finished "The Aleph" when he fell in love again, this time with a young writer called Estela

Canto, and his hopes of inspiration soon revived at the prospect of finding a new muse.

Borges became so besotted with Estela that he embarked on a turbulent on–off relationship that over its three main phases was to last ten years. Already in the first phase he proposed marriage, and Estela agreed – on condition they first had sexual relations. He went to a psychologist for help to overcome his inhibitions, but Estela came to resent what she saw as his fear of standing up to his interfering mother, and in July 1946, went off with another man.[22] Her desertion provoked an extraordinary outpouring: most of the stories collected in *The Aleph* (1949) were published between August 1946 and July 1947. In "The House of Asterion," for instance, the Cretan Minotaur is a lonely monster who longs to be put out of his misery by Theseus's sword. In "The Zahir," "Borges" is in love with Teodelina Villar, even though she is indifferent to him. After Teodelina's death, he comes across a coin – the Zahir – which obsesses and torments him to the point of madness.

Borges described "The Zahir" as "more or less 'The Aleph' once again."[23] Curiously, the date on the unforgettable coin was 1929, the year of Beatriz Viterbo's death, and the year of his final rejection by Norah Lange. But why do these women obsess "Borges" even beyond death? Their love might have led to a sense of the Absolute, as figured in the desperate hope that "behind the coin one might find God," or in the universal vision afforded by the Aleph. Each story is a version of the Dantean aspiration to find a muse who might inspire a masterpiece that could "summarize" his destiny. And yet, that destiny seemed ever out of reach, like the tortoise for the swift Achilles in Zeno's famous paradox, another favorite theme.

The 1950s were particularly difficult, with just flickers of hope lighting up a gathering darkness. Depressed by the authoritarian rule of Juan Perón (1945–55),[24] he published satirical and other pieces critical of Peronism, and stories like "The South" and "The End," which focus on destiny and identity, national as well as personal.[25] His affair with Estela Canto revived in 1954, but that same year an accident damaged his already weak sight and left him unable to read or write. A final parting from Estela came at the end of 1955, after which he wrote "*Inferno*, I, 32," a brief text about Dante's last days. In a dream, God reveals to the poet "the secret purpose of his life and work"; Dante "learned at last who he was and what he was, and blessed the bitterness of his life," but upon waking, he discovered that he could no longer recall that secret purpose (*CF* 323). In other words, even Dante had not found salvation through *The Divine Comedy*.

Following the fall of the Perón regime in 1955, Borges was appointed Director of the National Library, but it was a mixed blessing: he had failed

215

to find love, failed to engage fully with life, and here he was again, back in a library. In "Poem of the Gifts," he savored the "splendid irony" of being "granted books and blindness at one touch," and mused upon "this dear world losing shape, fading away / into a pale uncertain ashy-gray / that feels like sleep, or else oblivion" (*SP* 95, 97). His fate appeared to have been sealed, and he was running out of steam – after "The End" in 1953, he would not publish another story until 1969. He took to poetry again, and to short reflections in prose, which he would gather up (with some earlier ones) in a miscellany called *The Maker* (1960). Here he introduced a new device of impersonating great authors – Dante, Cervantes, Marino – in order to lament the failure of his fundamental creative endeavor. He assumes the guise of Homer in the title story and redefines the task of the writer – the pen was no substitute for the sword: the poet must sing the praises of the hero and not attempt to emulate him.

Even so, the old urge to capture something true and vital with his pen had not entirely died. In "The Other Tiger," he observed that all the tigers he had ever written about were but "literary images," "scraps remembered from encyclopedias," and yet, something imposed on him the "perverse adventure" of searching for the living tiger, "the one that is not in this poem" (*SP* 117, 119). Nor had the yearning to forge a literary destiny been extinguished. In "Borges and I," he splits his intimate self from a public self called "Borges," who has the habit of "distorting and magnifying" the things they have in common:

> Years ago I tried to free myself from him, and I moved on from the mythologies of the slums and outskirts of the city to games with time and infinity, but those games belong to Borges now, and *I shall have to think up other things.* (*SNF* 324, my italics)

As with the search to capture the "other tiger" in his writing, he must break free of the public "Borges" and pursue his quest to create the essential work that would "summarize" his destiny.

The late period (1965–1986): the author as weaver of dreams

Borges was largely unknown outside Argentina when he was surprised by the award of the International Publishers' Prize in 1961, jointly with Samuel Beckett. Within a decade he was being hailed as a great writer and invited to teach and lecture abroad. Yet, ironically, he had reached a dead end with the kind of fiction that was winning him such acclaim. From the mid 1950s he mostly composed poetry, although the poems he collected in *The Self and the Other* (1964) were very different from the work of his youth: they

216

were wistful, disabused compositions – sonnets more often than not – on time and loss and the enigmas of destiny, together with praise for heroic warriors, often set in a Norse or Anglo-Saxon frame, after he took up the study of Anglo-Saxon with a group of female students. All the same, poetry allowed a more direct expression of thoughts and feelings, and a more autobiographical focus in his writing, as in the work of his youth. In *The Self and the Other* he chose to include "*Two English Poems*," which are cries of anguish at the loss of a woman. Both were unpublished, written in English, and tellingly dated 1934, when he was still pining for Norah Lange.

He was no less tormented now by his failure in love. His confidant Bioy Casares noted in his diary: "Borges tells me about the misfortunes of his love life, the ups and downs, the analyses, the conjectures" (*Borges*, 996). Since his rejection by Lange, he had been deserted by a series of women – by Haydée Lange (Norah's sister), by Estela Canto, Cecilia Ingenieros, Margarita Guerrero, and several others. "That's what my whole life is like," he would complain; "A chain of women" (991). Bioy surmised that his relationships were invariably "platonic" because he thought of sex as "dirty": "He sees obscenity as an atrocious flaw: a *prostitute* is not a woman who is paid but a woman who goes to bed with a man" (1458). This prudishness, he believed, was the real obstacle: "Without understanding the reality, he talks about his *recurrent tragic destiny* and about how, by some perverse fate, a man always appears and takes them [his girlfriends] from him" (963, my italics).

Once more it was an upheaval in his personal life that was the catalyst for a new departure in his writing. He had fallen in love again – with María Esther Vázquez, a much younger woman. Mother, as usual, disapproved, but Borges was determined to stand up to her and marry his sweetheart. And yet he seemed unable to escape his "recurrent tragic destiny," for in November 1965 María Esther suddenly announced that she was to marry another man. Borges was devastated and, as had happened after Estela left him in 1946, there was an outpouring of new stories, later collected in *Brodie's Report* (1970). These were more personal and "realistic" than his admirers had come to expect, for he had shed many of the trappings of fantasy and metaphysics that had characterized the *ficciones*, and allowed the autobiographical dimension to come closer to the surface. As Arturo Echavarría argues in Chapter 12, the collection amounts to a bitter critique of Argentine society. And there is also self-critique. Indeed, *Brodie's Report* marks the beginning of a process of liberation. For example, the "The Elderly Lady" calls into question the sword of honor by portraying a snobbish woman (much like his grandmother), who clings to the memory of her illustrious military ancestor in order to distinguish herself from the invasive riff-raff of modern

Buenos Aires. In other stories he returned to the topic of the duel, but used it now to satirize his longstanding fascination with the dagger. The entrenched conflicts between the sword of honor and the infamous dagger, between hero and coward, self and non-self, were starting to dissolve. Two stories indicate the resulting emergence of a firmer sense of self. "Guayaquil" describes a mysterious act of renunciation whereby a patrician historian concedes to his immigrant rival, a German Jew, the honor of taking a copy of (fictitious) letters by Simón Bolívar. In "The Story from Rosendo Juárez," the protagonist explains why he refused a challenge to a duel. As Borges put it, the "seeming coward" saw through the romantic nonsense and childish vanity of dueling, and finally attained "manhood and sanity."[26] Both patrician and hoodlum gain a truer sense of self by accepting the reality of their everyday circumstances, rather than trying to live up to the expectations of others. (Variations on this theme also appear in "Unworthy," and later, in "Shakespeare's Memory" and "Blue Tigers.")

Borges's personal freedom, however, was so curtailed by blindness that in 1967 he resigned himself to marrying a widow whom his mother had chosen to care for him after her demise. It turned out to be a disaster. His despair is evident in the poems of *In Praise of Darkness* (1969), and in "The Other," a story in which he looks back at the naïve hopes of his youth from the lovelorn perspective of the present. In 1970 he obtained a legal separation and went back to live with his mother.

During his marriage he had found some distraction in the friendship of María Kodama, a Japanese-Argentine woman over forty years his junior. Having now separated, the prospect of a love affair prompted him to undertake a project he had been nurturing for many years. In 1955 he had referred to a "novel" he was planning to write called "The Congress," which he hoped "would sum up and would also be the resolution of everything I have written up till now."[27] In 1970 he took it up again and produced the longest story he ever wrote.

"The Congress" is a memoir written by an old bachelor, Alejandro Ferri, about a secret society dedicated to organizing a "Congress of the World" comprising delegates from all the nations of the globe. The aspiration to embrace the totality of the world is a familiar Borgesian theme (see "The Writing of the God," or "The Aleph"). The society's founder is a wealthy rancher called Alejandro Glencoe, and there is a Norwegian girl called Nora Erfjord who is its secretary, but power lies with a sinister character called Twirl, who exploits Glencoe's generosity: first, he recommends the creation of a reference library for the Congress, then he expands it to include the classics of each nation; next, he suggests the Congress adopt a universal language. Ferri is sent to London to research various such languages in the

218

British Museum and there falls in love with an English girl, "tall and slender" with bright red hair, called Beatrice Frost (*CF* 432).

When Ferri returns to Buenos Aires he finds that Twirl has extended the Congress to embrace practically any book in existence. Nora Erfjord has resigned in despair and Glencoe's house has become a chaotic library of uncatalogued books. However, shortly after Ferri arrives back from London, Glencoe has a mystical insight into the underlying oneness of the universe: "The Congress of the World began the instant the world itself began, and it will go on when we are dust. There is no place it is not" (*CF* 434). He orders all the books to be burned and tells the members of the society: "We no longer need the Congress" (*CF* 435). He then takes them for a coach ride around Buenos Aires "to contemplate the Congress," and all share his epiphany: "Mystics invoke a rose, a kiss, a bird that is all birds, a sun that is the sun and yet all the stars, a goatskin filled with wine, a garden, or the sexual act" (*CF* 435). After "that long night of celebration" they end up "exhausted but happy." Even the malign Twirl is forced to confess: "I have tried to do evil yet I have done good" (*CF* 435).

The story is a further Borgesian variation on the Dantean theme – love for a woman (Beatrice Frost) leads to the writing of a literary work (Ferri's memoir) which relates the discovery of the ultimate truth of things. There are conscious parallels with "The Aleph": Glencoe's initial aim to represent the world in a congress of delegates is as futile as Carlos Argentino Daneri's absurd attempt to describe the globe in his poem. And similar autobiographical allusions, too – Beatrice Frost has "bright red hair," like Norah Lange, while the Norwegian Nora Erfjord not only shares a first name with Lange but also a surname with Lange's mother, Berta Erfjord.

These references clearly recall Beatriz Viterbo in "The Aleph," and link back through her to Teodelina Villar in "The Zahir." But there is a difference: the "Borges" characters in "The Aleph" and "The Zahir" never enjoy the love of either Beatriz or Teodelina, and end up frustrated by the inadequacies of language or driven to the brink of madness. Ferri, however, makes love to Beatrice Frost, and eventually achieves self-acceptance and contentment, which allows him to write the story of the pantheist epiphany (of which his "congress" with Beatrice is, implicitly, the indirect cause).

At the time of writing "The Congress," Borges had not yet declared his feelings to María Kodama. He did so shortly afterwards during a trip to Iceland in 1971. This was the first time since the mid 1920s that a woman had not spurned his love. After Iceland, he wrote two new stories that point to a critical advance in his self-understanding. In "Ulrikke," an aging South American professor falls for a Norwegian girl, who unexpectedly offers him a night of love; this "miracle" reminds him of his youth, and of a girl, "fair and slim like Ulrikke, who had denied me her love." Once again, certain details allude to his youthful infatuation with Norah Lange. The story is set in York, a city founded by Vikings, Ulrikke is Norwegian (Lange was of Norwegian descent), and she tells the professor: "I will be yours in the inn at Thorgate." The word "gate" is derived from the Anglo-Saxon for "street," so Thorgate means "the street of Thor" or "the street of the Thunderer," which translates into Spanish as "Calle Tronador," a reference to the Lange villa on Calle Tronador where the young Borges had courted Norah before she rejected him for Oliverio Girondo.

All four stories, "The Aleph," "The Zahir," "The Congress," and "Ulrikke," are subtly haunted by shades of Norah Lange, which suggests that she had become the paradigm for the "chain of women" whose rejections appeared to have destroyed the possibility of writing the saving work that would clinch his destiny. Nevertheless, this intertextual web of allusions, so carefully contrived by Borges, evinces a progressive de-mystification of love and a recognition of its erotic character. In the first two stories, the protagonists' obsession with the two dead women sublimated sexual desire in futile metaphysical yearnings. But lovemaking *does* take place in "The Congress," and it is celebrated with orgasmic cries: "Oh nights, oh shared warm darkness, oh love that flows in shadow like a secret river, oh that moment of joy in which two are one, oh innocence and openness of delight" (*CF* 432). Nor does "Ulrikke" eschew sex, whether real or imagined, though it is primarily concerned with finding release from the memory of the thwarted desires of youth, for when the professor makes love in "Thorgate," he is said to have possessed the "image" of Ulrikke for "the first" but also for the "last time."

This acceptance of sexuality is taken still further in "The Night of the Gifts." It is a story about "first occasions that can't be forgotten," and deals with the initiation of an adolescent boy in a brothel. Since it is told to a group of men which includes Borges's father, it calls to mind Borges's own traumatic initiation in Geneva, when his father sent him to a prostitute shortly after he had fallen in love with his first sweetheart. After a gang of drunken *cuchilleros* bursts into the brothel, the frightened boy tries to flee but he is reassured by a young prostitute who rewards his "cowardice" by making love to him, and then shows him the way out of the brothel. As he leaves, he witnesses a policeman killing Juan Moreira, a gaucho outlaw much lauded by Evaristo Carriego. As in "The Story from Rosendo Juárez," then, this new tale amounts to the final unmasking and repudiation of the machismo that underpinned Carriego's "cult of courage," but it shows more clearly than before Borges's awareness that this "cult" had so fascinated him because of its pernicious association of sexuality with transgression.

Together with "Ulrikke," this story indicates that Borges was overcoming that deep-seated horror of sex which Bioy Casares had identified as the obstacle in his relations with women. Both the fair Nordic maiden and the dark prostitute offer to make love to the protagonist, a gift that is consummated in a spirit of wonder and awe, and which symbolically sets Borges free from the "recurrent tragic destiny" that had brought such misery to his life.

Argentina was afflicted in these years by hyperinflation, dictatorship, a vicious repression of urban guerrillas, and by a bloody conflict with Britain over the Malvinas/Falkland Islands in 1982, followed by a terrible economic collapse.[28] There were troubles in Borges's personal life too, stemming from the hostility of family and friends to his relationship with María.[29] As Jason Wilson shows in Chapter 15, a good number of the familiar themes appear in the poems of old age, such as time, identity, memory, nostalgia, loss, and world-weariness. Many express his disillusion with the state of the *patria*. Yet, even so, the poetry is punctuated by expressions of unwonted happiness, especially as regards the love poems, which infuse a new spirit of hope even at this late stage.

After his mother's death in 1975, Borges was more open about his relationship with María Kodama, and just as the experience of mutual love had de-mystified his idealization of women, so now would it lead him to de-mystify that ultimate Romantic illusion of his – the idea of a muse who would inspire him to write a saving masterpiece. A new story, "August 25, 1983," is a variation on "The Other" – a dialogue between two instances of himself.[30] Each version assumes he is dreaming the other: the older believes he's at home, waiting to die from an overdose; the younger has just checked into a hotel; both recall a time when a still younger Borges had planned suicide in that same hotel. They also recall a woman, whose memory still causes them pain. The older predicts that the younger "will write the book we've dreamed of for so long," but this "masterpiece," he warns, will turn out to be nothing more than a "museum" of hackneyed themes (*CF* 491). "That book was one of the roads that led me to this night," says the older Borges (*CF* 492).

The fact that the two Borgeses share the memory of a woman and the forlorn hope of writing "a masterpiece" implies a critique of "The Congress," which Borges had long hoped "would sum up and would also be the resolution of everything I have written up till now." And, in this respect, the new story may also be taken to represent Borges's realization that the Dantean dream of writing a saving masterpiece was a product of his solipsism, in as much as he had sought a woman's love not for its own sake but as a vehicle for the fulfillment of his literary destiny.

Stripped by experience of this mystical idea of love as the key both to his destiny as a writer and to understanding the universe, all he could do was surrender to his lover's intriguing "otherness." In "Music Box," he evoked the music of Japan (María was half-Japanese), comparing its notes to "drops of slow honey or invisible gold." Yet, what was the source of this mysterious music? "I shall never know. It doesn't matter. In that music / I am. I wish to be. I bleed away" (OC III 172). This letting go of the self in the "music" of the lover brought a new kind of happiness, and its source, he declared in "Happiness," lay in "the love wherein there is no possessor and no possessed, but both surrender" (SP 435).

The mutuality intrinsic to his new understanding of love began to shape his thinking about writing. He had never resigned himself to the "death of the author," and from the mid 1970s he embarked on a tentative process of "resurrecting" him. In 1981 he dedicated The Limit to María Kodama, and wrote that a true gift is "reciprocal": "The giver does not deprive himself of what he gives. To give and to receive are the same thing" (OC III 289). He developed this notion in the "Inscription" to Los Conjurados (1985), which he again offered to María Kodama: "We can only give what is already the other's. In this book are things that were always yours. How mysterious a dedication is, a surrender of symbols!" (SP 461). In the ensuing "Prologue" (SP 463), he extended the idea of the gift to embrace the process of literary creation. Writing was associated with dreaming: "In this book there are many dreams. I make clear that they were the gifts of the night or, more precisely, of the dawn, and not pondered fictions." The author, however, is not a passive vehicle for the transmission of these dreams: he realizes a form that was virtual in the subject matter itself: "Each work entrusts its writer with the form that it seeks." In other words, the author receives the "dream" as a gift of the night which he then shapes into "the form it seeks," and offers it in turn to the reader.

Who or what was the origin of the "gift" of writing? The search for the Absolute, or for God, had been an abiding preoccupation, but he could not overcome his agnosticism. In "The Long Search," he imagined "an invisible animal" existing "before time or outside of time," which "we men seek and which seeks us," yet which "eludes us from one second to the next" (OC III 486). Still, he explored the possibility that literary creation might offer salvation from nothingness. It strikes him in "The Lacquer Walking-Stick" that the stick had once been shaped to fit its owner's hand by an artisan about whom he knows nothing. And yet, the fact that he was thinking about that stranger created a link: "It is not impossible that Someone has premeditated that link. It is not impossible that the universe might need that link" (OC III 328). Similarly, "The Third Man" refers to a total stranger he happened to pass in the street and about whom he decided to write this poem. This was "to execute an irreparable act" – "I have forged a link" (*OC* III 486). Both poems were about "the secret bonds that unite all the beings of the universe" (*OC* III 338), a pantheist insight arrived at, not through a mystical revelation as in "The Congress," but through his creative will as an author. The "dream" (the virtual reality) of art could yet save us because it might signify a coincidence of the author's will with the Will of a "Someone" who might well exist beyond the realm of time.

In his final years, Borges had managed to find some means of justifying his life as a writer. In one of his last interviews, he professed a continuing skepticism about the existence of God, but sometimes, he observed: "I think it is not impossible that I may continue to live in some other manner after my physical death."[31] And he quoted an "admirable expression" of Bernard Shaw's – "God is in the making," implying that what the intellect denied might become accessible by other means. Still, he was not a thinker, he said, he had never "arrived at anything," he was just a "man of letters," "a weaver of dreams."

Conclusion

What gave direction and purpose to Borges's life was his quest to discover a "literary destiny." And love had always played a pivotal role in that quest. It had swept him to great heights of ambition in his youth, when he saw himself as an author-hero, capable of creating a new culture and identity for Argentina. But, conversely, its absence had plunged him repeatedly into a desperate sense of the "nothingness of personality." The second phase of his career corresponds to this kind of "death," figured pre-eminently in Pierre Menard, in which the author can be no more original or creative than his reader. Borges's *ficciones* thus represent varieties of solipsism, of the voided self, while registering an enduring desire for salvation by writing. In the third and last phase of his career, there is a renewal of the quest for a literary destiny, starting with a gradual process of liberation from his inveterate conflicts, leading to the actual experience of love as mutuality, and culminating in his late-flowering theme of the reciprocal "gift."

This final conception of writing as a gift synthesizes the ideas of the early and middle periods – it preserves the reciprocal trust on which the confessional poetics of his youth had rested, but acknowledges also, with Pierre Menard, that the author is not the exclusive origin of meaning, nor is there a single authorized interpretation of his texts. Borges did eventually arrive at a justification of his life as a writer, but it was not by writing a "masterpiece" that would "summarize" his destiny, not by "rescuing ... that which was fundamental to his life" (the gift for which Hladík had prayed to God in "The Secret Miracle"), it was through the "joy" of writing itself, in his activity as a maker, a "weaver of dreams." As he expressed it in the Prologue to his last book: "Nevertheless, I go on writing. What other fate do I have, what other beautiful fate do I have? The joy of writing is not measured by the virtues or frailties of writing. All human endeavor is perishable, Carlyle affirms, but carrying it out is not" (*SP* 463).

NOTES

1 Adolfo Bioy Casares, *Borges*, ed. Daniel Martino, Barcelona, Destino, 2006, 766. Subsequent page references to this diary by Bioy Casares are given in the main text. All translations into English in this chapter are my own, unless otherwise indicated.

2 Interview with Ronald Christ, *Paris Review*, 40 (1967), 155.

3 "An Autobiographical Essay," in *The Aleph and Other Stories 1933–1969*, ed. and trans. Norman Thomas di Giovanni in collaboration with the author, New York, E. P. Dutton, 1970, 211.

4 "An Autobiographical Essay," 211.

5 "Paréntesis pasional" ("An Interlude of Passion") [1920], reprinted in *Jorge Luis Borges: textos recobrados, 1919–1929*, Buenos Aires, Emecé, 2001, 32–33.

6 "Anatomía de mi Ultra" ("Anatomy of My Ultra") [1921], in *Textos recobrados, 1919–1929*, 95. See also, "Ultra Manifesto," in J. L. Borges, *On Writing*, ed. Suzanne Jill Levine, Penguin Classics, New York, Penguin, 2010, 3–4.

7 Edwin Williamson, *Borges: A Life*, New York, Viking Penguin, 2004, 125.

8 Williamson, *Borges: A Life*, 117 and 136–38.

9 See Borges's review article, "Ramón Gómez de la Serna," [1925], in *Inquisiciones*, Buenos Aires, Espasa Calpe/Seix Barral, 1993, 132.

10 "Invectiva contra el arrabalero" ("Invective Against the Slang of the [Poor] Suburbs") [1926], in *El tamaño de mi esperanza*, Buenos Aires, Espasa Calpe/ Seix Barral, 1993, 125–26. See also, Williamson, *Borges: A Life*, 137–42.

11 "Página relativa a Figari" ("A Page on the [Painter] Figari") [1928], in *Textos recobrados, 1919–1929*, 362–64.

12 See J. L. Borges, *On Argentina*, ed. Alfred MacAdam, Penguin Classics, New York, Penguin, 2010, 47.

13 "La felicidad escrita" ("Writing Happiness") [1926], in *El idioma de los argentinos* [1928], Buenos Aires, Espasa Calpe/Seix Barral, 1994, 41.

14 See Williamson, *Borges: A Life*, 149–74.

15 Epigraph to *El idioma de los argentinos*, 7.

16 "El idioma de los argentinos" [1927], a lecture reprinted in the collection of that title cited in note 13 above, 149. See also, "The Language of the Argentines," in J. L. Borges, *On Argentina*, 79–88 (87).

17 "An Autobiographical Essay," 219–20.

18 Roland Barthes, "The Death of the Author," in *Image-Music-Text*, ed. and trans. Stephen Heath, New York, Hill and Wang, 1977, 142–48.

19 "Commentaries," in *The Aleph and Other Stories*, 269.

20 Note the close parallels with Herbert Quain's two-act play *The Secret Mirror*, in which the writer Wilfred Quarles is jilted by the "haughty, Amazon-like" Ulrica in favour of the Duke of Rutland; the audience discovers in the second act that the whole of the first was an invention of a failed writer called Quigley. See "A Survey of the Works of Herbert Quain," in *Fictions* (*CF* 110–11).

21 *Borges en 'Sur', 1931–1980*, Buenos Aires, Emecé, 1999, 300–302.

22 See Williamson, *Borges: A Life*, chapters 9, 10, 19, 20.

23 Antonio Carrizo, *Borges el memorioso*, Mexico City, Fondo de Cultura Económica, 1983, 235.

24 See Williamson, *Borges: A Life*, chapters 20–23.

25 See Edwin Williamson, "Borges Against Perón: A Contextual Approach to 'El fin'," *Romanic Review*, 98 (2007), 275–96.

26 "Commentaries," in *The Aleph and Other Stories*, 282.

27 Interview with *Noticias Gráficas*, July 19, 1955, reprinted in *Jorge Luis Borges: textos recobrados, 1931–1955*, Buenos Aires, Emecé, 2001, 371.

28 See Williamson, *Borges: A Life*, chapters 28, 29, 30, 32, 33.

29 See Williamson, *Borges: A Life*, 438–40.

30 First published in *La Nación*, March 27, 1983, but dated "Buenos Aires, 1977." It was later included in *Shakespeare's Memory*.

31 The interview, with Amelia Barili, took place in November 1985. It was first published in English in the *New York Times Book Review*, July 13, 1986, and later collected in *Jorge Luis Borges: Conversations*, ed. Richard Burgin, Jackson, University Press of Mississippi, 1998, 240–47.

FURTHER READING

Works by Borges, in chronological order of publication
(Unless otherwise indicated, the place of publication is Buenos Aires. Anthologies
of other writers' works edited by Borges are not included.)

Fervor de Buenos Aires (poems), privately printed, 1923
Luna de enfrente (poems), Proa, 1925
Inquisiciones (essays), Proa, 1925. [Reissued by Espasa Calpe/Seix Barral,1993]
El tamaño de mi esperanza (essays), Proa, 1926. [Reissued by Espasa Calpe/Seix
    Barral, 1993]
El idioma de los argentinos (essays), Manuel Gleizer, 1929. [Reissued by Espasa
    Calpe/Seix Barral, 1994]
Cuaderno San Martín (poems), Proa, 1929
Evaristo Carriego (biography and essays), Manuel Gleizer, 1930
Discusión (essays), Manuel Gleizer, 1932
Las kenningar (essay), Francisco A. Colombo, 1933. (Later included in *Historia de
    la eternidad* below.)
Historia universal de la infamia (stories), Tor, 1935
Historia de la eternidad (essays), Viau y Zona, 1936
El jardín de senderos que se bifurcan (stories), Sur, 1941
Poemas (1923–1943), Losada, 1943. (First edition of collected poems, omitting a number of
    poems from earlier books and containing numerous variants on the original texts.)
Ficciones (stories), Sur, 1944
Nueva refutación del tiempo (essay), Oportet & Haereses (a fictitious publisher),
    1947. [Later included in *Otras inquisiciones* below.]
El Aleph (stories), Losada, 1949
Aspectos de la literatura gauchesca (originally a lecture delivered at the University of
    Montevideo, October 29, 1945), Montevideo, Número, 1950
Otras inquisiciones (1937–1952), (essays), Sur, 1952
Poemas (1923–1958), Emecé, 1958. (This marks the beginning of Borges's associ-
    ation with the publishers Emecé.)
El hacedor (poems and prose), Emecé, 1960
Antología personal, Sur, 1961
Obra poética, Emecé, 1964. (New title for collected poems. Includes new poems in
    a section called *El otro, el mismo*, later published as a separate volume under
    this title, Emecé, 1969.)

Para las seis cuerdas (lyrics for *milongas*), Emecé, 1965
Elogio de la sombra (poems), Emecé, 1969
El informe de Brodie (stories), Emecé, 1970
El Congreso (novella), El Archibrazo, 1971. [Later included in *El libro de arena* below.]
El oro de los tigres (poems), Emecé, 1972
Obras completas, Emecé, 1974
El libro de arena (stories), Emecé, 1975
La rosa profunda (poems), Emecé, 1975
Prólogos con un prólogo de prólogos (collected prologues to works by other authors), Torres Agüero Editor, 1975
La moneda de hierro (poems), Emecé, 1976
Historia de la noche (poems and prose), Emecé, 1977
Rosa y azul (first publication of two stories: "La Rosa de Paracelso" and "Tigres azules," which were later included in *Veinticinco Agosto 1983 y otros cuentos* below), Madrid, Sedmay, 1977
Obra poética (1923–1976), 10th edn., Emecé, 1978. (Last edition with variants on earlier texts. Henceforward new volumes of poetry will be incorporated without change in subsequent editions.)
Borges, oral (lectures delivered at the Universidad de Belgrano), Emecé/Editorial de Belgrano, 1979
Siete noches (lectures delivered at the Teatro Coliseo, Buenos Aires, in 1977), Mexico, Fondo de Cultura Económica, 1980
La cifra (poems), Madrid, Alianza, 1981
Nueve ensayos dantescos (essays, seven of which were first published in *La Nación*: six in 1948, one in 1951), Madrid, Espasa-Calpe, 1982
"La memoria de Shakespeare" (story). First published in *Clarín*, May 15, 1980, and subsequently incorporated as the title story of a collection forming part of the *Obras completas* (1989), below.
Veinticinco Agosto 1983 y otros cuentos (four stories), Madrid, Siruela,1983
Los conjurados (poems and prose), Madrid, Alianza, 1985
Obras completas, four volumes, Emecé, 1989
This Craft of Verse, Cambridge, MA, and London, Harvard University Press, 2000. (The Charles Eliot Norton Lectures, originally delivered in English at Harvard during 1967–68.)

Works in collaboration

With Adolfo Bioy Casares

Seis problemas para don Isidro Parodi (stories under joint pseudonym, H. Bustos Domecq), Sur, 1942
Dos fantasías memorables (two stories under joint pseudonym, H. Bustos Domecq), Oportet & Haereses (a fictitious publisher), 1946
Un modelo para la muerte (novella under joint pseudonym, B. Suárez Lynch), Oportet & Haereses, 1946
Los orilleros. El paraíso de los creyentes (two screenplays), Losada, 1955
Crónicas de Bustos Domecq (stories), Losada, 1967

Nuevos cuentos de Bustos Domecq (stories), Ediciones Librería de la Ciudad, 1977

With Delia Ingenieros

Antiguas literaturas germánicas, Mexico, Fondo de Cultura Económica, 1951

With Margarita Guerrero

El Martín Fierro, Columba, 1953
Manual de zoología fantástica, Mexico, Fondo de Cultura Económica, 1957.
(An expanded version published as: *El libro de los seres imaginarios*, Kier, 1967.)

With Betina Edelberg

La imagen perdida, 1953. (Unpublished script for a ballet; apparently lost.)
Leopoldo Lugones (essays), Troquel, 1955

With Luisa Mercedes Levinson

La hermana de Eloísa, Ene, 1955

With María Esther Vázquez

Introducción a la literatura inglesa, Columba, 1965
Literatura germánicas medievales, Falbo, 1966

With Esther Zemborain de Torres

Introducción a la literatura norteamericana, Columba, 1967

With Alicia Jurado

Qué es el budismo, Columba, 1976

With María Kodama

Breve antología anglosajona (translations of Anglo-Saxon texts), Santiago de Chile, La Ciudad, 1978
Atlas, Sudamericana, 1984

Obras completas en colaboración, Emecé, 1991

Collections of texts by Borges first published in journals, magazines, or newspapers

Jorge Luis Borges: Textos cautivos (Ensayos y reseñas en "El Hogar," 1936– 1939) (essays and reviews published in the magazine *El Hogar*), Barcelona, Tusquets, 1986
Borges en "Revista Multicolor de los Sábados" (articles, reviews, and translations first published in the literary supplement of the newspaper *Crítica*), Atlántida, 1995
Borges en "Sur," 1931–1980 (articles and reviews first published in the literary journal *Sur*), Emecé, 1999
Jorge Luis Borges: Textos recobrados, 1919–1929 (uncollected essays, poems, and reviews), Emecé, 1997
Jorge Luis Borges: Textos recobrados, 1931–1955, Emecé, 2001
Jorge Luis Borges: Textos recobrados, 1956–1986, Emecé, 2003

Borges in English

The most readily available editions are the three volumes published by Penguin:

Jorge Luis Borges, *Collected Fictions*, trans. Andrew Hurley, New York, Viking Penguin, 1998

Jorge Luis Borges, *Selected Poems*, ed. Alexander Coleman, New York, Viking Penguin, 1999

Jorge Luis Borges, *Selected Non-Fiction, 1922–1986*,* ed. Eliot Weinberger, New York, Viking Penguin, 1999

*The title of the British edition is *The Total Library: Non-Fiction, 1922–1986*, London, Allen Lane, the Penguin Press, 2000. The other two volumes appeared in the same year. The page numbers in the British editions are the same as for the US editions.

In Penguin Classics (New York, 2010), under the general editorship of Suzanne Jill Levine:

Jorge Luis Borges, *On Writing*, ed. Suzanne Jill Levine

Jorge Luis Borges, *On Argentina*, ed. Alfred MacAdam

Jorge Luis Borges, *On Mysticism*, ed. María Kodama

Jorge Luis Borges, *Poems of the Night*, ed. Efraín Kristal

Jorge Luis Borges, *The Sonnets*, ed. Stephen Kessler

Previously, Borges's principal writings were available to English-speaking readers in a variety of translations by different hands:

Ficciones, ed. with an introduction by Anthony Kerrigan, New York, Grove Press, 1962 (In the UK: Weidenfeld and Nicolson: London, 1962.)

Dreamtigers, trans. Mildred Boyer and Harold Borland, Austin, University of Texas Press, 1964 (Translation of *El hacedor*, 1960.)

Other Inquisitions, 1937–1952, trans. Ruth L. C. Simms, Austin, University of Texas Press, 1964

Labyrinths: Selected Stories and Other Writings, ed. Donald A. Yates and James E. Irby, New York, New Directions, 1964 (In the UK: Harmondsworth, Penguin, 1970.)

The Book of Imaginary Beings, written in collaboration with Margarita Guerrero. Revised, enlarged and translated by Norman Thomas di Giovanni in collaboration with the author, New York, Dutton, 1969 (In the UK: London, Jonathan Cape, 1970.)

The Aleph and Other Stories (1933–1969), ed. and trans. Norman Thomas di Giovanni in collaboration with the author, New York, Dutton, 1970 (Contains 'An Autobiographical Essay' and 'Commentaries'. See below.) (In the UK: London, Jonathan Cape, 1971.)

Doctor Brodie's Report, ed. and trans. Norman Thomas di Giovanni in collaboration with the author, Dutton: New York, 1971 (In the UK: London, Allen Lane,1974.)

Selected Poems, 1923–1967, ed. with introduction and notes by Norman Thomas di Giovanni, Delacorte Press: New York, 1972 (In the UK: London, Allen Lane, 1972.)

A Universal History of Infamy, trans. Norman Thomas di Giovanni, Dutton: New York, 1972 (In the UK: London, Allen Lane, 1973.)

In Praise of Darkness, trans. Norman Thomas di Giovanni, New York, Dutton, 1974 (In the UK: London, Allen Lane, 1975.)

The Book of Sand, trans. Norman Thomas di Giovanni, New York, Dutton, 1977 (In the UK: London, Allen Lane, 1977.)

The Gold of the Tigers: Selected Later Poems, trans. Alastair Reid, New York, Dutton, 1977 (Published in the UK as *The Book of Sand; The Gold of the Tigers*, London, Allen Lane, 1979.)

Borges: A Reader, ed. Alastair Reid and Emir Rodríguez Monegal, New York, Dutton, 1981

This Craft of Verse, Cambridge, MA, and London, Harvard University Press, 2000 (The Charles Eliot Norton Lectures, originally delivered in English at Harvard during 1967–68.)

With Adolfo Bioy Casares

Six Problems for Don Isidro Parodi, trans. Norman Thomas di Giovanni, New York, Dutton, 1981 (In the UK: London, Allen Lane, 1981.)

Chronicles of Bustos Domecq, trans. Norman Thomas di Giovanni, New York, Dutton, 1982 (In the UK: London, Allen Lane, 1982.)

Evaristo Carriego, trans. Norman Thomas di Giovanni, New York, Dutton, 1984 (In the UK: London, Allen Lane, 1984.)

With María Kodama

Atlas, trans. Anthony Kerrigan, New York, Viking, 1986

Borges in French

Œuvres complètes, ed. Jean Pierre Bernès, Bibliothèque de la Pléiade, Paris, Gallimard, 2 vols., 1993, 1999 (Contains informative notes, many of biographical and bibliographical interest.)

Critical studies of Borges's work

Aizenberg, Edna. *The Aleph Weaver: Biblical, Kabbalistic and Judaic Elements in Borges*, Potomac, Maryland, Scripta Humanistica, 1984

  Borges and His Successors: The Borgesian Impact on Literature and the Arts, Columbia, University of Missouri Press, 1990

Alazraki, Jaime (ed.). *Critical Essays on Jorge Luis Borges*, Boston, MA, G. K. Hall, 1987

Alazraki, Jaime. *Borges and the Kabbalah, and Other Essays On His Fiction and Poetry*, Cambridge University Press, 1988

Arana, Juan. *El centro del laberinto: Los motivos filosóficos en la obra de Jorge Luis Borges*, Navarra, EUNSA, 1994

Ashbery, John. "A Game with Shifting Mirrors." See Alazraki (ed.), 1987

Balderston, Daniel. *The Literary Universe of Jorge Luis Borges: An Index to References and Allusions to Persons, Titles, and Places in His Writings*, New York, Greenwood Press, 1986

  Out of Context: Historical Reference and the Representation of Reality in Borges, Durham, NC, Duke University Press, 1993

Balderston, Daniel, Gastón Gallo, and Nicolás Helft. *Borges. Una enciclopedia*, Buenos Aires, Grupo Editorial Norma, 1999

Barrenechea, Ana María. *Borges, the Labyrinth Maker*, New York University Press, 1965

Barth, John. "The Literature of Exhaustion." See Alazraki (ed.), 1987

Bastos, María Luisa. *Borges ante la crítica argentina: 1923–1960*, Buenos Aires, Hispamérica, 1974

Bell-Villada, Gene H. *Borges and His Fiction: A Guide to His Mind and Art*, Chapel Hill, University of North Carolina Press, 1981

Bioy Casares, Adolfo. *Borges*, ed. Daniel Martino, Barcelona, Destino, 2006

Block de Behar, Lisa. *Borges: The Passion of an Endless Quotation*, Albany, State University of New York Press, 2003

Bloom, Harold (ed.). *Jorge Luis Borges*, New York, Chelsea House Publishers, 1986

Bloom, Harold. "Borges, Neruda and Pessoa: Hispanic-Portuguese Whitman," in *The Western Canon*, New York, Harcourt, Brace, 1994, 463–92

Boldy, Steven. *A Companion to Jorge Luis Borges*, London, Tamesis, 2009

Blüher, Karl Alfred and Toro, Alfonso de (eds.). *Jorge Luis Borges: variaciones interpretativas sobre sus procedimientos y bases epistemológicas*, Frankfurt am Main, Vervuert, 1992

Bossart, W. H. and Hans H. Rudnick (eds.). *Borges and Philosophy: Self, Time, and Metaphysics*, Oxford, Peter Lang, 2003

Cahiers de L'Herne, "Jorge Luis Borges," Paris, Éditions de L'Herne, 1964

Calvino, Italo. "Jorge Luis Borges," in *Why Read the Classics?* Trans. Martin McLaughlin. New York, Pantheon Books, 1999

Champeau, Serge. *Borges et la métaphysique*, Paris, Vrin, 1990

Christ, Ronald. *The Narrow Act: Borges' Art of Allusion*, New York University Press, 1969

Cozarinsky, Edgardo. *Borges in/and/on Film*, New York, Lumen Books, 1988

Dunham, Lowell and Ivask, Ivar (eds.). *The Cardinal Points of Borges*, Norman, University of Oklahoma Press, 1971.

Echavarría, Arturo. *Lengua y literatura de Borges*, Barcelona, Ariel, 1983

   El arte de la jardinería china en Borges, y otros estudios, Madrid, Iberoamericana, 2006.

Fishburn, Evelyn and Hughes, Psique. *A Dictionary of Borges*. London, Duckworth, 1990

Fishburn, Evelyn (ed.). *Borges and Europe Revisited*, London, Institute of Latin American Studies, University of London, 1998

Flynn, Annette U. *The Quest for God in the Work of Borges*, London, Continuum, 2009

Frisch, Mark. *You Might Be Able to Get There from Here: Reconsidering Borges and the Postmodern*, Madison/Teaneck, Fairleigh Dickinson University Press, 2004

Gass, William H. "Imaginary Borges and His Books." See Alazraki (ed.), 1987

Genette, Gérard. "L'utopie littéraire," in Paris, *Figures*, Seuil, 1966

Helft, Nicolás and Alan Pauls. *El factor Borges. Nueve ensayos ilustrados*. Buenos Aires, Fondo de Cultura Económica, 2000

Irwin, John T. *The Mystery to a Solution: Poe, Borges and the Analytic Detective Story*, Baltimore, Johns Hopkins University Press, 1994

Kristal, Efraín. *Invisible Work: Borges and Translation*, Nashville, Vanderbilt University Press, 2002

Lafon, Michel. *Borges ou la réécriture*, Paris, Seuil, 1990

Lefere, Robin. *Borges, entre autorretrato y automitografía*, Madrid, Gredos, 2005

Lema-Hincapié, Andrés. *Borges ... ¿filósofo?*, Bogotá, Instituto Caro y Cuervo, 2012

Louis, Annick. *Jorge Luis Borges: Œuvres et Manœuvres*, Paris, L'Harmattan, 1997
Borges ante el fascismo, Oxford, Peter Lang, 2007

Macherey, Pierre. "Borges and the Fictive Narrative." See Alazraki (ed.), 1987

Man, Paul de. "A Modern Master." See Alazraki (ed.), 1987

Mateos, Zulma. *Filosofía en la obra de Jorge Luis Borges*, Buenos Aires, Biblos,1998

Modern Fiction Studies, Special Issue: Borges, 19 (1973)

Molloy, Sylvia. *Signs of Borges*, Durham, NC, Duke University Press, 1994

Nahson, Daniel. *La crítica del mito: Borges y la literatura como sueño de vida*, Madrid, Iberoamericana, 2009

Novillo-Corvalán, Patricia. *Borges and Joyce: An Infinite Conversation*, Leeds, Maney, 2011

Núñez-Faraco, Humberto. *Borges and Dante: Echoes of a Literary Friendship*, Oxford, Peter Lang, 2006

Nuño, Juan. *La filosofía de Borges*, Mexico, Fondo de Cultura Económica, 1986

Olaso, Ezequiel de. *Jugar en serio: aventuras de Borges*, Mexico, Paidós Mexicana, 1999

Olea Franco, Rafael. *El otro Borges, el primer Borges*, Buenos Aires, Fondo de Cultura Económica, 1993

Olea Franco, Rafael (ed.). *Borges: desesperaciones aparentes y consuelos secretos*, México, El Colegio de México, 1999

Richardson, Bill, *Borges and Space*, Oxford, Peter Lang, 2012

Romanic Review, Special Issue: Jorge Luis Borges, 98 (2007)

Rowe, William, Canaparo, Claudio, and Louis, Annick (eds.). *Jorge Luis Borges: intervenciones sobre pensamiento y literatura*, Buenos Aires, Paidós, 2000

Rowlandson, William. *Borges, Swedenborg and Mysticism*, Oxford, Peter Lang, 2013

Sarlo, Beatriz. *Borges: A Writer on the Edge*, London, Verso, 1993

Scholes, Robert. "The Reality of Borges." See Alazraki (ed.), 1987

Shaw, Donald L. *Borges' Narrative Strategy*, Leeds, Francis Cairns, 1992

Sosnowski, Saúl. *Borges y la cábala: La búsqueda del verbo*, Buenos Aires, Hispamérica, 1976

Sturrock, John. *Paper Tigers: The Ideal Fictions of Jorge Luis Borges*, Clarendon Press: Oxford, 1977

Sucre, Guillermo. *Borges, el poeta*, Monte Avila: Caracas, 1974

Steiner, George. "Tigers in the Mirror." See Alazraki (ed)., 1987

Tanner, Tony. "Borges and American Fiction 1950–1970." See Alazraki (ed.), 1987

Toro, Alfonso de (ed.). *Jorge Luis Borges: Ciencia y filosofía*, Hildesheim, Georg Olms Verlag, 2007
(ed.). *El laberinto de los libros: Jorge Luis Borges frente al canon literario*, Hildesheim, Georg Olms Verlag, 2007
(ed.). *Jorge Luis Borges: Translación e historia*, Hildesheim, Georg Olms Verlag, 2010

Toro, Alfonso de and Toro, Fernando de (eds.). *El siglo de Borges: Homenaje a Jorge Luis Borges en su centenario* (2 vols.), Frankfurt am Main, Vervuert; Madrid, Iberoamericana, 1999

Updike, John. "The Author as Librarian." See Alazraki (ed.), 1987

Waisman, Sergio. *Borges and Translation: The Irreverence of the Periphery*, Lewisburg, PA, Bucknell University Press, 2005

Williamson, Edwin. *Borges: A Life*, New York, Viking Penguin, 2004

   "Borges y Bioy: una amistad entre biombos," *Letras Libres*, 81 (2008), 30–37

Wilson, Jason. *Jorge Luis Borges*, London, Reaktion Books, 2006

Yates, Donald A. "Behind 'Borges and I'," *Modern Fiction Studies*, 19 (1973), 317–24.

See also *Variaciones Borges*, the journal of the Borges Center at the University of Pittsburgh. Its informative website is at: www.borges.pitt.edu/

SUBJECT INDEX

234

INDEX OF BORGES'S WORKS

INDEX OF CHARACTERS

Cambridge Companions to...

AUTHORS